D1544893

Anne McCaffrey

Anne McCaffrey

A LIFE
WITH DRAGONS

ROBIN ROBERTS

UNIVERSITY PRESS
OF MISSISSIPPI
Jackson

Willie Morris Books in Memoir and Biography

www.upress.state.ms.us

The University Press of Mississippi is a member of the
Association of American University Presses.

Illustrations courtesy of Anne McCaffrey unless
otherwise noted

First edition 2007

∞

Library of Congress Cataloging-in-Publication Data

Roberts, Robin, 1957–
Anne McCaffrey : a life with dragons / Robin Roberts. — 1st ed.
p.   cm.
Includes bibliographical references and index.
ISBN-13: 978-1-57806-998-9 (cloth : alk. paper)
ISBN-10: 1-57806-998-X (cloth : alk. paper) 1. McCaffrey,
Anne. 2. Novelists, American—20th century—Biography.
I. Title.
PS3563.A255Z846 2007
813'.54—dc22

2007003696

British Library Cataloging-in-Publication Data available

To my mother, Shirley Moore Roberts—
without her unwavering support and encouragement,
this book would never have been written or published

CONTENTS

ACKNOWLEDGMENTS

I am grateful to Anne McCaffrey for opening her papers and her circle of family and friends to me. Her three children, Alec Johnson, Georgeanne Kennedy, and Todd McCaffrey, were very open and helpful. All of those I interviewed were forthcoming and enthusiastic about the project: Susan Allison, Marilyn and Harry Alm, Maureen Beirne, Jean Bigelow, Derval Diamond, Annett Francis, Vaughne Hansen, H. Wright Johnson, Virginia Kidd, Kevin and Marcia McCaffrey, Andi McCaffrey, Pota Meier, Antoinette O'Connell, Elizabeth Ann Scarborough, Shelly Shapiro, Richard Woods, Betty Ballantine, Jody Lynn Nye, Pamela Melroy, and Elizabeth Moon.

I thank Pat Dyer and Rachel Albert from the Radcliffe Institute for their help in obtaining Anne McCaffrey's college records, Stuart Hall in Staunton, Virginia, for sending me Anne McCaffrey's file, Mrs. Nancy Brown at Montclair High School for help in obtaining high school records, the New York Public Library for sending me a copy of Anne McCaffrey's undergraduate thesis, and Princeton University for sending me H. Wright Johnson's thesis. Keith Stokes supplied the photographs from the Grand Master Ceremony. At University Press of Mississippi, Seetha Srinivasan provided much needed enthusiasm and commitment to this project. Walter Biggins, Anne Stascavage, and Karen Johnson were also extremely helpful and professional in the editing process. My thanks to a very generous and insightful Jane Dona-werth who made a number of useful suggestions.

The work of many years, this biography has benefited from the critical insights of a number of colleagues in my writing groups. Angeletta Gourdine has been a mainstay, and her own work and standards continue to provide me with inspiration. Rosan Jordan, Frank de Caro, Carolyn Ware, Sharon Weltman, Jennifer Jones, and Susannah Monta all read portions of the book and supplied helpful advice. Geoff Clayton, Rachel Kahn-Fogel, and Joe Ross have been good friends and stalwart supporters of this project. Keith Kelleman bought me a trilogy of Anne McCaffrey novels in 1983, thus starting the journey to this biography.

My two Louisiana State University Chancellor's Future Leaders in Research, Erin Jackson and Daniel Devillier, provided invaluable research assistance. Erin was there at the beginning, and Daniel at the very end. My grateful thanks to both of them. A sabbatical in 2002 enabled me to begin the research for this biography, and a travel grant from the English Department provided funds for a research trip to Washington. The LSU Office of Research supported a crucial data-gathering trip to Ireland. I am grateful to the university, college, and department for their support. My colleagues in the College of Arts and Sciences Dean's Office have been supportive in ways they don't even realize: I am particularly grateful to Dean Guillermo Ferreyra and Russell B. Long Professor of Political Science Wayne Parent. Rebecca Caire, Lois Edmonds, Tina Fos, Mark Hovey, Brian Landry, Carolyn Landry, Bronwyn Lawrence, Brenda Macon, Ginger Martinez, Margaret Parker, Michelle Perrine, Tianna Powers, and Ann Whitmer have made administrative work easier and this book possible.

Finally, but most importantly, I want to acknowledge the love and support of my family. My mother, Shirley Moore Roberts, insisted that we journey to meet Anne McCaffrey in 1996, and the rest is history. My sister Linda Roberts-Drake provided invaluable help when I interviewed Virginia Kidd. My father, David Roberts, and sisters and brothers Gayle Roberts and Greg, Jenny, and Bryan Pisklo, Kim Roberts, David, Russell, and Leni Roberts, Richard, Laura, and Alison Roberts, Roger and Mary Ellen

Roberts and Jonathan Kohanim, Scott Roberts, Ian Drake, and Rev. Bill and Laura Ellen Wade also provided support. Dylan and Chelsea Wade and Darcy, Bobcat, and Blackjack offered a respite from work when needed. Brooke and Kiva Pierce completed a bigger job than this book when they welcomed Amelia into the world. I look forward to Amelia's reading Anne McCaffrey's works. My sister-in-law Marylane Koch, herself a writer, supplied endless encouragement, as did her husband, Robert Koch, and daughter, Meredith Koch. My thanks to Lottie Nash Wade, an educator for five decades and a wonderful role model. My husband, Leslie Wade, supplied a firm belief in the biography's merit and completion. I owe him more than I can express.

Anne McCaffrey

Introduction

TO MILLIONS OF READERS AND her legion of fans, Anne McCaffrey is an icon, a magical presence, a writer whose books they devour, whose appearance at conventions they treasure, and whose fiction, Web site, and fan clubs dominate their lives. Literary critics know Anne McCaffrey as a member of a ground-breaking group of women science fiction writers who forever changed the field, humanizing it through their emphasis on women's issues and plots. Librarians and book sellers know Anne McCaffrey as an extremely popular writer, one who is "review proof," and whose name alone is enough to sell her latest book. Anne's struggles and triumphs as a woman writer reveal much about women's lives, particularly how to balance work and children, career and romance, and how to find meaning in a world that still values women more for their appearance than for their creativity. This biography will trace her development into a tremendously successful science fiction writer, and her impact on a genre that had, up to the mid-1970s, been dominated by men. The emphasis here is on this remarkable woman's life, rather than on literary analysis of her works. And while this book would not have been possible without Anne McCaffrey's full cooperation, and that of her family and friends, it is not an authorized biography; she neither asked for nor received any advance notice of the book's contents. Based on years of research and hundreds of hours of interviews, this biography charts the life of a remarkable woman writer.

Although she writes about other worlds, Anne is very much grounded in a particular place, Dragonhold-Underhill, the estate she built in rural Ireland. Dragonhold-Underhill's rural setting gives it a quality of timelessness and separation, and its many features reflect the essence of what the writer has created in her fictions and in her life. The forty-seven-acre estate is set in County Wicklow, known as "the Garden of Ireland" for its gently rolling hills and lush gardens. Dragonhold-Underhill is a comfortable contemporary home, built in 1990 with every modern convenience. The estate is secluded on a tiny, narrow country road crowded with dense, towering green shrubbery. The house blends into the landscape and appears deceptively small from the road; its two chimneys are the only clue to its extensive layout. Two large wrought-iron gates display the relief of a large bronze dragon. On one side, a white plaster wall topped with black wrought-iron spikes contains a wooden plaque announcing "Dragonhold-Underhill" in black letters.

To anyone familiar with her books, Dragonhold-Underhill seems a modern version of the "Hold," the central social and geographical unit in Pern society. The Holds are communities organized around a lord and his family, and based primarily on agriculture or another practical activity. Just like the lord of a Hold in one of her Dragonriders of Pern books, Anne is the center of all the activity at Dragonhold. The estate exists because of her, and fans journey from all over the world to visit her there. The center of this activity is Anne herself. Paradoxically, the very quiet and private act of writing has lead to the hustle and bustle of a large enterprise, including a working horse stables, extensive gardens, and staff, friends, and family. Yet, for all that focus, she seems reluctant to talk about herself. Only by persistent questioning can an interviewer succeed in getting Anne to finally talk about herself. Despite the very tangible signs of her success as a writer, she downplays her own importance.

Anne's modesty may be a pose of self-abnegation, but it seems genuine. It is an attitude sharply at odds with her children and friends, who are protective of her. They warn visitors (and this biographer) not to tire Anne out or ask troubling questions. To family and friends, Anne is a writer whose work and time must be shielded from those who would distract her or waste her time. In the local pub in Kilpedder, just a few miles from Dragonhold-Underhill, the local men pretend not to know who I am talking about when I ask if they know Anne. "*Ian* McCaffrey?" one asks. When I correct him, and explain where she lives, he says, "Oh, that crazy American with all the horses."

Anne's insularity is more than that of a landowner in rural Ireland; it is also another way that she has re-created the isolation and sense of being an outsider that shapes so much of her fiction. As the middle-aged and now older woman who refuses to play by traditional gender roles, as, for example, the "crazy" American who built the first heated barn for horses in the area, Anne has remained outside the society where she lives. As a consequence, she has faced some hostility, especially in the 1970s and 1980s. At one point, there were even rumors that Anne was running a coven, so she bought a traditional witch's broom to display outside her home. She still owns that broom, displays it in her living room, and proudly tells visitors the story. But the surrounding community has long since accepted her, and she has made many friends who make Dragonhold-Underhill a warm and welcoming place.

Anne's writing allowed her to escape a confining life, and she has created a comfortable, extended, but very self-contained household in Ireland. The house shows that, despite Anne's success, she is very practical, designing her home for use rather than for conspicuous display. Its open layout, large rooms, and high ceilings suggest an openness, as do the animals who wander freely about the house. Anne clearly cares a great deal for the animals who share her home. They go where they please, moving through the bustle of visitors and of kitchen work. When I ask to take her photograph, Anne takes her aptly named orange Maine Coon cat, Pumpkin, in her arms, unwilling to have her photo taken by herself. The only portrait of her in the house is an oil study that depicts her with her favorite horse, Mr. Ed. Her study opens up

3

with a large picture window to a horse pasture. No longer able to ride, she can still enjoy seeing her favorite creatures gambol in the fields. Her desk is positioned against a wall—if she looks to her right, she sees the outdoors, to the left is her study door, rarely shut, so she can see and hear what is going on in the rest of the house.

Although, when my mother and I visited Anne in June 1996, she could hardly walk because her arthritic hip (replaced only a month later) was giving her trouble, she swept into the hallway, beaming a large delighted smile, as though we were long-lost friends whom she was eager to see. With a wave of her hand, she directed us to the dining room, offering us tea or coffee. Her speech is characteristically American, with only a few words or inflections to remind you that she has lived in Ireland now for over thirty years. She has the immediate warmth that many Americans notice in the Irish: she puts you at ease. A friend and collaborator, Elizabeth Moon, recollected her first impression of Anne: "A blazing fire in a big fireplace. Gracious, warm, kindly—and the loveliest smile and laugh. I felt like I found another aunt. Oh, and that upright elegant look, too."

During one of our interviews, Anne reminds me that while writing is her life, it is not her only life. While every day is filled with mail or visits from fans, and she appreciates the contact, she does not expect or court adulation. Sitting in her dining room in rural Ireland, I am aware that after she made her fortune in the 1980s, she could afford to live anywhere. Her choice to live far away from the hustle, bustle, and pressure of New York City, or any other major publishing venue, has helped her to stay grounded. As dragons provide a leavening sense of the corporeal for their riders in McCaffrey's fiction, so horses have given Anne a grounding in the everyday world. In her words, "Horses help you keep your perspective. You have a lot of hard work keeping a horse, and there's nothing like shoveling shit every morning, or getting tossed, to keep you slightly humble."

As we sat down with drinks at her table, she showed me with delight a globe of Pern. As pleased as a child with a new toy, she pointed out the scientific detail of this representation, created by astronomer Steven Beard, who often helps her with the science in her books. It had been an unexpected present from him, and she repeated a few times, "It was such a surprise!" Holding the globe in front of her, she beamed at me across her dining-room table, her green eyes reflecting the green of the land masses on the globe. "A whole world in my hands," she said with a chuckle. The oddly shaped continents and the much larger expanse of blue sea reveal that it is an imaginary world she holds and controls and in which she is most comfortable. Where it echoes elements of Pern, Dragonhold-Underhill is another imaginary or dream world.

Like all writers, Anne transmutes the features of her life into art. Charting her life course reveals the frame from which she built her art. In many ways, her family's story is the story of an American family: Irish immigrants to America make good. But her story twists and turns, with Anne herself ending up an immigrant back to Ireland. In the motif of a journey, grounded in the story of her great-grandparents' immigration and her own repatriation to Ireland, Anne found the fodder not only of her science fiction novels, but also of her Gothic novels. From her great-grandparents, grandparents, and parents, she also learned a family tradition of honesty and even rebellion in service of justice. Anne's passionate nature, as well as her desire to impress a high-achieving father from whom she was separated due to World War II, amplified the usual traumas of adolescence; she has never forgotten the emotions of this time, and one of the hallmarks of her novels is her ability to evoke in the reader the intense longings of adolescence. These longings are often satisfied by love by and for animals. Anne transformed this affection for animals into fictional creatures who have egalitarian relationships with humans: for example, the Dragonriders of Pern benefit from their dragons' unconditional love and acceptance and telepathic communication. Anne's very basic need for love and connection, as well as respect, shapes her fictional worlds. At the same time, her innate instinct to perform, perhaps also a part of her Irish heritage, but also very much a part of her nature, appears in her literary creation of "Talents." Many of her characters have special skills, such as singing or second sight, that she develops in her fictions into scientifically plausible qualities. In this regard, Anne can be said to have performed the quintessentially science fiction act of extrapolation, taking an idea—of an animal friend or the power of a singer's voice—and developing it along a continuum.

Her success as a writer can be measured not only by her sales, but also by her fans' devotion to her and to the worlds she has created. While the stereotype of a best-selling author might be the egotistical, solitary creature, isolating herself from human contact to write imaginary worlds, Anne's life challenges this idea: she seems to thrive on a large, dependent household. This arrangement repeats her family life as a child, with a housekeeper and a grandmother, and her sharing a large mansion on Long Island with another couple and their children and pets in the late 1960s. Like most women, Anne defines herself in relation to others: in her unpublished autobiography, a sketch of about fifty pages, she begins by listing all the people who have influenced her, including her parents, teachers, other science fiction writers, and her agents. She even gives credit to her ex-husband, despite an acrimonious divorce: "*He* didn't believe what I wrote had any merit: I *had* to prove it all to him. Often that sort of negative response is even more instrumental to success than positive support." It is worth noting here that even decades after their divorce Anne still wants to give her ex-husband some credit.

There is much truth to what Anne says—that a writer's career is shaped by the people she encounters, especially those whose approval she seeks. Paradoxically, in seeking to gain approval from a demanding father and an unsupportive husband, Anne ended up instead with the uncritical affection of millions of readers. Shadowing Anne at Dragoncon (a science fiction convention) a few years ago, I witnessed her interactions with fans. Waiting in line for hours, hoping to get their books (or stuffed dragons, programs, or badges) signed by their favorite author, were a thin twelve-year-old girl in gold-rimmed granny glasses and a large, burly man with a shaved head, his big muscles encased in black leather pants and vest. Holding out a silver chain-mail bracelet, the man placed the bracelet on Anne's wrist saying, "I made this for you." A young woman with long, dark hair, black jeans, and numerous body piercings bounded up to Anne and cried, "I loved dragons so much I had one tattooed on my back. That's how much you have influenced me." With tears in her eyes, another woman writer, Laura Curtis, stopped signing her own books to come over and give Anne a big hug. "Thank you for writing *Dragonflight*. I started writing because of your books," she declared. This kind of devotion has fueled Anne's tremendously successful writing career, and along the way she has affected not only innumerable readers, but also the genre.

This adoration, too, comes with a cost, as Anne's son, Todd, and daughter, Georgeanne (Gigi to family and friends), also writers, struggle to protect their mother at conventions and other public events. Anne herself acknowledges how draining such admiration can be, and she wears a protective crystal under her shirt when she makes public appearances, "to absorb the energy" of her fans' demands. The tremendous pressure on her to write more books, especially more books set on Pern, weighs on her. In addition to the fans' hunger for more stories, Anne still has practical considerations for writing: no longer worried about surviving, she now has hefty bills and many people dependent on her. Generous to a fault, she supports her children, friends who have fallen on hard times, a niece, staff people, even friends from New Orleans who had to evacuate due to Hurricane Katrina.

One of the twentieth century's best-loved and most widely read writers, Anne has made immense contributions to fiction. In 1968, she was the first woman to win both the Hugo (an award bestowed annually at the World Science Fiction Convention) and the Nebula (awarded annually by the Science Fiction Writers of America), the genre's most prestigious awards. In 1978, she became the first science fiction writer to have a book on the *New York Times* best-seller list. In 1999, the American Library Association recognized her work with the Margaret A. Edwards Award for Lifetime Literary Achievement. Anne has also collected the Ditmar Award (Australia), the Gandalf Award, and the Streza (the European Science Fiction Convention Award). In 2005, she was named a Grand Master by the Science Fiction and Fantasy Writers of America, an honor bestowed only on twenty-two other writers, of whom just two are women. In 2006, she was inducted into the Science Fiction Hall of Fame. Her books have been translated into fourteen languages and have sold more than twelve million copies. These distinctions and statistics are important because she was a leader in the feminist revolution in science fiction, and she also focused on female protagonists and women's issues—child rearing, for example—at a time when strong women were largely absent from the genre. Sarah Lefanu, the author of one of the first books on women and science fiction, *Feminism and Science Fiction*, praises Anne's contributions: "It is great to have Anne's girls and women with their skills and strengths and emotions."

One of the most popular writers of a group of women who began publishing science fiction in the 1960s and 1970s, Anne came to writing later than her peers and was older than many of the other famous science fiction writers who began publishing in those decades: Ursula K. Le Guin and Joanna Russ, among others. And also unlike those writers, Anne faced the struggle of trying to support herself and three children by her writing. Yet like them, Anne became an award-winning writer who helped feminize the genre. Anne brought great emotional depth to her writing. While not as overtly political as Russ or Le Guin, Anne nevertheless challenged traditional ideas about women and science and women as heroes. Her novels' strong emotional appeal can be traced to Anne's own preoccupations and concerns as a member of a generation who came of age during World War II. Disappointed by the opportunities available to her as a highly educated and intelligent young woman, she gravitated to science fiction for the alternatives it offered to an unsatisfactory real world. But she found limited roles for women in the pulp magazines she read, and she consciously wrote her first novel, *Restoree*, "as a tongue-in-cheek protest, utilizing as many of the standard 'thud and blunder' clichés as possible with one new twist—the heroine was the viewpoint character and *she* is always Johanna on the spot."

Like that of other women science fiction writers, Anne's work champions strong female characters, and she positions women in worlds where they have greater opportunities than in the real world. As literary critic Jane Donawerth notes, these women, including Anne, moved the figure of woman as alien in science fiction "from margin to center." At the time Anne began writing, feminist anthropologist Sherry Ortner, in a famous essay, "Is Female to Male as Nature Is to Culture?" (1972), analyzed how women's association with nature was presented as a reason for women's subordination. Taking women's stereotypical association with the natural world, Anne and a number of other women science fiction writers inverted this association, making it into something positive, a strength for their female characters. Anne's dragons, for example, are genetically engineered, telepathic creatures that bond with their humans. The dragons enable humans to live on Pern, providing an alternative to machine transportation and a way for the colonists to fight a life-threatening spore. In making dragons, that had heretofore been featured primarily as evil beasts, into attractive companions, Anne reshaped our cultural image of them. Significantly, she did so in a structure in which queen dragons were the species' leaders. Bonding with female humans, the dragons enable women on Pern to assume positions of leadership; and, as Jane Donawerth explains, "the dragons offer an alternative model for relationship," one that is more positive than traditional masculine domination of women. Similarly, Vonda McIntyre's eponymous character Dreamsnake, for example, is a natural healer who uses genetically altered snakes to cure illness. There are many other instances of feminist science fiction writers who reclaim animals as special partners with women, from Joan Slonczewski to Octavia Butler, but Anne was one of the first, and her Dragonriders of Pern are surely one of the most enduring and most popular of such creations.

A number of women science fiction writers use strong female protagonists whose position as outsiders enables them to connect not only with other beings, but also with other humans. Again Donawerth describes a pattern central to Anne's novels: "the hero intuits the intelligence of another life form" and "establish[es] communication with the aliens before 'developers' destroy them and their planets." Donawerth cites *Dinosaur Planet Survivors* as a prime example.

In Anne's case, her sense of her family as being different, and herself more so, contributed to her sense of sympathy for outsiders and a strong desire that such characters should eventually be appreciated and rewarded for their difference. Her parents, for example, stood out in her suburban New Jersey hometown by their level of education and by their odd habits. Anne's father marched the children in military formations, keeping in practice for the second world war he knew would come, and her mother took the children out of school to see movies. Both parents believed in second sight, or premonitions, and they have family stories of such experiences. So it is no wonder that Anne helped popularize the mental powers, such as telepathy or telekinesis, known as psionic powers, that have become one of science fiction's mainstays. Anne's creation of characters with psionic talents in her Tower and Hive series, or powerful voices, as in the Crystal Singer series, depicts misfits who become valuable to their societies and who find self-worth in their usefulness through their special powers. The short story that later developed into the Tower and Hive series reveals Anne's view on such qualities: it is entitled "A Womanly Talent."

Her first novel, *Restoree,* was a space gothic romance, a new hybrid that few reviewers recognized. Anne wrote the novel because, she said, "After seven years of voracious reading in the field, I'd had it up to the eyeteeth with vapid women." Anne's willingness to write about love, sex, and emotion became her fiction's identifying characteristic. As she later explained, "Emotional content and personal involvement are *expected* in stories by me. In fact, I have had stories returned to me by editors because they lacked these elements." Anne sees these elements as essential to the transformation of the genre during her writing career: "With the injection of emotional involvement, a sexual jolt to the Romance and Glamour, science fiction rose out of pulp and into literature." While there may be other formulations of science fiction's rise to respectability, Anne and other women science fiction writers undoubtedly helped the genre achieve more acclaim through their insistence on characterization and attention to writing style. In the early twenty-first century, we may minimize the extent of this transformation of science fiction, but Justine Larbalestier, who has written an in-depth study of early twentieth-century science fiction, comments that, after reading through fifty years of pulp science fiction, "it became much easier to understand what it was that Russ and Wood and McCaffrey were reacting to." Larbalestier found the misogyny of magazine science fiction overwhelming.

Women science fiction writers often depict the integration and acceptance of feminine values in other societies with a very strong, if implicit, message about the relevance of the feminine in the real world. Dismissed as "diaper copy" in the 1960s, the fiction that Anne and other writers published brought feminine values such as mothering into science fiction. Judith Merril, a strong supporter of Anne's work and an influential editor as well as a writer, in 1947 published a famous story, "That Only a Mother," about a father's and mother's very different reactions to a child's radiation-induced deformities. But Anne's work moves beyond conventional gender roles (there are very few diapers in her fictions) to deal with the emotional needs of girls and women. Excluded herself from any active role in World War II, while her brothers and father were off fighting, Anne depicts female characters who are successful combatants and strategists in her Dragonriders of Pern series, where male and female Dragonriders battle the dreaded Thread, and in the Tower and Hive series, where humans with special psionic talents combat an utterly alien species who threatens the existence of humanity, among many other examples.

Anne repeatedly depicts outcast characters who radically change their circumstances by discovering they have a special skill. Communicating with dragons, singing crystal, or having psionic powers, all may function as stand-ins for what really happened in her life: she felt abandoned as an outsider as a young girl at camp and as a young woman exiled to a southern boarding school, and she lived through a desperate and depressing life of dependency on an abusive husband. Just as Mary Shelley's miscarriages influenced her creation of the novel *Frankenstein*, so Anne McCaffrey's relationships affected what she depicts in her science fiction worlds. Like all writers, I suspected, and this biography confirms, that Anne lived a life that shaped her writing, though Anne's traumas were transformed in her writing.

As soon as I met Anne, I knew I wanted to write her biography. The biographical chapter I had written for my critical study, published in 1996, only made me want to know more; the bare outlines of her life hinted at a depth that just could not be covered in one brief chapter. Though her son Todd had published a brief memoir of his mother, *Dragonholder*, when I pointed out that it would be well augmented by a traditional biography, she granted me permission. Serious setbacks with her health, including a heart attack and a minor stroke, made McCaffrey realize her own writing time might be limited. She wanted to spend her time with fiction, not the more painful subjects that would emerge from dealing with her life history. Finally, in 2000, Anne gave permission for the first extended interview for this biography. She did not ask to see the manuscript before its publication or put any person or subject off limits. Her full cooperation in opening her records and papers to me made this biography possible, and I am grateful to her for her understanding the importance of full access to write a proper biography.

Licensed by my role as biographer, then, I plied her with questions about her life. She deflected the questions from her life to that of her daughter and brother, who had both faced and conquered serious, life-altering illnesses. Anne's unwillingness to talk about herself reveals her unease with her fame and her subscription, even as a very successful writer, to the convention of femininity that requires women to minimize their own struggles to focus on people who have really suffered. She told me that she hasn't even read the Young Adult biography of her, *Anne McCaffrey: Science Fiction Storyteller*, written by Martha Trachtenberg, because, in her words, "I bore myself." But her life has been anything but boring.

A strong and determined woman herself, Anne creates and recreates her fictions in part by drawing on her own life, and even in a brief sketch her biography reveals a fascinating and complex figure: a beautiful young girl too smart to fit into a traditional gender role in high school; a restless young mother who wanted to write; an American and an expatriate writer who became an Irish citizen; an equestrian and animal lover who dreamed of fantasy worlds with perfect relationships between humans and beasts; a wife trapped in an unhappy marriage just as the women's movement took hold.

After I met Anne, I began to see in her the qualities of her many heroines: Helva's passion, Lessa's autonomy and fearlessness, Nimisha's intrepidity, the Rowan's housemotherliness, Masterharper Robinton's skill with people and love of life. In a 1999 visit to New Orleans, the author's regal side emerged, a startling contrast to her Dragonhold persona. My mother and I met her at the elegant Antoine's Restaurant in the French Quarter for dinner, and Anne was every inch a grande dame, charming and elegant. Then a few years later at Dragoncon, a science fiction convention, I saw her use all these skills to charm, negotiate, and survive a four-day event in which she was bombarded by fans, participated in panel discussions, and generally was on display. What I gradually began to see was the complex, contradictory, and engaging personality that had generated the many diverse characters she created.

Anne had been the guest of honor at Dragoncon in 1989, and her presence was a major reason the attendance doubled to over three thousand. She also attended the convention in 1999, traveling there briefly from New Orleans, where she had received the lifetime literary achievement award from the American Library Association. In the intervening years, Dragoncon had exploded into a media con, emphasizing comics, gaming, and film more than print and expanding to over twenty thousand attendees. Yet a "Pern Track," named for McCaffrey's most popular world, continued to be a mainstay and an annual event for many members of the more than two hundred McCaffrey fan clubs. Anne's decision to appear at Dragoncon 2003 was her public statement that, despite her heart attack, stroke, and a number of debilitating falls, she was still very much alive and kicking. She also wanted to promote her first new Pern book in three years, *Dragon's Kin*, which she coauthored with her son Todd. In 2002, she had sent

Todd to Dragoncon to represent her; in 2003, they were there as a team, with Anne loudly proclaiming Todd and her daughter, Gigi, who was back in Ireland, the heirs to her fictional worlds. It was an emotional handing over of the kingdom (or rather, kingdoms, since Anne has created a number of worlds besides Pern).

As Todd was explaining the changes they had made in the first draft of *Dragon's Kin*, a dedicated fan and helper, Lea Day, came in with a cart stacked with books for Anne and Todd to sign. Todd grabbed a handful and began signing the ones his mother had already signed. Lea complimented Anne but explained that she thought Anne was too nice. McCaffrey admitted, "I feel like I am fraudulent and I don't think what I do is all that great." Todd burst in, "That's because you had a shit father." And McCaffrey agreed, saying, "That's a part of it," but she then turned the conversation to the book she was signing for a coffee expert who had helped her with the Freedom series. While the private Anne is open, she also clearly has subjects she would prefer not to discuss.

The wide-ranging discussion and bustling room reminded me of the kitchen table at Dragonhold-Underhill, where similar conversations had taken place during each of my visits. I suddenly realized that it wasn't the place, but Anne herself who created an exciting environment wherever she was. Dragonhold, then, wasn't so much a physical place, but a world that Anne carried with her. It is this world view that she creates in her books—a place where ideas matter, where women and men are equal, where hard work can lead to success, worlds, in short, that are better than what we have today. Yet, there are shortcomings even in McCaffrey's imaginary worlds, where heroines like Moreta die saving others, where loss of life, due to the lack of technology and the harsh conditions on Pern, is common. Anne's own deep feelings of loss when her father and then mother died, when her marriage ended, when a love affair concluded, all fuel her fictions, which many readers unashamedly admit make them cry.

As she lived her own life, Anne also imagined alternatives to her difficult times and wrote her joys and pleasures into her characters' lives. She drew on her family history and her ethnic heritage to create alien worlds. When she lost a family member, when her marriage disintegrated, she drew on the same creative powers to "rewrite" her own life. Yet she has never lost sight of the "dragons" of earlier years, her feelings of insecurity as an adolescent, her frustrations at not being able to sing as she wanted or write as she wanted, the end of her marriage, her emigration, her tumultuous love affairs.

Though she has tamed them—as Lessa Impressed tamed her queen dragon or Menolly tamed a clutch of fire lizards—Anne's emotions, passion, and energy remain near the surface. Her courage in beginning her own life again, in wrestling with her own private dragons, helped her imagine and create characters who could do the same. The only formidable dragons in evidence at Dragonhold-Underhill are artistic representations on her gates and interior walls. Just as Anne turned dragons from feared monsters into humans' best and most intimate friends, she has taken the joys and travails of her life and turned them into art. It is this transformation that this biography will explore, beginning with her family heritage and following her to the Grand Master Award Ceremony in 2005.

CHAPTER 1

An Irish Family Heritage

A family trait—bucking the system.
—Anne McCaffrey, e-mail

FROM A FAMILY CAULDRON of Irish heritage and a tradition of iconoclastic beliefs and behavior emerged a wild child who was a loner. Anne McCaffrey's family background, explored in this chapter, provided much of the raw material that would, decades later, be transformed into science fiction. Like most families, Anne's provided contradictory experiences for her, but she always had a sense of being loved and being special. Even as a very young child, Anne was aware that she had family qualities and traditions against which she would be measured.

Her Irish family heritage, her unusual parents, and her brothers provided her with a strong sense of identity. The qualities that were needed to produce her writing began in her family traditions. Anne's Irish heritage encouraged storytelling and a trust in psychic power. As a middle child and the only daughter, she struggled to create an identity that would impress her father. She learned about military discipline and structure from her father and about using writing to deal with her emotions from her mother, while her grandparents' and her parents' distrust of conformity and their belief in "bucking the system" allowed her to create heroines who did the same. Anne felt that she was different in some way, but when she was a child, this sense of difference did not present the problems that it would for her in adolescence. A happy and well-loved child, she acquired a sturdy sense of self from her family. That self-image incorporated the freedom to be different, the importance of excelling at something, and the determination to succeed, even at a cost. These qualities, along with boisterousness and a belief in psychic phenomena, would at first cause Anne trouble, but those same traits would also enable her, years later, to become a successful author.

Anne's sense of her Irish American heritage came mainly from her grandfather McCaffrey and her grandmother McElroy (née McCann), her other grandparents having died before she had a chance to know them. Three of her four grandparents were Irish American in a time and place, nineteenth-century Boston, when bias against the Irish was common. In the middle of the nineteenth century, job ads placed in the newspapers often read "Help Wanted: Irish need not apply." Requests for domestic servants advised that only "Protestant foreigners" would be considered. Anne's grandparents and parents lived through the NINA (no Irish need apply) times, and they were bitter about the rampant prejudice. While the blatant discrimination would disappear later in the twentieth century, at the beginning of it, the Irish in Boston were "still concentrated in low-status, blue-collar jobs." As they struggled to survive economically amidst virulent anti-Irish prejudice, her grandparents displayed patient resistance, determination, and hope. Anne's grandfathers were typical Irish Americans, one working as a policeman and a boat purser, the other as a journeyman engraver. However, they wanted more for their children than secure but dead-end jobs. Most Irish Americans remained a part of the working class usually for a second and third generation, but Anne's grandparents succeeded in pushing her parents into the upper middle class by means of education.

The one exception to the family Irishness was grandfather McCaffrey's wife, but Anne never knew her. Selina died before Anne McCaffrey was born in 1926, but she has pictures of her; each one has her tall grandfather seated to minimize her grandmother's shortness. They had three daughters and a son, George Herbert, who became Anne McCaffrey's father. A photographic portrait of Anne's grandfather George Hugh, dated 1882, was the first picture he ever had taken. The print shows him in his State of Massachusetts military uniform, tall and thin with large hands, standing erect and unsmiling. A picture of him as an elderly man reveals a shock of white hair, big bushy eyebrows, a large unruly mustache, and a severe expression. There are no photographs of him holding his grandchildren, and Anne doesn't remember ever playing with him.

She was afraid of him. He towered over her, his large bristly mustache protruding toward her, and he was gruff. His house was scary, with enormous dark furniture. It smelled funny. He was her grandfather and a cop. Anne knew that everyone walked carefully around her grandfather McCaffrey: "My grandfather McCaffrey was an imposing man—I was scared stiff of him." While he was not particularly prosperous, he kept a home that seemed large and spacious to young Anne: "The old house in Boston, Roxbury, was not far from where my cousins, Rita and Junni, lived. It was what was known as a railroad house, one room leading into the next. Two stories, clapboard and quite spacious, though dark with huge heavy furniture which scared me for some reason. It had been a farmhouse before the city closed around it." When Anne was a young girl, until she was eleven, she spent a lot of time at her grandfather's. Because her father was doing doctoral research in Boston, the family frequently visited Grandfather McCaffrey in a nearby Boston enclave, 285 Thornton Street, West Roxbury. Her grandfather's home was a place where children were to be seen, not heard, but Anne and her wild cousin Tony McElroy would run madly around the house, playing hide-and-seek and other games while the adults sat and talked. Anne enjoyed playing with her cousins and traveling with her father, but she dreaded encounters with her formidable grandfather.

While young Anne found her grandfather remote and unaffectionate, she also learned to respect him for his toughness and his uncompromising honesty. Family stories about her grandfather's integrity taught her values that she internalized, values that in later years informed her creative work. Over the years, Anne repeatedly heard stories of her grandfather's struggles with authority. He didn't relate these to his granddaughter himself, but her father would talk to her about the family on the long drive from New Jersey to Boston. From these stories, Anne learned the importance of showing tolerance toward others, even when there was a price to pay. Her grandfather never advanced in the Boston police force because he refused to misuse his power. In those days many Irish Americans stuck together, reinforcing their group identity by harassing newer immigrants of other nationalities and showing favoritism toward other Irish Americans, no matter their conduct. George Hugh abhorred such discrimination.

At the end of the nineteenth century and the beginning of the twentieth, Bostonians saw a wave of increased hostility between the older immigrants, the Irish, and the newer Jewish refugees. Historian Dennis Ryan documents that in Boston, "Irish policemen in the early 1900s harassed Jewish peddlers and grocers, charging them with violation of the blue laws, and disrupted their weddings on the pretext that unionized musicians violated city ordinances prohibiting work on Sunday." In answer to this pattern of persecution, Anne's grandfather not only enforced the laws equally on his beat on Salem Street, but also objected to the racial and cultural bias at the core of such discrimination. By treating the Jewish merchants as equals under the law, George Hugh broke with most of his colleagues and countrymen, a truly extraordinary and brave action. "No one persecuted anyone on George McCaffrey's beat," Anne boasts today, echoing her father's words many years ago. She also learned that virtue often reaps unexpected rewards. As a show of gratitude for George Hugh McCaffrey's fair treatment, Jewish merchants (among them prominent shoemakers named Wolf and Sandler and a few tailors) endowed a scholarship to send Anne's father, George Herbert McCaffrey, to the elite Roxbury Latin Grammar School. He took full advantage of the opportunity, applying himself and excelling academically, eventually obtaining a scholarship to Harvard. George Hugh's "bucking the system," then, worked to his son's advantage in ways no one could have anticipated.

From the stories told about Grandfather McCaffrey, Anne also learned the virtue of being confident and assertive, of standing up for what she believed in, even against overwhelming odds. She remembers, "Grandfather, as a police officer, had a high integrity, and got under the skin of some of the politicians with various of his complaints." Another story she often heard at her grandfather's house was the one about how he arrested Honey Fitzgerald, an influential Irish American politician, for electioneering. Honey Fitzgerald later founded an influential Irish American political dynasty through his daughter Rose, who married Joseph P. Kennedy. Fitzgerald had been lobbying hard too close to a polling booth in violation of election laws, and George Hugh arrested him. That George Hugh had the evidence and made the charge stick made the experience all the more galling for Fitzgerald, and likewise gratifying to Anne's grandfather. The McCaffreys often told the story. It's "a family trait—bucking the system," she says. "My father did it as well, so did my brother and so has my older son." Certainly it is a trait that Anne shares and values enough to recreate in many of her fictional characters: Lessa in *Dragonflight* and Killashandra in *Crystal Singer,* for example. And as happened in her family, these characters usually find an unexpected reward.

Her grandfather, as she recalls, "had also been a purser on the Boston-Providence ferry boat, and I remember being taken on that ride with my brothers and my cousin. There is still, I think, a photo of us, taken while in a lifeboat." In the photograph, all four children look delighted to be in the lifeboat, attached to the side of the ferry. Only three years old, Anne adventurously leans over the side, an enormous smile lighting her face.

After her father finished his doctorate, the family traveled less often to Boston, especially after 1938, the year her grandfather died. Although he had not been ill, George Herbert McCaffrey decided he knew without a doubt the day he was dying. He summoned a priest to give him the last rites and promptly expired. His dominant personality, even in death, impressed Anne tremendously. Grandfather McCaffrey's prescience about his death gave impetus to a family belief in second sight or mental powers, a belief common in Ireland and among Irish Americans. Grandfather's foreknowledge of his own death became the marker for a special gift running in Anne's family.

Anne's maternal grandmother and her stories and beliefs also had a profound impact on Anne's life. Like her paternal grandmother, her maternal grandfather died before Anne was born, and Grandmother McElroy spent summers with her son John in Winthrop, Massachusetts, but she lived the rest of the year with Anne's family. Perhaps because she was financially dependent on her children (and resented it), Grandmother McElroy was fiercely independent in her social and political views.

Her grandmother McElroy knew how to make wonderful taffy—if she was in a good mood and inclined to make it. Anne was supposed to help her in the kitchen, but when she did, grandmother McElroy would criticize her father, and, just as bad, she would scold Anne for her character flaws. Anne thought she was a witch. A short woman, she had a long oval face, prominent nose, determined chin, and the beautiful white hair that she passed on to her daughter and granddaughter. Despite Grandmother McElroy's reputation for being stern, family photographs show her smiling at her grandchildren. Grandmother McElroy stressed her family's reputation and accomplishments to her grandchildren. Katie McCann McElroy was full of stories about the McCann family's romantic and impressive past. Katie's grandmother (Anne's great-great grandmother) had been educated at a private convent school in County Wexford, Ireland. An education like that in early nineteenth-century Ireland signals that the McCann family had once been Irish gentry. While she and her husband had even less money than the McCaffreys, her grandmother's social standards were high, due in large part to her family's past. Not only had Anne's great-great-grandmother attended private school in Ireland, but also her great-grandfather had attended college. So while Anne's father was not only a college graduate but eventually received a doctorate, Anne's grandmother was not much impressed.

Because of her grandmother, Anne McCaffrey learned to value education and once again, independence. Katie McCann had been a grade-school teacher, and she was proud of it, but she was even prouder of her parents and grandparents. She talked a lot about her father, who had been "a hedgerow teacher, a Blackrock College student who escaped being jailed by the British for teaching Catholics" during the Protestant ascendancy in the early nineteenth century. Barred from government and military employment and from careers in the law, Irish Catholics of that era were also forbidden to educate their children, except in religious schools that promoted Anglicanism. Like the priests who surreptitiously offered Mass, however, many teachers educated Catholics outside the law, though they faced imprisonment for doing so. Catholic Irish Americans of her grandmother's age valued education so highly because it was a privilege that had been denied them. After his Irish "school" was discovered, Anne's maternal great-grandfather traveled first to Roseneath, Scotland, and from there emigrated to the United States. His McCann brothers, Anne's great-uncles, were also rebels, union organizers working in the Pennsylvania coal fields. In an unpublished essay, she describes them with pride as "Molly Malloys," as Irish American labor organizers were known. Risking their lives to organize workers to fight for better conditions and pay, her great-uncles were heroes to young Anne. The exploits of her great-grandfather and his brothers find new expression in her characters, those who frequently resist occupying forces (as in the Doona and Freedom series). In Anne's novels, too, emigration often appears as a road to a better life, except that in her fiction, her characters emigrate to other planets, not countries. The positive side of hearing about immigration in her youth affected her imagination. It also undoubtedly made it easier for Anne herself to immigrate back to her family's original homeland decades later.

This is not to say that she admired everything about her grandmother. Anne's great-grandfather McCann's staunch Catholicism mutated to something less admirable in Katie McCann McElroy's beliefs. Judgmental and critical, she listened to the radio broadcasts of Father Coughlin, an ultraconservative and anti-Semitic priest. Coughlin opposed the involvement of the United States in European affairs, including World War II, while Anne's father was convinced that the United States would have to enter the war. Anne rejected Grandmother's McElroy's religious and political beliefs, choosing to side with her beloved father. If this wasn't enough to alienate her from her grandmother, Grandmother McElroy would commandeer the radio to listen to Coughlin when Anne and her brothers wanted to listen to the Lone Ranger.

While Anne rejected her grandmother's political beliefs and dogmatism, she did learn from her the joys of cooking. A cosseted youngest daughter, Katie McCann had not been allowed to cook before she married. She and her husband were never prosperous enough to hire kitchen help. Katie found not knowing cooking such a handicap she was determined that her daughter and granddaughter would never suffer. Like her mother, Anne grew up learning how to make meals. She says, "I cannot remember NOT knowing how to cook. Grandmother made Irish potato pancakes (from leftover mashed ones) and also was a dab hand [with] molasses taffy, the making of which appealed to all us kids when we could talk grandmother into concocting it. Lamb stew was also a favorite of hers which I learned to make early in my life. I think those two Irish dishes were the last Irish in her capacity. She always made jellies and preserves which I had to help her with. An atavistic sense of providing for the bad season which still plagues me." A fear of imminent catastrophe is understandable in the daughter of an Irish family driven to the New World by the Famine. One of Anne's most famous creations, the mycorrhizoid spore, called Thread, that falls periodically on Pern, dislocates populations and destroys all organic life. Thread surely draws on Anne's awareness of the "late blight disease" that caused potato famine and an Irish diaspora. Making and preserving food in her life and fiction reflects a need to prepare for difficult times, but all who have eaten at Anne's table agree she has turned this drive into art.

Mary T. Brizzi was one of the first critics to note the emphasis on food in her fiction, explaining that in McCaffrey's novels, "Bad food is a disgrace or a warning. . . . Good food is evidence of thrift, good deeds, and industry." Anne has edited two cookbooks, *Cooking Out of This World* and *Serve It Forth*, and is known for her own excellent cooking, especially her pies. Anne believes that her grandmother passed on not only her cooking skills, but also a tendency to second sight, which ran in Anne's father's family. Katie's dead sister (also named Anne) appeared to her, and when a somewhat frightened Grandmother McElroy asked her sister what heaven was like, her sister replied that "it would do." Unfortunately, second sight did not protect Anne's grandmother from financial misfortune and bitterness. Her husband, Anne's grandfather, had saved five thousand dollars, an impressive sum in the year he proposed to Katie McCann, Anne's grandmother. She refused him, and James McElroy then spent a year on Mississippi River steamboats, gambling away his savings. He returned home and proposed again. This time he was accepted, but told no one he'd lost his fortune. This legend of financial disappointment, which had lifelong consequences for the McElroys, may explain some of Katie McElroy's bitter temper. As for Anne, the way she reacted to her grandmother's sharpness was with the determination not to be so unpleasant. Indeed, a bad temper is often a sign of an evil character in Anne's novels.

Grandfather McElroy died before Anne could remember him, but she respects him as the source of the family's artistic talent. According to family accounts, Anne's mother and brother inherited their ability to draw from him; he was a journeyman printer and an engraver in New York and Pennsylvania. Both Anne and her brother Kevin's widow, Marcia, still own copies of an engraving of his, of a ship in a storm-tossed sea. She also treasures a spoon and small bronze pitcher he crafted. More significantly, Anne's musical interests and talent, which are repeatedly reflected in her books, seem to be descended from Grandfather McElroy's other art, skill with a fiddle. He was a characteristically Irish musical performer.

Although they were another generation removed from Ireland, Anne's parents, too, manifested the passion, dramatic flair, love of storytelling, and respect for extrasensory powers that are often associated with the Irish. Anne loved both her parents, but she was always aware that her family wasn't quite normal. Her parents, she says, failed to fit in suburban America not because of their Irish ethnicity, but because of their idiosyncrasies. Her mother scribbled stories; her father maintained his military status after the war ended; neither parent attended church, and they traveled all over the world when few other middle-class couples went for extensive international travel.

Anne McCaffrey's parents were remarkable people and crucial influences on her writing. She has said: "If I were asked to choose which influence was the most important in my life, I'd have to answer that it was my parents. Neither fit the patterns of style and behavior in the 1920s, '30s, and '40s for our middle-class status." Her father, who had fought during World War I, kept up his army reserve commission. He would call his children using his "parade ground voice," and after 1938 he practiced his command voice by having his children march up and down their driveway. It is a measure of her love for her father and her own quirkiness that after recounting this story of her father having his children march, she is still unsure why her family was seen as strange. Anne remembers that the neighbor children thought that her parents were "different though I never sussed out [*sic*] why. Except that Dad was a Harvard graduate [and PhD] and mother was taking courses at the local Teacher's College which struck a lot of kids as 'odd.'"

In the 1930s and 1940s, the McCaffreys' educational interests and attainments were unusual. In 1936, according to the 1939 *Statistical Abstract*, only 2,768 doctoral degrees were awarded in the United States, when the country's total adult population was approximately 75 million. Only 270,000 women attended college in that year, out of an adult female population of approximately 37 million. Yet perhaps Anne's parents' most distinguishing quality was a willingness to embrace difference. In her words, "My parents insisted on our tolerance for others and were exceptionally broad-minded about race, creed AND color." Although they considered themselves Catholic, her parents did not attend Mass regularly. At their grandmother's insistence, Anne says that she and her brothers "were sent off for Mass every Sunday and holy day but [she] never attended with [her] parents." Her parents' behavior and what the Catholic Church taught were at variance, so she chose to follow her parents' example: "I learned more of tolerance and understanding from my parents' attitudes toward things than I did from church teaching which . . . I could ignore." Her parents had other distinctive qualities. For example, Anne's father was a fanatical gardener, and she remembers with fondness the family's annual neighborhood Tulip Party, after which each lady left with a dozen tulips from their thousands of tulips. She remembers that, after her brother Hugh broke his arm, her father encouraged them all to play cards every Sunday and included the neighborhood children in their games. The exercise of hand and eye in a card game called Multiple Canfield improved Hugh's co-ordination, but playing cards on a Sunday in suburban New Jersey in the 1930s caused comment among the neighbors.

Anne has modeled many of her characters' relationships on her parents—two extraordinary, feisty, and original individuals. From their marriage she had an example of a realistic, working long-term relationship. She notes: "Once we were grown up . . . I know they had a very good time together. . . . Tolerance I think and great intelligence worked where other things might not." "Dad and Mother were well matched," Anne said. "He had the 90% perspiration to make a genius, [and] she had the 1% in-spiration. They respected each other." At one point, when Anne was fourteen, her mother was quite exasperated by her husband's oddities and complained to a family friend, a doctor. The friend pointed out that perhaps she herself wasn't so easy to live with. She repeated this story to Anne, explaining that married people had to accommodate each other's peculiarities. Most often in Anne's fiction, her characters develop compatibility and mutual respect over the course of an entire novel. Her characters above all seem to have to learn to respect one another's opinions and work, just as her parents did.

Both parents cared deeply about literature and one or both of them read aloud to Anne every night. McCaffrey's mother tended toward Rudyard Kipling's novels and short stories and the sci-ence fiction of A. Merrit; her father declaimed poetry by Kipling and Henry Wadsworth Longfellow. Anne recalled that her father "had a marvelous voice in which to roll out those phrases." Those literary preferences had an effect on their daughter's work, for Anne's writing has the epic range and exotic settings of Kipling's, the magical science of Merrit's, and the storytelling and lyricism characteristic of both Kipling and Longfellow.

Anne's father, George Herbert McCaffrey, was a commanding presence, both in the army during both World Wars and as the head of his household. His determination to be colorful and unique can be seen in his nickname, reflecting his title, but spelled phonetically, "the Kernel." He loved his children, but he also treated them as if they were his minions. Anne remembered that "he had a series of cussings . . . Damn it, Goddamnit, and Goddamnitall to hellingone . . . the severity of which indicated to us [his children] when to make ourselves scarce." She recalled him as "a precise and neat man, as an officer often is, and he hated confusion and disorder."

A hard taskmaster who never took a holiday, he nevertheless devoted time to his children, reading to them, supervising their schoolwork, assigning them chores. But he also took his daughter on trips, not only to his family in Boston but also to his job in New York. She acknowledges, "As the only daughter, I was sometimes my father's pet." While she and her father were more distant when she was teenager, as a young girl, she could be spoiled and included on his journeys. Anne remembers, "Dad worked in the Battery area and it was great fun to take the train to Jersey City, the ferry across the Hudson [River] and walk up to his building. . . . Dad would often take me to his office and his secretary, Mary Duggan, would keep an eye on me. Then we'd have lunch at Schrafft's where I would have chocolate fudge for dessert. That usually was my birthday treat from my father, going to the office with him." Anne experienced Take Your Daughter to Work Day long before it was commonplace. Being taken to work by a parent encourages a girl to take herself seriously and to think about having a career. Of course, in the 1930s, the idea of taking one's daughter to work and, further, encouraging her to think of a career was almost unheard of. Nor was it just any job Anne conceived. When she applied for jobs after college, she would seek to follow her father's path by applying for work, whether in the government or a corporation, that would take her abroad.

Tough and feisty himself, the Kernel expected his children,

including Anne, to be aggressive. G. H. taught all his children to swim by throwing them in the pool—literally "sink or swim." Anne, whose father called her "Puss," wasn't frightened when she learned to swim this way because the "lesson" took place at the Montclair Athletic Club in an indoor pool. She remembers floundering over to the side and grabbing the side wall. As tough as he was with his children, G. H. was tougher with himself. Anne's brother Kevin remembered his father hiking in a Montclair Park, toting a forty-pound pack at age fifty, preparing himself for what he saw as the next war, which he saw as inevitable. "He pushed himself hard," Kevin recalled. And the children responded, though the boys were more able to achieve in ways their father could appreciate. Both Kevin and Hugh earned more achievement points than any other Boy Scouts in their respective troops, but Anne had to try to find other ways to impress her father. She did so in part by playing games with her brothers and being a tomboy. This made sense because Anne's father taught her the same skills he taught his sons: "how to set a screw or drive a nail, saw wood, run properly, even [to] clean weapons. He *expected* much of his children." He did not, however, praise them, an absence Anne attributes to generational differences: "He was of the generation which felt the younger one should do its duty without the need of praise." Anne desperately wanted her father's approval, as did her brothers, but none of them felt they achieved the high standards he had set for them. G. H. McCaffrey often quoted a phrase that exemplified his standard; it was supposed to explain the difference between Harvard graduates and the graduates of other, inferior universities: Harvard graduates had "the ineffable consciousness of effortless superiority." Unfortunately, and perhaps understandably, with such a domineering father, the McCaffrey children never developed that strong sense of self-assurance that their father had.

G. H. McCaffrey himself made a good job of living up to his rather overbearing creed of superior achievement, but at least he did so with a sense of humor. His grandson Todd, Anne's second son, describes him this way: "Gruff, stern and insistent were the qualities most remembered by his children. GH or the 'Kernel,' (for Colonel), as he was now [during World War II] signing his letters, was a disciplinarian of the old school. . . . He ha[d] a dry sense of humor." He liked puns, and his correspondence with his family is peppered with witticisms. One his grandson Todd quotes in *Dragonholder* is his alliterative response to a similarly worded telegram Anne sent him (about post-surgery recovery): "PATERNAL PARENT POSITIVELY PURRING PLEASURE PAST PERFORMANCE . . . PRESENTLY PEEING PERFECTLY."

Only one of George Herbert McCaffrey's photo portraits shows him smiling. Taken sometime during his graduate school days, the picture shows a handsome and self-assured young man in a suit. Another, from a campaign card, shows him in a starched collar with gold-rimmed glasses like a young H. G. Wells. In almost every other family photo, he is in uniform and stares directly at the camera. Trim and fit throughout his life, G. H. himself exercised the self-discipline and control he demanded of his children. Intense and hard working, he throve on challenges. Though he taught for three years at Harvard, he found he needed a more active career. Managerial and organizational skills were his forte, and it was a point of pride for him to make substantial improvements whenever he was in charge. His more notable achievements include revising the New York State tax code, overseeing a bridge being built in Italy (Ponte Caffreo is named after him), and introducing new farming methods in the American zone around Vienna after World War II.

Anne's father was a person of importance in the larger world. "My Dad was the famous one," she says. He graduated from Harvard with high honors, and he expected high achievement from his children, though none of his offspring equaled his formal educational accomplishments. Although he moved well beyond his father's standing in society, G. H. retained from his upbringing an interest in and respect for the police and the military. After earning a master's degree in government in 1913, he received a fellowship to study police systems in Ireland and elsewhere in Europe. Continuing his graduate study, he was awarded a Harvard University doctorate in 1937. His dissertation was titled "The Integration and Disintegration of Metropolitan Boston." His interest in urban planning demonstrated a commitment to organization and structure, and how their design could be used to benefit people. Anne's creation of fictional societies and worlds can be seen as achievements paralleling his accomplishments.

G. H. McCaffrey held a reserve commission in the army while he was employed by the Commerce and Industry Association of New York. Then, during World War II, he served in a number of prominent positions. On December 7, 1941, after the attack on Pearl Harbor, Hawaii, he had volunteered to serve his country in any capacity, so in January 1942 he was posted to Georgia at his reserve rank of lieutenant colonel. Because he had been trained in a Military Governor's course at the University of Virginia, he was sent overseas in May 1943. Anne remembered, "Whatever bonding might have occurred later [between her and her father] was scotched by the war because Dad was away from the time I was fifteen until the year I graduated from college. I wrote him often and he would find time to write back. Every letter from him was much treasured by me." Having a successful father who was a public figure affected Anne in many ways: she admired the values he stood for, and she wanted to live up to his accomplishments. She also realized that his commitment to the military took precedence over his family's needs.

During World War II, G. H. McCaffrey had a distinguished career in the army, where his courage and independence served him well. He "was the first man off the first LCT to land at Licata, Sicily," Anne says. "There were only kids on that LCT, scared of their first sight of combat with planes trying to strafe the stone wharf . . . so Dad walked up and down like a Sunday stroller, smoking a cigarette and encouraging the orderly landing of troops." While Anne's proud recounting of this story reveals her admiration for her father, she was nonetheless jealous of his military affiliation and his devotion to his garden. He "was a gruff, undemonstrative man, with rigid standards requiring excellence and obedience. I used to complain that he cared more about his (damned) Army and his wretched garden than his kids," she recalls. His final assignment was as military governor of Agrigento, Italy. There he displayed some characteristically Irish intuition when one dark night he suddenly ordered his driver to stop, sensing trouble. Sure enough, just ahead a bridge had been destroyed. G. H. was also involved in the rescue of the Lipizzaner mares from the Soviets as they advanced on Czechoslovakia. All through his military career, G. H. had hidden his heart attacks and diabetes from his superiors. Eventually, however, his hard work and stress resulted in a bout of illness that could not be ignored, and, unhappily, he returned to his old job at the Commerce and Industry Association. He did better after the war, welcoming a chance to help the Japanese with their tax system, and he and his wife lived in Japan from 1950 to 1952. G. H. also volunteered to work for the United Nations in Korea but was forced back to a stateside hospital by a prostate operation and, later, tuberculosis.

As a teenager and a young woman, then, Anne was separated both physically and emotionally from her adored father. This left her desperately wanting to prove herself to him. Because becoming a published writer was an accomplishment she thought he would respect, she went to tell him when she got her first paycheck (a hundred dollar check from Sam Moskowitz for her first story, "Freedom of the Race"). Arriving at her parents' house, she found him doing yard work. When she told him her good news, she says, "I think my father grunted. He was, at the time, busy trying to fix a bare spot in the front lawn. Being him, he wanted to have a perfect front lawn. . . . So, when he discovered that a huge boulder was protruding up out of the ground, too big for him to dig up, he got a blow-torch and heated the top of the rock, then poured cold water on it, causing the stone to crack. He continued these exercises until he reduced the upthrust some eight inches, which would allow grass to grow and flourish on the spot." Her father's faint acknowledgment of what was, to Anne, an important moment—the publication of her first story—was typical of their relationship. She wanted encouragement and praise, and her father was incapable of giving them.

The Kernel died on January 25, 1954, when Anne was twenty-seven and not yet a famous writer. His stature was evident in his *New York Times* obituary, which filled a twelve-inch column. "G. H. McCaffrey, 63, OFFICER IN TWO WARS," runs the headline of a piece detailing his many achievements. Anne McCaffrey's father is very clearly her hero and, as she would admit years later, "I got a father fixation." Anne dedicated what she describes as her favorite book, *The Ship Who Sang*, to her father. Words in the novel's dedication to him, "soldier, citizen, patriot," appear to be a model for many of her heroic male characters, from F'Lar to Master Robinton. G. H. did not live to see Anne McCaffrey become one of the most popular writers of her time, yet it may be his very absence that influenced her creation of male characters and her use of military conflicts in plots. With her real-life hero gone, she recreated her father in her fictional heroes.

His death, quite early on in her writing career, might also have enabled it emotionally. Like Leslie Stephens, the father of another remarkable female writer, Virginia Woolf, McCaffrey dominated his daughter. Of her father, Leslie Stephens, Woolf writes, "His life would entirely have ended mine. What would have happened? No writing, no books; —inconceivable." Anne does not describe her father in such harsh terms, and, indeed, he may not have been quite so forbidding, but his death did mean she could never prove herself to him. As she says: "My father's death was a catastrophe for me. . . . I now know why. . . . We had different standards and principles and he never allowed me to have mine. He had very high ones and I wobbled." Yet her father's death meant also that Anne would not be burdened by his lack of support. She would still live up to his high standards by working very hard on every book, but she would do it with her mother's enthusiastic encouragement, and without her father's characteristic indifference. Nor was indifference G. H.'s worst fault. He was judgmental. His will provides a salient example. After college, Anne had borrowed some money from her father when it appeared she would go abroad for a job. When he died, she had not yet repaid the money, and she was therefore cut out of his will. Outraged by her husband's provision, Anne's mother blacked out those sections of the will, sparing Anne's feelings. She used her own money to make sure Anne received her just inheritance.

Despite his exacting nature, she loved her father very much, and her loss affected her stories. Losing a father figure or a male mentor is a pattern that often appears in her fiction. For example, in *The Ship Who Sang*, Helva, the human who is the "Brain" of a spaceship, must cope with the devastating loss of her male partner. She watches him die, unable to save him. The loss is the substance of the first of the collection's tales, while the subsequent stories detail Helva's healing and, eventually, learning to love again. So, too, has Anne healed from the loss of her father by finding other individuals to love and admire.

While Anne McCaffrey's father endured great hardship and performed heroically in the line of duty, Anne McCaffrey's mother modeled another type of bravery, a feminine strength that would appear in all of Anne's heroines. She recounts her mother's bravery during World War II, when she coped with having her husband and son Hugh overseas while her son Kevin was seriously ill. Even before World War II, Anne's mother often ran the household. In the late 1930s, her husband was working on the New York City Building Code and often had to stay over in Albany, the state capital. Anne's mother was stalwart and independent, and she encouraged her daughter's fortitude. Of Anne Dorothy McElroy McCaffrey's example, Anne writes, "Is it any wonder I write about strong women?"

Throughout Anne's life her mother was more supportive than her father. The children called their father the Kernel, while their mother was Mum. Yet Mum was no more conventional than their father. Anne's mother had beautiful hair that turned a bright white while she was in her thirties. She modeled a wild and free femininity, due in part, her son Kevin thinks, in reaction to her own mother's school-teacherly primness. It is perhaps not surprising that the neighbors called her "the white-haired witch." Anne would depict independent and wild female characters over and over in her fictions, and she also modeled her mother's behavior in her own life. Unlike her father, who is almost always stern in family photos, her mother fairly scintillates in family photos. Her hair charmingly tousled, she beams at the camera. She seems well aware of her reputation for beauty. She welcomes the camera's gaze. A natural charmer, she exudes self-confidence. Tall and full-figured, Anne's mother was a lively presence. She laughed more often than her husband, telling jokes to break family tension. When her mother caught Anne and her brother sneaking her unusual Puerto Rican cigarettes, she used reverse psychology. She told Anne and Kevin that they were welcome to smoke. After this invitation, smoking cigarettes no longer seemed as much fun to them. A strong but very feminine woman, she liked Blue Grass, a perfume by Helena Rubinstein, and usually wore a well-cut suit or skirt and sweater combination—often the sweater was one she had knitted herself. Her mother doted on Anne but found her tomboyish proclivities a bit frustrating. While her father would raise his voice and swear when he was angry, her mother had subtler but even more compelling ways of showing her children she was angry. Tightened lips and a certain tense expression let her children know they were in trouble. Yet even when she reproved them, they knew she loved them.

Anne's mother had a tremendous amount of energy and intellectual curiosity. She studied French at a nearby college and tried unsuccessfully to teach the language to her children. Active in the League of Women Voters, she had a wide range of friends and usually went out in the afternoon, often with others to see movies. A devoted movie-goer, she pulled Anne and Kevin out of school to go see *Gone with the Wind*. Her mother's endorsement of popular culture helped Anne see the value of science fiction at a time when it was still dismissed as "pulp fiction." Her mother believed that popular culture was important. Though Anne's mother had her mother to assist her, she also had hired household help. There was still a lot of housework to be done, with three children and a big house. But Anne's mother always found time to read for pleasure and often scribbled ideas in a notebook. A voracious reader of mystery novels, she devoured books by Josephine Tey, Ngaio Marsh, and Agatha Christie, and even wanted to write mysteries herself. Her mother's love of mystery novels gave Anne familiarity with that genre, and, indeed, many of her books have a puzzle or a mystery at their centers. Her mother also encouraged her to write, in Anne's words, "because it kept me busy and out of trouble, and also because she knew that writing things down that bothered me would get them out." Thus encouraged,

Anne found therapeutic or cathartic writing a strategy she would employ throughout her life.

Anne's mother, Anne McElroy McCaffrey, was energetic and positive, qualities thrown into sharp relief by the fortitude with which she managed the consequences of an accident she sustained. While Anne's mother was unconscious under anesthesia in a dentist's office, her foot slipped into a heating vent, and she badly burnt two of her toes. The injury was serious; one toe had to be amputated, and, in Anne's words, Mum "was in pain a great deal of the time after that but learned to walk again and take up her life." Because of this injury, she always had to wear special shoes and couldn't walk or run very well. Watching her mother uncomplainingly deal with an injury made a big impression on Anne—and on her brother Kevin, who for years coped bravely with a life-threatening illness. Not surprisingly, courage, perseverance, and the ability to face physical hardship are distinguishing qualities among many of Anne's heroines. This is especially true of Helva in *The Ship Who Sang*.

While her grandfather and father occasionally experienced second sight or precognition, it was her mother in whom "the sight" manifested itself most strongly and strikingly. In fact, Mum's precognition was, perhaps, directly responsible for the family's ability to hang onto its middle-class lifestyle during the Depression. As Todd J. McCaffrey explains, "The Depression was not the major trauma to the McCaffreys that it was to so many others in that era. Mrs. McCaffrey had 'had a feeling' about the stock market a few days before the crash and had pulled all her money out. For the next few days GH had chided her foolishness—but he got very quiet when the market crashed." According to family lore, the gift of the sight appears primarily in her female line. Her mother's confidence in second sight fueled her daughter's belief in the power of her own intuitions. As a teenager Anne herself had a psychic experience: the phone rang, and though her mother assumed something had happened to her husband, young Anne McCaffrey somehow knew that it was her grandfather Hugh who was ill. On another occasion, when she was at boarding school during World War II, Anne woke up in the middle of the night, worried to death. Her mother telephoned to report a similar feeling the next day, and six months later they found out that George Herbert's ship had been attacked and that he had spent an hour and a half in a lifeboat on that very night, at that very time. These experiences, then, are the personal background underlying the scientifically explained telepathy appearing in many of Anne's series. From *Dragonflight*'s Lessa to *The Tower and the Hive*'s Rowan and Damia, her heroines rely on their psionic powers to save not only their families, but even entire planets or planetary systems. Anne has taken a family legacy of second sight and, by putting it into science fiction settings, transformed it into psionics: mental powers accepted and powerful in their worlds.

Her mother, in fact, gave her daughter many gifts. Mum was a lifesaver to her, always there when Anne needed help. Indeed, after her daughter's divorce, Mum helped Anne and her family cope by splitting expenses with them. As Anne describes it, "Mother paid half the rent and money towards the food since Dublin was more expensive to live in than I realized. I couldn't have survived those early years without the financial support." Fortunately, unlike Anne's father, her mother lived to see her daughter's writing career blossom. She acknowledged her mother's importance to her in the dedication of *Dragonquest* to Anne Dorothy McElroy McCaffrey.

Anne's girlhood was also strongly shaped by her two brothers: Hugh, called "Mac" by his family, and Kevin. Anne was born on April 1, 1926. Hugh "Mac" McCaffrey, born on August 17, 1922, was almost four years her senior. Her brother Kevin, born September 8, 1927, was her baby brother. Anne McCaffrey occasionally experienced the classic fate of a middle child, feeling lost and neglected between two other siblings. She describes her childhood as being defined in part by having "two brothers on either side to knock me about." Anne was molded by her birth order and by her sex, both factors that had an impact on her upbringing. According to studies, middle children are "the most likely to be neglected." Almost the very words Anne uses appear in articles about birth order: "middle children often feel kicked around." A psychologist describes the middle child in terms that fit Anne McCaffrey: "They're not the fighters that the first ones are, and they're not the babies who need to be taken care of." Mac was a fighter in a number of ways; sent off to military school for discipline, he later joined the CIA. And Kevin's severe illness reinforced his birth order as youngest—he required special care for years. Anne's response to being one of a few women writing science fiction in the 1950s and 1960s is characteristic of the middle child, as described by a psychologist: "'I always felt like I had to do it better,' says a middle child, 'because that's the only way I was going to be seen. I had to be different, so I am different.'"

Something of a tomboy, Anne enjoyed playing traditionally masculine games. She played with her brothers as much as they would let her. For example, she was "allowed to kick goals for her brothers' team." While her brothers were making and painting lead soldiers, she was occasionally permitted "to melt lead and pour them [the soldiers] in the molds. Keve was good at painstakingly painting them [the soldiers], but the boys didn't like me homing in on 'their' toys," she explains. Kevin and Hugh were quite fond of each other, and their games were much rougher and more physical than the games girls were supposed to play. Hugh was very fond of Kevin, especially as he never ratted on Hugh, even when Hugh nearly blew his brother's leg off when the boys were playing with their father's .38. The bullet went off inches from Kevin's leg, as Kevin sat at the old teak desk in the boys' room. The family regularly played Canfield (a Solitaire-like card game with multiple players) and Monopoly together, games that stress competition and aggression. The family was fond of chess, but Anne didn't do as well at it as her brothers did. When she teamed up with her mother, however, they would beat her father and brother Kevin, even though Kevin was the best chess player of the family. This is one example of how Anne would learn the importance of women working together, a lesson emphasized in her novels. As most girls do, she learned traditionally feminine games; she played with paper dolls and doll clothes, a popular girls' activity in the 1930s. As she dressed her dolls, McCaffrey created stories for them. She also enjoyed dressing up the family

37

cat, Thomas, and wheeling him around in a baby carriage. While many children treat their pets as dolls, in Anne's case we can see the beginning of a lifelong treatment of animals as part of the family. This enduring attitude results in the creation of fictional dragons that are part of intimate relationships in the world of Pern.

She was always closer to the brother she calls Keve. When I asked her what it was like growing up with two brothers, she replied, "I'll give you an example of that problem. When I got to Radcliffe, Hugh wouldn't introduce me to friends because he didn't think I was good enough. Keve, on the other hand, didn't think his friends were good enough to associate with me." (The boys attended Harvard while Anne went to college at Radcliffe, which at that time was a separate women's school). Hugh and Anne had a tumultuous relationship until both were adults. She understands it as classic sibling rivalry: "I think it was pure sibling rivalry. . . . [H]e was the elder and had been displaced by the girl." As is often the case, Hugh, older than Anne by four years and older than Kevin by five, lorded over the younger two. Anne remembers, "Hugh would skite off to stay with friends across the street and Kevin and I knew it, but never would have dared peach on him." Kevin was more willing to play with his older sister, whom he admired. When they were in their early twenties, he and Anne even had first- and third-floor apartments in a building owned by their mother in their hometown of Montclair. Proud of his sister's writing, in 2002 Kevin had a whole wall in his home devoted to leather-bound copies of his sister's books. Though it took a number of years, Anne and Hugh eventually reached an amicable understanding. Anne helped her brother Hugh with his first and only book, *Khmer Gold*, published posthumously in 1988. In his dedication of the book, his words typify a family tendency toward blunt speaking: "To my sister, Anne McCaffrey, who kicked me in the ass until I started to write."

In one childhood photo, Anne looks like she is squealing with happiness. She has a huge grin on her face and has her arms crossed out and forward. In another picture, a somber Anne stares straight at the camera, her arms straight down at her side. When I asked her which pose was more characteristic of her early childhood, she replied, "I was definitely a volatile temperament so both were characteristic, depending on the circumstances." This self-characterization fits almost all her heroines, from Helva in *The Ship Who Sang* to the Dragonrider Moreta. Like their creator, these characters can be temperamental, but they are always good-hearted and generous. Anne's earliest memory reveals her daring and exuberance. The memory, she acknowledges, was probably reinforced by her parents retelling the tale, but that it was retold so often means the story reflects how her parents saw and reinforced her identity as a hell-raiser. She says, "I remember the lighting in the back room of our first house on Bellevue Avenue, so some of it has to come from me. . . . The sun coming in, all the lights on in the room and the smell of wall-paper paste. I remember facing the windows, with a dark loom to one side and my mother's hands on my shoulders as I say, 'Oh, I am a bad girl!' With my own hands shielding my buttocks. I had evidently fallen into the tub of wall-paper paste and my father was trying to finish repapering the room. It was on a Sunday so the paste I had dripping on me might have made the difference of him finishing the job or having to hold it over." This anecdote suggests that Anne was a much-loved child because her antics were considered amusing, if not encouraged.

Another early memory concerns a more serious escapade. Anne's grandmother was watching the children play at the beach while Anne's parents were at a party. Rambunctious Anne ran up a seawall and fell off it and into the water, breaking her arm and fracturing her skull. She was only five years old, but she vividly remembers her grandmother being angry at her, pulling her up the long walk to the hotel, and calling her parents to come get their injured daughter. Her parents drove her to Children's Hospital in Boston, where Anne received seven stitches. On the long drive to the hospital, her mother held her tightly, not realizing that her daughter's arm was broken and that she was crying from the pain of the tight embrace. Anne was also a bit of a rapscallion in other, less dangerous matters. Her brother Kevin remembered how much she despised liver and that she "devised a scheme to hide it in the joints of the table" during dinner.

Anne fondly recalls her childhood as a happy and healthy one. She remembers having mastoiditis (a swelling in the lower region of her skull), but no other serious childhood ailments. Her brother Kevin recalled that she sucked two fingers on her left hand into childhood, and her "parents tried to do everything to break the habit. . . . [H]er fingers actually developed ridges and they were afraid that she would cause her teeth to protrude. . . . They even had some metal caps with sleeves tied onto her wrists." Indomitable, however, Anne escaped this contrivance and stopped sucking her fingers only when she was ready to stop. She describes her younger self as "a godawful, ego-centric extrovert," and adds that at school, "I made a career of bucking the system and spent a good deal of my time either in the corridor, for talking too much, or at the principal's office waiting to have an 'interview.' I probably would have been considered hyperactive in today's psychological profiles." Anne's best friend was Virginia Hamilton, the daughter of a principal and a former teacher. Virginia "had a room over an attic, a sort of eyrie, and she was strong enough of will that I would compromise with her. There were other girls, but they only 'tolerated' me and I knew it." McCaffrey's solitude is typical of middle children, who in one study were found to be "the least popular." Anne's description of her childhood also fits her heroines, such as Menolly from *Dragonsinger* or the Rowan from the Tower and Hive series. Gifted and precocious, these protagonists have few friends until they discover their place in life and how to use their great talents constructively.

Children who are advanced for their age often look to adult role models, in part because they are ahead of their peer group. Like other such children, Anne had significant relationships with adults. She admired her fifth-grade teacher, Mrs. Butler, who was notable for being a Quaker, a nonconformist, and tolerant. She once made a quilt using pieces of clothes from all the children in her class. Her other close childhood confidante (besides her best friend, Virginia Hamilton) was a housekeeper. While there were a number employed during Anne's childhood (one she recalls only as Fat Catherine), Ella Patella lasted the longest. While Anne's mother did the cooking, Ella would prepare food, and young Anne would help her peel potatoes or scrape carrots. There was a semi-private space, a landing up a few stairs from the kitchen, where Ella would iron. While she was ironing, Ella, who had no children, would listen as Anne confided in her. In Anne's words, "[I] would talk my heart out to her because I really was such a difficult child . . . [and] she was always kind and supportive. She was a significant personality in my young life." Like many a precocious child, Anne found that supportive adults understood her better than her peers could.

While Anne loved to read, she also had many other childhood activities or adventures that shaped her love of science fiction. When Anne and her brothers had done their garden work properly, they were allowed to go to children's matinees. She was influenced by the texts that shaped many science fiction directors and writers: "I remember *The Lone Ranger* serial and Buster Crabbe in *Flash Gordon*—also Roy Rogers. I used to listen to the radio serials of the Lone Ranger, lying on the floor, head under the desk in which the radio was housed, because the speaker was underneath it, and we had to keep the volume low not to bother Grandmother." Anne McCaffrey didn't just listen to exciting adventures—she also created her own. She recalls "skiving out of the house to go climb in the quarry—it wasn't something I was allowed to do, but could pass a lot of time for me. I was as popular with my peer group as pimples so playing by myself was frequent. I did love climbing on old granite faces. Dangerous, but then, fun!" Again, her heroines never shy away from physical danger, but relish it as young Anne did.

In addition to being physically active, Anne began writing adventure stories. At age nine, she wrote a Western novel called *Flame, Chief of Herd and Track*, the eponymous character being a horse. Unfortunately, no copy of this juvenile fiction exists, but the title and genre reveal her interest in adventure fiction and horses. She had already begun taking horseback riding lessons at the South Orange Arsenal, and she kept up her riding at Girl

Scout camp in the summers. The thrill of being in charge of a large, powerful animal and the affection she received from horses would later develop into her most popular creation, the dragons of Pern that humans could ride. Anne's dramatic and storytelling impulses merged in her habit of telling herself stories, out loud, to put herself to sleep. Sometimes, as she acted out her story, she got quite loud, and her father, whose bedroom was next to hers, "would thump on the wall" to shut her up. As she grew older, the stories became more romantic and less action oriented, but she remembered, "It was such fun that I'd go back and retell the story over and over and eventually fall asleep. . . . It was one reason I hated to sleep with anyone because I couldn't 'think' the stories: they had to be acted out, out loud, with me playing all the parts and sound effects. . . . It was, however, a habit that marriage eliminated completely." But this habit marked her writing. As her editor Shelly Shapiro explained, even today, "When Anne writes it, she lives it."

While she knew that she could not follow her father's footsteps into the military, Anne was also aware of the threat of war. More than other children her age, she understood how politics could influence what a person could do in this world. As a child growing up in the 1930s and 1940s, with politically astute parents, Anne McCaffrey was knowledgeable about the problems in Europe. Her beloved father "was always aware of [political] affairs . . . and [he] deplored the German movement, especially after my Uncle John, going in the capacity of a cotton-mill superintendent, came back from Germany and said that all the machinery he had seen could be retooled for munitions." Despite his age, her father began preparing himself for war, surely affecting his children's view of the world. She says, "I remember that, after that, Dad started long hikes to get himself fit and went to ALL of the meetings of his reserve officer group." McCaffrey says also that she "remember[s] him and Mother arguing about Chamberlain's compromise and the fears they had for the future." Anxiety about war dominated the adolescence of Anne's generation, but with her father's early awareness of war and his determination to be prepared, she surely was affected more strongly than other girls her age. While conflict and external threats have been staples of science fiction for decades, their appearance in McCaffrey's fiction can also be explained by the political conflicts during her childhood and adolescence. In her fiction she depicts the pain and suffering caused by violent conflict, yet her protagonists always rise to meet its challenges, just as Anne and her family did.

But Anne's ability to convey emotion stemmed not just from the anxiety of pre–World War II tensions, but also from how this backdrop shaped her adolescence. A girl of great passion and intensity, Anne struggled to find an outlet for her feelings in a time when world war made individual angst seem petty. Although she tried to do so, Anne couldn't deny her need for attention and her need to be loved. Her intelligence and her unorthodox family made it likely she would have trouble fitting in. Throughout her adolescence, she found solace in horseback riding, singing, and, most importantly, reading and writing.

CHAPTER 2

Adolescence and a Time of War

That McCaffrey girl, she's a brat. I am sick of her and I don't know
how Claudia stands her. Let Claudia keep her under control.
—Overheard by young Anne McCaffrey

ANNE MCCAFFREY'S WRITING celebrates adolescence. Her award-
winning Young Adult series, the Harper Hall Trilogy, explores
the trials of youth, but her adult fictions also convey the intensity
of emotion special to the teenage years. Inspired in part by her
own experiences as a young woman, she captures and re-creates
the powerful longing, confusion, and desire of adolescence. Her
editor Susan Allison explained that Anne "writes movingly and
well about people who feel themselves different from others in
the world, who feel like they don't fit in." Anne's ability to give
life to such characters derives from her own adolescence. Like
many young girls, she had to navigate the perils of thinking she
was unattractive, feeling herself to be an outsider, trying to develop a talent to make herself stand out from the crowd, looking
for adventure, and finally discovering ways to find love and acceptance. As a teenager, Anne McCaffrey desperately wanted to
be loved. Her adolescence was marked by separation from family
members, worry about the health of her beloved younger brother,
the looming threat and then reality of world war, and the much
more common adolescent anxieties about appearance and identity. These experiences marked her life and her writing.

At fourteen years old, she was sent to Girl Scout camp when her
younger brother, Kevin, was recovering from the first of many op-
erations to cure his potentially fatal bone disease, osteomyelitis.

Meanwhile, her older brother, Hugh, was off at Boy Scout camp. She loved camp; it gave her the opportunity to ride horses, and for the first time she found an audience for her creative endeavors. Selected by the counselors to direct the camp play, Anne wrote a piece based on a Rudyard Kipling story, "The Butterfly That Stamped." One of Kipling's *Just-So Stories*, the tale depicts King Solomon and his wife, who overhear a male and a female butterfly arguing. Through clever manipulation, the queen uses the butterflies' marital conflict to correct the king's 999 other wives, who have also been quarreling. The title refers to the male butterfly's boast that if he stamps, the palace and garden will disappear. She dramatized the story's message about the importance of not showing off, a moral close to her heart. Because it was a rainy summer, the play got more time and attention than it would have otherwise. At camp, she discovered a love of performance and theater that would only grow in years to come.

At Girl Scout camp, Anne admired one of the counselors tremendously, twenty-eight-year-old Claudia Capps. An athlete and a superb rider, loved by all the campers, Claudia was someone Anne wanted to emulate. It is often said that eavesdroppers hear no good of themselves, and for Anne this was decidedly the case. While she was in the infirmary with an infected mosquito bite that needed tending, she overheard another counselor in a nearby room explain that the rest of the staff counted on Claudia to "keep the McCaffrey girl under control." Chastened, Anne realized she needed to tone down her self-centeredness. Desperately seeking her role-model's approval, she tried to be more like Claudia in temperament, more considerate of others and less clamorous. Her gratitude to Claudia persisted for decades. In a letter to a young student years later, Anne would recall, "I KNOW I became easier to deal with after that. B.C. (Before Claudia), you wouldn't believe what a mess I was." In a 1985 interview she gave while she toured Colorado, Claudia's home state, Anne credited the camp counselor with mentoring her and helping her become a more considerate, self-aware individual. The newspaper located Claudia Capps, then seventy-three, who confirmed that she was tapped to bring the McCaffrey girl "'under control.'"

This humbling camp incident affected Anne's self-image for years. Fortunately for her readers, Anne's self-depreciation did not permanently change her character. Not long afterwards, her college professors and dorm staff would also describe her as too boisterous and enthusiastic. Like many very intelligent, talented young women, she had difficulty finding her place. And growing up in a time when young women were supposed to be decorous and decorative didn't make the task any easier.

Anne's successful play at summer camp brought a moment of triumph to an otherwise typically turbulent adolescence. Despite her adventurous spirit and independence, she also experienced the classic "crisis of confidence." At or around puberty, many American girls lose their pre-pubescent confidence. They begin to believe that they are unattractive and unintelligent, realizing that they must conform to gender stereotypes to be considered feminine and desirable. They doubt themselves, losing their tomboyish energy and zest. Her brother Kevin explained that she was critical of her girlhood self: "she gives herself the worst press." He also recalled that as a teenager she was "upset that she didn't have more girlfriends." Always at home with books, Anne was less comfortable in a crowded high school cafeteria. She vividly remembers not being invited to eat with people during lunch period at Montclair High School. Anne's friends were also outsiders both in appearance and attitude. Her two close high school friends, Barbara Currie and Gladys Gravitz, were "also not interested in following the 'crowd.'" Anne explains, "None of us was pretty in a conventional way. Gladys was blond and Barbara's hair I admired, dark, and it was always so nice in a pageboy. Mine still wasn't much." The standard of feminine beauty at that time involved thick hair curled in pageboy haircuts. Anne's hair (like most women's) would conform only after a lot of effort on her part. Her dramatic features were not conventionally pretty in the 1940s, which favored petite women like the actress Veronica Lake. Feeling unattractive diminished Anne's self-worth.

Anne's memories reveal how appearance and *perception* about appearance shaped her self-image. The correlation between an adolescent girl's appearance and her feelings of inadequacy about herself are classic. As Mary Pipher and others have documented, "adolescent girls focus on their changing bodies. . . . Girls feel an enormous pressure to be beautiful and are aware of constant evaluations of their appearance." A self-help book, *Let's Talk About You*, written for girls in 1943 and reprinted frequently during that decade, reveals that girls experienced feelings of inadequacy and were expected to define themselves by their appearance and attractiveness to men. The book advises, "With your own brother overseas it seems as if you shouldn't think of yourself so much as you do. But you can't keep your mind on the risks of battle all the time." The book offers a great deal of practical advice, including a suggestion that its readers date younger boys since the older ones are off at war! Another similar book, *The Girls' Daily Life*, published in 1944, is a school text that has a chapter entitled "The First Impression," and the penultimate chapter is "Marriage: A Career." The concluding chapter reveals that in the 1940s especially, young women were socialized to see their worth residing in marriage. Young women during the war were reminded (as young women are today) that most of their value resides in their looks and their malleability. In her novels and stories, Anne creates characters who must learn that having a Talent (emphasized with capitals in her novels), such as the ability to cut rare crystal by singing or controlling mental powers, is more valuable than society's idea of conventional physical beauty.

Anne describes her adolescent self as "not a pretty girl," a surprising revelation to anyone who knows what Anne McCaffrey looks like. Pictures of her from 1940 to 1948 show a dramatically attractive young woman, with green eyes, full lips, and lovely hair. Her brother Kevin explained that "one of Anne's problems was that she wasn't as beautiful as Mother," but again photos reveal a different perspective—a strong resemblance between Anne and her extremely beautiful mother. But sometimes, especially in the teenage years, perception is more compelling than reality. Named for her mother, Anne was called Annette by her family until junior high. Then, because there were nine other Annes in high school, she asked to be called Lee Ann both at school and at home, because she thought it sounded "much nicer." Of course, a name change involves more than aesthetics, as she acknowledges: "I wished even then to be distinctive." She admits, "I think that I disliked me [more] than the name and felt that a change of name might help. It didn't but it seemed a good idea at the time." Anne changed her name at a time when she really desired to change her identity and to control her own destiny—a need shared by many of her heroines, who likewise take new names as they struggle to find their identities.

Her brother Kevin recalled that Anne spent a lot of time reading; his most vivid image is of her coming home from the library loaded down with books. Like her fictional heroines, Anne was a bit of a loner. She would escape her adolescent anxieties by reading. Her favorite writers took her to strange new worlds where unusual people had exciting adventures and found purpose and meaning in their lives. Anne especially enjoyed fiction set in ancient Rome and Greece; one particularly favorite writer was Caroline Dale Snedeker, whom Anne describes today as being "a good, accurate writer." Snedeker's novels contain some of the elements that characterize Anne's own writing: strong female characters who resist forces that try to oppress them, innovative use of mythology, history brought to life, belief in the power of music, and romance. *The Forgotten Daughter* (1929), for example, so affected Anne that she bought a copy in a used bookstore three decades after she first read it. Snedeker's main characters are two women abducted from the Isle of Lesbos—one an adult, one a young girl—who declaim, "We are Lesbians—no man shall be our master." The narrator proclaims a philosophy that defines Anne's books and her life: "Unselfishness, insight into the rights of others, was and is the only cure" for resolving conflicts.

She also learned from Snedeker's novels that romantic relationships were not the only thing that could be important, that art could have redemptive powers, and that love could take many forms. All were liberating ideas for young Anne, who struggled with pressures to conform to traditional roles for girls. Snedeker's novel *The White Isle* (1940), for example, features a young heroine, Lavinia, who is jilted; but she travels with her family to Britain, in Roman times the equivalent of traveling to another planet. In Britain, Lavinia finds a new life and discovers that she has telepathic powers, an artistic gift that compensates her for the loss of her first love. In another Snedeker novel, *The Spartan* (1936), music bridges cultural difference. Through music, characters communicate across linguistic and cultural barriers. Snedeker's depiction of music as a powerful force resonated with Anne's own talent and love of music, themes that would appear in Anne's Harpers of Pern and Crystal Singers. In *The Spartan*, Snedeker openly portrays the love of men for men, and the author's sympathy for homoerotic relations between men undoubtedly affected Anne. Years later, she would see and depict homosexuality on a continuum of acceptable sexual behavior.

Her first novel was inspired by Snedeker's work. Written in a black school notebook when she was fifteen, the novel, appropriately enough, was written during Latin class. Unfortunately, no copy of it exists today; it did not survive Anne's many moves. Her focus on her novel may explain the slip in her Latin grade from C in 1941 to D in 1942. She describes the novel, titled "Eleutheria, the Dancing Slave Girl," as being "about a very pretty (natch) [naturally] talented (natch) girl whose Patrician father had fallen into debt and all his belongings, including his children, were sold. Eleuetheria dances and meets a young Roman and falls in love and he buys her freedom. Typical early teenage transference. But it started me enjoying the practice of writing and that's when my addiction started." She didn't share the novel with her parents: "It was sort of my 'private' thing, daydreaming in another time and place."

A voracious reader, she also devoured Rudyard Kipling's work. A Nobel prize winner who wrote of exotic adventures in other lands, Kipling embodied many values that Anne would later emphasize in her own work. He frequently championed an underdog, an outsider (as he did in Anne's favorite Kipling work, *Kim*). Although he did so in a way that can appear offensive and patronizing to modern readers, Kipling did advocate the mingling of different cultures, an attitude Anne witnessed in her parents. Kipling's belief in technology colored her own faith in science, and his use of poetry and ballads provided a model for her use of ballads in *Dragonflight* and the inclusion of songs throughout the Dragonriders of Pern series.

Kipling's vision of benevolent colonialism, adventure, and heroism is one present in the works of another of Anne's favorite writers, Zane Grey. Many people prejudge Grey's novels as merely potboiler Westerns, filled with clichés and racism. While Grey certainly trades on the racist stereotypes of his time (especially the stereotype of the noble but savage Indian), there are some elements of his work that nonetheless appealed to the nascently feminist Anne McCaffrey. Grey was an innovator because "he wrote Western stories—particularly *The Light of the Western Stars*—from a woman's point of view." In his most famous novel, *Riders of the Purple Sage*, a Mormon woman of wealth and privilege battles the sexist and xenophobic Mormon hierarchy, aided by her riders. She declares, "I'll die before I ever bend my knees." This Zane Grey character, Jane Withersteen, could easily be the model for Lessa or Killashandra. Both Jane and another female character dress in men's clothes and rebel against traditional female roles. In a pattern typical of Grey's fiction, the women in this novel renounce their power for the love of a man. It remained for the adult Anne to re-imagine these endings, taking Grey's strong female characters and allowing them to hold onto the power they have gained. Horses play an important role in Grey's books, enabling life in the West even as Anne's dragons enable the settlement of her fictional world, Pern. In Grey, Anne found a writer who shared her love of horses and who appeared sympathetic to her adolescent sense of being an outsider. His novels deal with loners who reluctantly make connections with other people and enthusiastically bond with animals, elements that define most of McCaffrey's novels.

While she read widely, if one novel can be said to have had an effect on her, it was the cult classic *Islandia* (1942). In interviews, she frequently credits this book by Austin Tappan Wright for making a strong impact on her. She remembers reading and rereading *Islandia* when she was fourteen—no mean accomplishment, as the novel runs over one thousand pages. While Anne's other favorite novelists wrote historical fiction, Austin Tappan Wright's book is pure fantasy. Islandia is a fictional country set on an imaginary continent. His work has been compared to J. R. R. Tolkien's *Lord of the Rings* for its rich and vividly detailed description of an imaginary society and place. Part of the power of *Islandia* stems from its detailed realism, an approach that Anne would take in creating Pern and other fictional worlds. *Islandia*'s frontispiece is a fold-out map, and Wright explains in detail what the Islandians wear, eat, and plant. Their world, like Pern, is isolated, feudal, and pre-industrial. A book of fables helps chart the Islandians' course, as ballads are crucial to Pern society. Pern's open and tolerant sexuality has its antecedents in Islandian sexual freedom. Islandians' love of music and dependence on horses appears not only in Pern, but also in Anne's other fictions, where animals and music (and other arts) are highly esteemed.

Islandia's plot focuses on an American who tries to open Islandia up to foreign trade, but when he fails, he decides to become an Islandian. In the course of a year spent on the island, he learns that foreign trade would be as damaging and as oppressive as the physical invasion threatened by the Germans (Wright was prescient in his choice of invaders). The protagonist, John Land, is a loner (as Anne was during adolescence). His gradual integration into another society suggests that it is not that he is defective, but that Americans lead miserable and distorted lives because of our society's emphasis on capitalism. Like Charlotte Perkins Gilman's *Herland, Islandia* depicts the gradual acclimation of an American man to a more agrarian, sexually liberated, and gender-balanced society. Anne was drawn to the narrator John, who learns to see women as human beings entitled to sexual desire and who, like men, need a purpose or career. This radical and innovative world view delighted and entranced Anne, who already felt that the world she lived in was greatly flawed. The flight of the protagonist John from his country foreshadows her own exile to Ireland decades later.

Islandia's frank discussion of human relationships made it an appealing book to Anne, who at fourteen was trying to figure out sexuality, especially since the contradictory and restrictive dictates directed at girls in the 1940s were confusing at best.

51

Through the Islandians, Wright presents radical and powerful arguments against corporations and business, in favor of environmentalism, sexual freedom, and feminism (though he does not call the Islandian philosophy "feminism" per se). Wright's novel deals frankly with male and female characters' sexual desires. He depicts an Islandian house of "prostitution" without condemning the practice or the women involved. His social vision is progressive and radical, and it had a strong influence on Anne's similarly utopian creation of alternative societies. That Anne would read a book with such adult themes at fourteen reveals her maturity compared with other girls of the 1940s. (Significantly, another prominent feminist science fiction writer, Ursula K. Le Guin, also cites *Islandia* as an important influence.) While the book contains a few romantic subplots, these are well subordinated to the almost anthropological creation of an alternative society. Almost every aspect of American society is questioned and found wanting. *Islandia's* radical challenge to America showed Anne that alternatives to the real world could exist in fiction. Immersing herself in the world of *Islandia*, she could escape the contemporary world in favor of a better place, one where she could finally fit in, as the book's narrator discovers he does.

Both Wright's and Grey's novels, however, contain overtly racist elements. In addition, *Islandia* is also a classist society. While they mostly remain in the background, an evil "black" race threatens the Islandians. In the opening pages, the protagonist, a Harvard freshman, quickly abandons a conversation with another freshman when he discovers the boy attended a local (public) high school. Islandia's feudal society is based on nobility, a concept the American narrator quickly adopts. Fourteen-year-old Anne, however, with a father from Harvard and destined for Radcliffe herself, would not recognize the elements of class bias. While her experiences at school in the South and with Ella Patella, her parents' African American housekeeper, would enable her to reject racism, classism would remain an unexamined element in her life and work.

In her reply to a sophomore questionnaire at Radcliffe, Anne describes her hometown of Montclair, New Jersey, as "a normal suburb with all of the advantages of a progressive community and lack of financial worry, a stimulating group of people to associate with." Quite surprisingly for 1940, Montclair High School, where she began and finished high school, was integrated. Anne and her brother easily accepted their integrated school. As Kevin McCaffrey wryly pointed out, he didn't attend any other high school, so he didn't realize his school was unusual. Kevin McCaffrey ascribed the integration to the fact that the town didn't have enough students to have two separate high schools, but as we all know, scarcity of resources has never prevented segregation. Of her integrated high school, Anne has this to say: "The school could not—nor would it afford—two high schools. No one thought anything about it. They had a different color skin. So what? We all had different colored eyes. I was aware of racism and such biases but I was very firmly taught that they should make no difference."

The Interracial Committee of the New Jersey Conference of Social Work published a 1932 report, *The Negro in New Jersey*, that sheds some light on the racial situation that surrounded Anne in her adolescence. That three members of the committee came from Montclair suggests the town's involvement with and concern for racial equity. New Jersey had provided for the gradual abolition of slavery in 1804, but the state certainly followed the nation in racist legislation thereafter. During the 1930s, the African American population in Montclair was above the state average, at 15 percent versus 5 to 10 percent throughout Northern New Jersey. The McCaffrey's African American housekeeper, Ella Patella, typified black women's employment in New Jersey at the time, as "eighty-six out of every 100 [black women were] engaged in personal and domestic service compared to 16 out of 100 white women." While Montclair followed many national trends of discrimination, the report demonstrates a more favorable climate for blacks there than in other New Jersey towns. Montclair is one of five towns singled out for favorable mention for having an integrated community center. African Americans' rent there was the second highest paid by African Americans in the state; this statistic reveals Montclair's affluence and also its attraction for

African Americans, who were willing to pay higher rent to live there. Other statistics, such as the numbers of books about African Americans available in the town's library, rank Montclair fifth in the state.

The McCaffreys' lack of overt racism can be traced to their parents. Kevin recalled that his mother was appalled by the restrictions that racism placed on Ella, who was college educated. Anne's mother encouraged Ella Patella to take the civil service exam, telling her that she was too smart to stay in domestic service. She took the exam, did extremely well, and worked for the postal service as a supervisor until she retired. Anne recalls, "Ella had gone to college and had far more brains than many white people mother had to work with." Having a relationship with Ella forced Anne to face racism early in life. Perhaps most shocking to Anne, who always wanted to have children, was Ella's determination not to have children because they would be second-class citizens in racist America. Ella's husband "also had a college education . . . but they did not have any children. Said they wouldn't bring up any black children to struggle the way they had." Even Montclair, which a statistical report suggests was relatively more progressive in terms of race, did not alter Ella's opinion about American racism. Through Ella's eyes, Anne was able to see the oppressiveness of racism. A few years later, Anne would observe her father's distaste for racism, which he saw as parallel to his negative experiences as an Irish American in Boston. When he managed an army base in Georgia, her father "decided there would be no racism problems where he was the ranking officer— and there weren't." Anne's exposure to race bias, which began with her relationship to Ella, reinforced her sympathy for people treated by the world at large as outsiders.

Anne's family had a sense of the forthcoming war, and while other American girls from 1940 to 1942 might have been oblivious of looming political conflict, her family kept the subject alive in their home. More than other girls her age, she was aware of the possibility of war. Although she lost no family members in the conflict, both her older brother and her father served overseas— her brother as a soldier and her father as a military governor in Italy. Anne picked up on her parents' keen interest in international politics and could not help being aware of the military buildup in Germany. While her brothers played with toy soldiers, the McCaffreys realized that the boys might have to become real soldiers, as their father had during World War I. For a girl, the implications of war were very different. Although Anne wanted to play with her brothers' toy soldiers, she was not allowed to be fully a part of their war games, just as women were not fully a part of the U.S. Army. Her brother Hugh went off to war, and she stayed home and baked tollhouse cookies for his care packages. While she claims she never wanted to be in combat, she gives her female characters more central roles than the one she played during World War II. In her novels, women often engage in guerrilla warfare, use their psychic powers to battle enemies, or both, perhaps a fictional compensation for Anne's real-life exclusion.

Despite being barred from combat, women played a key supporting role during World War II, and many historians identify the war years as a time of upheaval and change for American women. Anne identifies women's work during wartime as crucial to her understanding that "women could do more than their conventional roles of marriage and children." In July 1944, just after Anne began college, women's labor force participation expanded to an all-time high, with 19 million women employed, a 47 percent increase from March 1940, when Anne was a freshman in high school. Even more remarkable was the increase in married women's workforce participation, which accounted for over 70 percent of the increase in working women. Many of these jobs were in the high-paying manufacturing sector. Anne also had the example of her mother, who held a number of professional jobs before and during the war, making her a minority, especially among middle-class women. But the war meant that more mothers from all socioeconomic groups were working outside the home, many of them in factories. The war years were marked by women joining the workforce in record numbers and by the absence of men, a combination that resulted in less surveillance and control of children. While Anne's mother did not engage in war-related work, she was completely absorbed by her son Kevin's illness and was less available to her daughter. Anne remembers that all her friends had relatives in the army, but few had fathers in the war. Most of her friends' fathers (like Anne's father) were exempt because of their age.

But her father volunteered. Anne's father was away from home during her adolescence, a critical time in her development. Like her heroines Lessa, Rowan, and Killashandra, among others, she may have felt orphaned, or at the very least abandoned, by her parents, a natural response, no matter how unavoidable her brother's life-threatening illness and world war were. During Anne's adolescence, everyday life was prosaic and marked by wartime economies. Because they were comparatively well off, the McCaffrey family had to deal more with separation and illness than with financial deprivation. For example, wartime rationing meant that the McCaffreys had to conserve gasoline, but the fact that they had a car separated them from many American families at that time. According to a 1941 World Motor Census map, there were only 31 million cars registered in the United States when the adult population was close to 84 million people. Anne recalls wartime shortages, but because of Kevin's illness, her family received extra gas and meat coupons. Her mother wrangled a pair of real silk stockings for her to wear to her dancing lessons, another rarity in wartime America. While she never felt deprived, Anne remembers the restrictions on items like shoes and sugar. Their family always preserved a lot of summer fruit from the McCaffrey garden, including peaches, pears, tomatoes, and even concord grapes from which they made jelly. In this way, Anne's chores were characteristic of most American women's during the war years. To conserve resources, almost every family had a "victory garden" (so-called because they meant more food could be sent to the troops, ensuring victory) and canned and preserved their own fruits and vegetables.

Before the war, the McCaffreys were famous for an annual garden party, from which every woman in attendance would exit with an armful of tulips. There were over five thousand tulips in their garden, a number that gives some idea of the garden's size and splendor. Their father and the children did all the work.

In Anne's words, "we just manicured the ants' toenails on the weekends," referring to her father's meticulousness. The garden was a tribute to their father's military mentality, practiced on his children before he was a postwar administrator, in charge of reconstructing European societies. Before the war, such a large and beautiful garden marked a difference between the McCaffreys and their neighbors. Once World War II got underway, though, even affluent families made their yards into valuable resources— for those at home and abroad. In addition to the garden, Anne's father had reconstructed a courtyard patio on their property, directing his sons to dig out old stones and create new paths. Anne was involved in the gardening, too, and she remembers that she would be relieved from gardening duty on cold days when she was menstruating. While she didn't enjoy the subordinate status of girls, she found pleasure when her feminine qualities provided an excuse to escape yard work. But at a southern girls' boarding school, she found the restrictions of femininity more irksome.

During Anne's high school years, her mother was occupied full-time with Kevin, staying in a rented room and spending all her time at the hospital. A niece of her mother's friend Mab Beckwith had gone to Stuart Hall, a prestigious girls' boarding school in Virginia, so Anne's mother "sort of waved the flag (dad was back in service) and leaned on their honor to take [Anne] in." It wasn't Anne's decision; she would have preferred to live with family friends, as she ended up doing the next year. Then she could have graduated on time with her high school class. But Anne accepted the disruptive change with good grace. She didn't particularly like Stuart Hall, but she understood the circumstances that had sent her there. Part of her adolescence was spent coping with all the attention that her brother Kevin required from her mother. Anne says, "I wasn't as nice to my mother as I should have been, considering what a good mother I now know she was." Her flexibility in the face of a difficult situation is a quality that would serve her well in coming years. She drew on her independent spirit when she was sent from New Jersey to Virginia by herself. Her father and older brother were already serving in the army, and Kevin was too ill to be left alone, so Anne's mother packed her off on the all-day train trip. Although she was only sixteen, she says she was "pretty self-reliant and the trip was an adventure. I remember the Dean of Women for Stuart Hall met me at the train station and did not think much of a girl my age . . . being allowed to make such a long trip by herself. But I did fine."

It was hard for Anne to make friends because most girls had been there since freshman year. Her forward-looking ideas about race were one reason she didn't fit in at Stuart Hall. Her creation of the annoying Kylara in *Dragonquest*, whom Brizzi describes as "a 'southern belle' from Southern Weyr," owes a great deal to her experience with southern young ladies at Stuart Hall. She says, "It was difficult but I wasn't as bad a kid then as I was earlier. And I had my own room as well [and I] did a lot of creative writing in study hall when I'd finished my assignments." Because the school was already fully enrolled, Anne's room was a converted music room, apart from the other girls' rooms. Except for Christmas vacation, she spent school holidays at Stuart Hall. Her mother was still intensively nursing Kevin, so Anne stayed at Stuart Hall with a couple of other girls whose families were also far away.

Her courage in facing a traumatic relocation is admirable, but her fiction reveals that the move also entailed emotional upheaval. Her experience at boarding school explains a pattern in her writing, that of the orphaned protagonist. Lessa, Rowan, Helva, to name just a few characters, struggle with abandonment, with parents who have either died or abandoned them. Through these characters, Anne recaptures her own alienation and painful adjustment to being alone in a strange place, without family. She confronted racism again at Stuart Hall. The school was all white when she attended, in contrast to her integrated public high school in Montclair, New Jersey. She explained "When our history class [at Stuart Hall] dealt with the Late Great Unpleasantness all those Southern girls of good family hied them to the infirmary with a variety of ailments so they wouldn't have to use his name (Abraham Lincoln's) in class." Despite cultural differences, she reveled in the intellectual challenges at Stuart Hall. Because of excellent teachers, she especially enjoyed history, French, and Spanish. While Anne didn't fit in because she was a Yankee and "not an Old Family," she enjoyed dining with Mademoiselle or Senorita (according to which language the teacher was speaking) and conversing in the languages she was studying. Anne also shocked her peers and teachers by wanting to go see the latest Tarzan movie. That form of popular culture was not supposed to appeal to the young ladies of Stuart Hall. Here her insistence on seeing the movie foreshadowed her "insistence" on writing science fiction, both considered "outside the pale." Anne's determination to see a popular film harked back to her mother's influence. Anne's mother, after all, had taken her children out of school so that they could see *Gone with the Wind*, which she considered an important cultural event.

Anne had high test scores, and her grades at both schools run the gamut from A to one F. Otherwise, she received mostly B's with the occasional C and A in a time well before grade inflation. Anne's academic difficulties were brief; for example, after a first report of F she finished with a solid A in a Bible course. In the end, she didn't have the mandatory two years of Bible courses to graduate from Stuart Hall. Her Stuart Hall records reflect an atmosphere of anti-Irish and anti-Catholic prejudice. The school principal, Ophelia A. Carr, writes of Anne, "In a group as small as a private school, a single Roman Catholic is accepted very naturally by the others unless she makes herself conspicuous. Lee Ann boasted a good deal about her Irish ancestry, and about her faith, and while she has not antagonized the students, she has made herself a little ridiculous by doing so." Those comments are from Stuart Hall's files, but more damaging and revealing are the principal's comments in a report to Radcliffe. In an otherwise positive report, Carr writes of Anne, "She has some of the racial pugnacity which might be expected." Fortunately, Carr also recognizes and compliments Anne's considerable gifts: "She is gifted musically and writes very well. Like most embryo writers, she undertakes very ambitious sorts of literary work, and loses interest before she completes them. However, she has been the Pres. of the Writing Club this year, and has made many creditable contributions to the club publication, mostly short stories and poems." It seems clear that at Stuart Hall Anne was able to develop her writing, while at Montclair the year before and after her energies were not so directed or fulfilled. To Carr's credit, she appears to have captured Anne's character. "She is a very cheerful, forgiving girl, and has entered whole-heartedly into the life of the school with no evidence of resentment."

While Anne experienced dislocation in her move to Stuart Hall, she did have a fairy godmother of sorts to make up for it. Her aunt, Gladys McElroy, helped her cope at Stuart Hall. Aunt Gladys paid for piano instruction and horseback-riding lessons, both of which Anne loved. She was "very much a tomboy and rode horseback whenever there was money available." Piano lessons and riding went far to compensate for Stuart Hall's lack of field hockey, a sport she had enjoyed at Montclair High School. Anne was a good dancer, a capable horseback rider, and a competent field-hockey player. She says that field hockey was "a sport where my aggressiveness was useful and I was a pretty good player." She recalls, "We were young ladies [at Stuart Hall] and restricted in what rough sports we could play." Anne, the tomboy, had other, more conventional loves of dancing and music. In the 1940s, women's physicality was class based: working-class women were encouraged to direct their physical energies toward factory work; middle-class girls like Anne, especially at private boarding schools, were being turned into "ladies," women whose primary object was to be ornamental and charming. She resisted this conditioning, and in an era long before girls were encouraged to be physically active, Anne McCaffrey gained poise and physical self-confidence. Atop a horse, she felt strong and powerful. And her fictional heroines invariably exhibit physical prowess, confidence, and mastery.

While her brothers battled war and illness, respectively, Anne struggled to earn enough credits so she could graduate from high school on time. To matriculate from high school with the rest of her peer group, she signed up for summer school at Montclair High School. Her Montclair High School transcript shows a more consistent pattern of achievement and an interest in languages.

(She studied Latin and French.) During her senior "year," an accelerated program, she received all A's except a C in typing. At Montclair she participated in Glee Club, the Riding Club, and the Dramatic Club. Her senior yearbook portrait appears over the name Lee A. I. McCaffrey and this couplet: "The Army calls her ducky! But she's really just a quack."

Anne had many classmates who were young men, boys finishing their high school work before they went off to fight in the war. She remembers, "I knew quite a lot of boys who went to war and did not return, . . . John Huntley and Jerry Pangborn, both of whom were killed on D-Day, from shell concussion rather than a direct hit. . . . John was an only son and his parents never really recovered from his death. Mabel Pangborn had her son's body brought home and I remember going to his funeral. She, too, was devastated though she had one remaining son who survived the war and the Army totally unscathed." She was fortunate not to lose her brother or father in World War II, but she lived with the fear for the duration, anticipating their deaths, and she saw firsthand the cost of war to others. In McCaffrey's novels, the heroines never shirk from combat—emotional or physical. The strong presence of war or the threat of war shapes many of her plots, providing a backdrop of crisis for her characters. In addition, when Anne kills off a major character (such as the eponymous protagonist Moreta), the character dies heroically, saving others, embodying the legend of World War II soldiers.

Her brother Kevin's struggles with a life-threatening illness made an indelible impression on her. One night, Kevin's leg had to be secured so that he couldn't injure it; and as he tossed and turned, Anne, who had relieved her mother, struggled to stay awake. Yet when he became still, she somehow knew that he would recover from the crisis, and he did so. Once when Kevin had to be moved from one hospital to another, the ambulance men tried to keep him from seeing a hearse drive up; Kevin then bravely quipped, "Never mind, I'll be there soon enough." What finally saved Kevin's life was a then new and unproven drug, penicillin. "The Smallest Dragonboy," one of Anne's most popular short stories, is a tribute to Kevin's bravery. Anne's belief in the power of science was bolstered by Kevin's eventual recovery due to emerging medical research.

Mrs. McCaffrey insisted that young Anne have a good social education, despite the pressures of Kevin's illness and the looming war. She was sent to "dancing school in Upper Montclair, ballroom dancing . . . and while I was good dancer, I was not a popular partner and sat out a great many hours. Mother made my clothes which were comparable to what the other girls had but 'I' knew they were homemade. Still, it was fun to design a new dress with mother." Anne says her mother was "a good seamstress and we were limited to how many formal gowns could be bought for me [because of] Kevin's illness." She never had to wear the same dress more than once, and she enjoyed the rare time spent with her mother. Sewing was one of the few traditionally feminine activities that she enjoyed. Because Kevin needed so much of their mother's attention, Anne was grateful for any opportunity to be with her. Sewing, while enjoyable, was something done out of necessity rather than a loved hobby. Cooking, a practical activity, was also something she shared with her mother (and grandmother), and at this activity Anne excelled.

Anne remembers sitting out many dances at her weekly ballroom cotillion, but she was by no means a wallflower. It was at those dances that she encountered the stirrings of romance. Her first crush was on a boy from Glen Ridge named Bobby Dunne. They met at her dancing class, and he danced with her frequently. "He was the captain of his school's football team, and he was the first boy to kiss me." She remembers, "It was nice, but I kept thinking there should be more. We were good friends so maybe the necessary hormones weren't exercised." "I was 14, and he was allowed to take me out to the movies." Her father didn't think that she was old enough to date, "whereas every girl [she] knew had at least one date—how could he be so antediluvian!" Anne's father was very protective of and strict with his daughter. "I don't think Dad ever went to bed unless he knew I was safely at home," she remembers, but after 1942 he wasn't home to watch over her anymore. Her father's position in the army in the 1940s also enabled her to be the belle of the ball—literally. Her father's status guaranteed male attention, but her own maturity and friendliness, as well as her attractiveness, would have secured a full dance card, too. She visited him at his army base in Moultrie, Georgia, for Christmas 1944, and while his rank as colonel kept her from having to worry about sexual advances, it also ensured that every dance would be claimed by an attentive soldier. Anne said, "I had a wonderful time at Moultrie because everyone would dance with the colonel's daughter. I learned a great deal about how to carry on without being a simp at Moultrie."

Anne's talent for singing and acting developed. She wrote, "[I] enjoyed High School Choir most—but that gave me a chance to show-off. My voice was loud, even penetrating {grin} so I was a useful soprano. (I did try out and got the part of Margot in the *Vagabond King* in the Montclair Opera Society.)" Her remarkably strong singing voice, like her aptitude for dancing, created opportunities for socializing. Music also provided her with relaxation and confidence; she remembers all forms of music being fun and good for her. When she was at Stuart Hall, she again sang in choir, in addition to the piano lessons paid for by her Aunt Gladdie. At the time, she wanted to become a concert pianist; she had "strong hands and a wide reach [and] played something by Scriabin for [her] spring concert." With her talent as her entree, Anne was able to mix with adults of many ages. Not surprisingly, her characters, especially in the Rowan series, use "Talent" (psychic power) to found new communities. Like Anne, these characters see themselves as outsiders until their Talent is discovered, and then they become sought after by the members of another society. In her books, she always depicts music as an important career. For her characters, music provides a sense of identity, purpose, and even a tool with which to save lives (as when Helva sings to deafen her kidnapper in *The Ship Who Sang*). In the Dragonriders of Pern, her most famous series, music is the main form of communication and it captures the history of the planet Pern, where harpers are among the planet's most respected and powerful inhabitants.

Anne remembers "lunch time in the cafeteria where no one

would invite [her] to join them," but that nightmare was balanced by her pleasure in the high school choir. The choir master, Mr. Arthur Ward, was extremely popular with everyone, and to Anne's delight, he chose her to be the choir librarian. During Anne's last full year at Montclair (1941), the very popular annual Christmas concert was canceled because of a flu outbreak. The highlight of the concert was always the Hallelujah Chorus. As the choir librarian, she was able to get hold of copies of the music, and she arranged for as many of her fellow students as possible to join her in front of Mr. Ward's house; there they performed an impromptu Hallelujah Chorus. The motivation may have been that it was going to be Mr. Ward's last concert, but she recalls that she felt it was "imperative that we show him how much we appreciated his direction." She remembers the event as "the brightest spot of my high school career," but we can easily imagine that it was also the brightest spot of Mr. Ward's career. Whatever her doubts about her high school popularity, her organization of an impromptu concert demonstrates that she could be a leader and that her peers responded to her generous nature.

Anne's adolescence was both typically and atypically traumatic. She struggled with self-acceptance, a girl's complicated coming-of-age, and the typical adolescent feelings of inadequacy. But she also had to deal with a father and brother away at war, a brother with a deadly illness, and leaving home herself to go away to a boarding school in which she didn't fit. But where most people choose to forget the struggles of adolescence, Anne McCaffrey still draws on them, in all their intensity and pain. Anne re-creates the passion of youth through her characters. In her young adult novels, like the Harper Hall Trilogy, the main character is an adolescent. That award-winning series has been much acclaimed for its accurate and compelling depiction of young adults. Indeed, Vaughne Hansen, one of her literary agents, declares that its main character, Menolly, "*is* Annie." However, one of Anne's signal achievements as a writer is her ability to communicate a similar intensity of emotion even in mature characters like Masterharper Robinton in the Dragonriders of Pern series and Yana Maddock in the Powers series. Her high school years were filled with tumultuous events, but she coped well, and she brings her hard-earned adaptability and optimism to her novels. While she tried to "keep under control," her enthusiasm and passion shone through even her own efforts to subdue herself. Transmuted in a science fiction setting, her teenage years provide a source for the great heart and fundamental optimism that create the appeal of the fictions.

CHAPTER 3

College Days and Marriage

Anne has calmed down from the most hoydenish days. She seems
better adjusted here this year and better liked. There is with all her
loudness a great delicacy in her understanding of others, in artistic
matters and a sensitiveness of recognition. She is warm and deep.
—Radcliffe college file

IF AS AN ADOLESCENT ANNE struggled to fit in, at college she finally came into her own. At Radcliffe College, she made lasting
friendships, satisfied her intellectual curiosity, and fulfilled her
desire to perform. Radcliffe offered her a challenging intellectual environment, and during and following the war, it had an
Ivy League coeducational easiness. She was able to pursue her
academic interests, and she developed a social life that can only
be described as hectic. Thus, her move to Cambridge for college
was a crucial step in her journey to personal and professional
happiness.

Like most young women at that time, Anne was expected and
pressured to marry soon after college, and marry she did, in
1950—not as quickly as a number of her own friends but still
less than three years after graduation. Beginning well, her marriage was a partnership that flourished in the vibrant life of New
York City. Then, as the children began coming, she moved to the
suburbs. Even though Anne's life then came to look like that of
other American homemakers, the strictures supplied by the era
could not suppress her drive to express herself, to perform. She
found outlets in singing and in musical theater. Later she began
to develop as a writer. Eventually, her writing became her refuge
from a controlling and sometimes abusive husband.

If her adolescence gave her much of the emotional experience she was to translate so effectively in her books, her college years opened her to broader vistas, taught her much about research, and developed in her the self-confidence she would need to take her writing seriously, to believe in it, and stick to it in the face of what would be active and ongoing discouragement from her husband. (But, then, life with her father must have taught her something about getting on with things even without support or approval). Radcliffe was one of America's best women's colleges as well as the sister college to Harvard, America's oldest institution of higher learning and a men's school. Because of her father's association with Harvard, the McCaffreys never considered any school other than Radcliffe College for Anne or Harvard University for her brothers. Anne describes Radcliffe as "the right college for me," but she also acknowledges Harvard might not have been a good fit for her brother Kevin. Her sympathy for Kevin may stem from her own experience at Stuart Hall, which was not exactly the right school for her. However, the McCaffrey children did as they were told, even as young adults. Anne's application for admission to Radcliffe indicates that she applied to no other schools and that her educational goal was "to have knowledge usable in postwar abroad." Even at seventeen, she was already looking to travel overseas. However, it would be years before she could go abroad.

It was in February 1944 when she graduated from high school. She had only a month to wait before beginning college, but, with typical industry, she kept busy. Though she had received only C's in typing in high school, she could type quite fast, and she spent a month working for the local board of education, typing and mimeographing their list of supplies. This may have improved her accuracy, which wasn't exactly perfect. At any rate, whatever skill she developed in typing, she certainly has had the opportunity, as a prolific writer, to use it.

Anne entered Radcliffe in March of 1944. The war was still in full swing, and it was an exciting place to be. Her classmate Pota Lewis Meier recalled that Radcliffe students were encouraged to be independent thinkers. For that time, Radcliffe was a progressive institution, operating on an honor code. After a semester of passing grades, students were allowed to stay out past the dorm curfew of 10 p.m. The young women felt they were quite sophisticated, studying hard, partying hard, and socializing with each other by playing bridge and smoking and conversing. Anne enjoyed being at Radcliffe because there her intelligence and writing skills were appreciated. As she says, "I REALLY enjoyed campus life and the challenge of studying." She made the dean's list every semester except her first. One of her classmates, Freddie Brennerman, described their experience:

> We landed, that summer and fall, squarely on top of the wall dividing Radcliffe As-It-Was from its beginning to Radcliffe As-It-Was-To-Become. Some of our organizations were still single sex (Idler), some became integrated even as we watched (Radio Radcliffe into the Crimson Network). Our freshman classes were all women and all in Radcliffe Yard on Garden Street. Some of us took courses in our third semester just in order to sample integrated classes in Harvard Hall, and by the time we were juniors, nearly all of our classes were integrated. We bowed to strict parietal rules that freshman year, but they were relaxed as we became upperclasspersons.

In Anne's years there, Radcliffe and Harvard were bustling. Dorms were crowded with refugees and WAVES, and like Anne's high school, Radcliffe offered an accelerated program so students could take classes without a summer break. She took advantage of this option in order to graduate in three years and finish with her class, the class of 1947.

Reports by Radcliffe residence hall heads describe Anne's energy and vitality in these years. These official reports depict an attractive and lively young woman, perhaps a bit too lively to fit a 1940s idea of a "lady." A pamphlet distributed to the class of 1947 reveals the college's traditional expectations: "Poise is doing and saying the right thing at the right time without being obvious. All girls need it." The pamphlet advises students, "Don't sit like an octopus," and informs them about regulations governing the wearing of hats (required for teas) and pants ("In public . . .

slacks, shorts, blue jeans are tabu"). The Anne McCaffrey her advisors describe did not fit that model of decorum. She had too much energy and high spirits and describes herself as breaking most of the rules, "especially the dress code. One rainy day, for example, she took a barefoot stroll down Brattle Street and was caught by the dean of women, who was not amused. McCaffrey shrugged it off; she had only one pair of shoes and did not want to ruin them."

At college, Anne was still known as Lee Ann or Lee. Miss Rose Cabot, head of her first residence hall, commented on her: "She seems better adjusted here this year and better liked. There is with all her loudness a great delicacy in her understanding of others, in artistic matters and a sensitiveness of recognition." As in the reports from Stuart Hall, this perceptive analysis highlights Anne's empathy and artistic sensibility. Her junior year hall head, Miss Florence Gerrish, is perhaps a little bit less understanding, but she describes a woman still identifiably Anne McCaffrey: "still too boisterous and self-assertive. Kind-hearted and conscientious." In a letter of reference, Miss Gerrish is kinder, but she still characterizes her as being out of the bounds of propriety. She writes that Anne is "too show-off & noisy to be very popular—tries too hard to be funny and clever—If her great vitality & good spirits could be toned down she could go far—At present she is an irrepressible St. Bernard puppy—but a nice one." In his notes, her sophomore tutor, Professor Cross, says something similar to Gerrish: "A little bumptious and flashy, with less performance than good-will. No serious deficiencies." These descriptions provide some insight into the writer-in-training, and they also outline the obstacles that an unconventional young woman would face. In the mid-1940s, the expectation, hardly unique to Radcliffe, was that a young woman should be quiet and demure. These comments of those entrusted with her well-being show that even as Anne challenged traditional gender roles that decreed women should be quiet and unassuming, she earned her instructor's grudging respect. Furthermore, Miss Gerrish's last letter, written a few months before Anne graduated, shows that Radcliffe did not succeed, in Gerrish's words, at "trimming her down." But the note of caution about her boisterousness shows that she could not, or more likely *would not*, conform. (This is the kind of behavior that Anne endorses in almost all her main characters, from Lessa in *Dragonflight* to Nimisha of *Nimisha's Ship*).

The academic choices she made also reveal her inclination toward the unconventional. She took a wide range of courses, including Russian, Slavic, Celtic, and French language courses, Political Philosophy, Chinese Philosophy, Cartography, History, Geography, and Government. You might expect that a young woman who wrote "novelist" as her first choice of a vocation would have selected literature and writing courses, but, characteristically, Anne McCaffrey chose an untraditional path. She encountered some resistance to her major, as Radcliffe's head of the college did not think Anne could handle such a difficult course load. But Anne persevered, obtaining the department head's approval. This professor, Sam Cross, had known her father at Harvard, and when he granted her approval to major in Slavic languages, he commented, "Of course you can! You're George McCaffrey's daughter; where is the bastard—oh, I can't say that to you, can I?!" In her course work, Anne "bucked the system," following a family tradition. Despite the warnings about difficulties, she persisted and graduated with honors. From this experience she learned the importance of following her own instincts. She also developed the foundations of a broad world view, as well as the perspective and skills to create believable alien cultures and worlds.

Her decision to major in Slavic languages was dictated in part by her second vocational choice; after novelist she listed "diplomatic service." Her ambitions are further defined by a side note to these two, "preferably combined." Her third choice, almost obligatory for a young middle-class woman in the 1940s, is listed as "housewife." Anne would manage to do all three, first becoming a housewife, then a writer. Her middle choice, the diplomatic service, she accomplished vicariously through characters in her fictions. Her interest in other languages and cultures was ostensibly about preparing herself to do graduate work abroad or to work in the diplomatic corps, but it would pay off years later, in ways that she could not imagine during college. Quite without knowing it, at Radcliffe she was gathering skills that would make her an accomplished and successful writer.

Organized religion is not a feature in Anne's fictional worlds, except when she occasionally depicts oppressive religious institutions that must be opposed or destroyed. Though she personally believes "in God/The Force or whatever you want to call it" (and was, years after college, to associate herself with Presbyterianism), the lack of organized religion on her most famous world, Pern, is often discussed by critics. Living in the travails of war, and enduring her brother's long and dangerous illness and her own adolescent angst, she found the Catholic Church of little help to her, and she associated her grandmother's Catholicism with a controlling, censorious piety. Thus, in college she rejected "the trappings and the rituals" of religion and stopped attending Mass. She remembers thinking, "God did not like hypocrisy and my continuing to observe Mass etc. was hypocritical." The grandmother who had been so insistent on her children's and grandchildren's Catholicism was gone; she had died in 1939. As for her parents, they accepted her rejection of Catholicism with equanimity, as they themselves had philosophical differences with church doctrine. Unfortunately, Anne's godmother, Inez McCaffrey (who, despite her last name, was no relation, but a college friend of Anne's father), was hurt that Anne did not come to her with questions about her faith. Inez had invited her to attend Mass, and after she refused, Inez and Anne never met again, even though Anne wrote to her and apologized. It was a sad loss; Anne took her middle name from her godmother, and Inez had recommended her to Radcliffe.

Ever going her own way, Anne also synthesized her own literary canon in college. She did not read contemporary American or English novelists, nor did she read American or English science fiction writers. She continued to read Rudyard Kipling and Zane Grey and studied Russian writers, most notably, Eugene Ivanovich Zamiatin, whose utopian novel *We* was the central focus of Anne's undergraduate honors thesis, "The Utopian Novel with Special Emphasis on Eugene Ivanovich Zamiatin and His Novel

WE." Now considered a classic, but still rarely taught in literature departments, in 1947 *WE* did not fit into any of the conventional literary categories. In working with this novel and topic, Anne researched several science fiction writers and, quite unknowingly, took another step in the direction of her own career as a science fiction writer. Indeed, Anne's own work is far better known and read than that of Zamiatin or the other writers she discusses. (Further, the thesis is quite critical of Huxley's *Brave New World*, finding it inferior to Zamiatin's *WE*. Here again we see her resistance to authority and her faith in her own judgment. *Brave New World*'s pessimism had no appeal for her).

The thesis, a respectable fifty-eight pages, exhibits Anne's keen intellect and interest in unorthodox literature and—with its detailed description of Russia in 1920—her ability to convey setting and ambience. It was a work of which she could justifiably be proud, and it was the thesis that earned her the distinction of graduating cum laude. (It is a little sad, then, that one of its acknowledgments cites her father "for his criticism and corrections," and not, alas, for his "support and encouragement"). The thesis is well written and researched, especially the first section, a survey on utopian thought and literature. In the light of Anne's subsequent career in science fiction, it is interesting that her analysis of various utopias divides them into two camps: escapist or reconstructionist. Her own fiction rather avoids these two extremes; there are always elements of redemption and hope in the relations of the characters, but there are always dangers to be faced as well, such as the invasion of Thread on Pern or the hostile alien Hivers in the Tower and the Hive series. The elements she admired in Zamiatin's work she would later produce in her own writing: a strong female character, the celebration of passion and deep feeling, and an upbeat attitude toward change. Yet Anne was not uncritical of Zamiatin, faulting the paucity of his work, remarking that, "unfortunately," Zamiatin was not prolific, "because of the pains he took with his work." In her own writing, she would err rather to the other extreme, to the extent that her literary agent, Virginia Kidd, would beg her to slow down!

All in all, Radcliffe gave Anne the tools and the rigor that would enable her to create the novels that she would later write. Anne did not study science—in fact, in her reply to the Radcliffe College jobs-placement questionnaire, under "subjects disliked" she answered "science." But Anne did learn the importance of research, and she did acquire the skills to do it. (This same training also taught her to respect and value librarians. Later, she would consider getting a degree in library science herself.) When she finally settled into her career as a writer, she found that the skills she learned at Radcliffe would help her locate the information she would need to know, whatever the subject.

In 1944 and especially 1945, men who had been released from military service started to return to Harvard, changing the atmosphere at Radcliffe considerably. She began to meet and date men who had working-class backgrounds. Because of the GI Bill, many men were able to attend Harvard who otherwise could not have afforded the university's steep tuition. Anne felt that some of the men would have been happier elsewhere: "To be frank, some of them . . . would have achieved more if they'd gone to their own local universities. Harvard could be overpowering with its traditions and requirements. I knew two boys who suicided—[from] loss of self-esteem and/or the pressures of their war experience." This blunt assessment of class difference has no suggestion that the institution should change, reflecting her upper-middle-class bias. Anne had not dated much her first three semesters, but "once the lads started coming home, I'd beg off a date so I [could] stay in and wash my hair or my clothes. Too much of a good thing." She brags, "I was also known for being able to drink even the 'fly' boys under the table. It was usually I who walked them back to their dorms to be sure they got there safely. However, Cambridge was a reasonably secure town so walking the mile back home was never a problem. I'd meet up with other girls." The rigid dorm rules that had marked her freshman year were gone, and the men who returned from war felt entitled to a new sexual freedom, which the Radcliffe students enjoyed, too. But of course, for the women there was the worry of an unplanned pregnancy. More than one of her classmates married during college, but for many others, there was a huge sense of relief when a menstrual period arrived.

About such matters, Anne was more open and direct than some of her classmates. Her mother's honesty about sex had conditioned Anne to see sexuality as nothing to be ashamed of or hidden. One day, she even raced through the hall, rejoicing rather loudly that she had gotten her period. But her classmates admired her frankness, even if many of them couldn't quite emulate it.

Among the men who returned to Harvard were her two brothers. She recalls picking up their laundry and doing it for them, thinking nothing of it at the time. This experience may have been unconsciously resented, as it appears on Pern, when drudges have to do housework for others, or in Anne's first novel, *Restoree*, where the main character, Sara, resentfully does her family's housework. Anne still didn't get along as well with Hugh as she did with Kevin, and she didn't rely on her brothers to get her dates.

One man Anne met reinforced her lifelong idealism. She often saw Bobby Kennedy, who went to one of the college coffee shops, Hazen's. Bobby would hang out there with his fellow football team players: "He would drift among us 'Cliffies' to see if we had some spare government paper that could be redrafted and submitted by the football team. They had to maintain a decent grade or they couldn't play football and with Bobby as captain of the team, it was sort of up to him to help. He was the best of the Kennedy lads as far as I was concerned." Bobby Kennedy's charm and enthusiasm overshadowed for Anne the casual appropriation of women's work and the specter of cheating. A positive attitude toward "helping" other writers or collaborating would appear much later in Anne's extensive work with other writers, discussed in chapters 6, 7, and 8. Not only Kennedy's charm, but also the liberal attitudes of classmates and professors opened Anne's political views. Already tolerant and a free-thinker, Anne's experiences in college confirmed her lifelong liberalism and idealism. In this regard, she began to develop independence from her family, who were all Republicans.

At Radcliffe, she participated in a number of extracurricular activities that bolstered her self-confidence and poise. Cabot Hall, a new dorm at the time, was a lively place, with sixty students who made the atmosphere rather clubby, calling each other by their last names as men did in the army, so that Anne was "McCaffrey." With her friend Pota Lewis, Anne belonged to the French Club, which had both Radcliffe and Harvard students. She lists the Radcliffe Entertainment Unit as one of the activities in college that gave her the greatest pleasure. A musical performance group, the Radcliffe Entertainment Unit was a high-prestige club. The group sang at the army camps in the area, working up a show. One of the girls danced, and Anne usually sang two songs, one of which was the romantic ballad "Chloe." She wore a nightclub-style black dress and "plenty of makeup," thus reinforcing her advisors' image of her as too boisterous. Being in the Radcliffe Entertainment Unit was her favorite activity, she says today, because before the war ended "[she] had a chance to show off and get to the army bases. Most of the male student population was pretty 4-F or underage, so we tried to meet more suitable dates when we could. Nothing ever came of it but it was fun." The Radcliffe Entertainment Unit was, however, excellent preparation for the musical theater work she would devote herself to until turning primarily to writing in 1965. The musical theater work was not merely a sideline, but an integral part of her desire to create and perform. Another outlet for her, these entertainments provided practice for seeing group dynamics, especially leadership, development. But she reveled in the performative aspect. In Oscar Wilde's *The Importance of Being Earnest*, Anne played the comic role of the butler (as a maid). She remembered, "I was always going to be a writer. It was just that I wanted also to be a film star or a singer in an opera—or you know, a lot of other things. The writing was always there."

Anne also worked on the school newspaper, the *Idler*, and the Harvard Radio Workshop, both activities that polished her social skills more than her writing skills. She did little writing for either group, although she remembers writing some poetry, including an ode to drinking coffee. Not surprisingly, coffee (or its alien equivalent) appears often in her novels. Anne wrote an operetta based on the *Dream of Angus*, which she had studied in a Celtic course she had taken. Included was a whacky song, "Chickory, chiggory chill / There's an awful lot of coffee in Brazil." In an upper-level composition course, she was required to write two thousand words a week, and it was in this course she began a story that decades later she turned into *Mark of Merlin*. She had taken riding lessons to complete a gym requirement at Radcliffe, so the heroine in this early version had a horse rather than a dog as the character of Merlin. But the genesis of a workable plot was there from her college days. Significantly, it was the idea for the book rather than the actual writing that she gained from the experience.

One of the most valuable parts of her Radcliffe years was the socializing; she learned how to express herself publicly. In Cabot Hall, Anne spent a good bit of time in the smoking room, playing bridge with her friends Jean Davis and Pota Lewis. She didn't spend all her spare time in the smoker, though. She spent time with her Russian roommate, Kira Kalachevsky, practicing her conversational Russian. Like other Radcliffe students, the young women talked about their hope and fears, cute boys, their classes. To Pota, who was four feet and eleven inches, Anne was "an imposing presence, very fun-loving . . . a bit of a character." Jean, who was in the Radcliffe Choral Society, remembers Anne singing as others played the piano in their dorm. In addition to a common interest in music, Jean and Anne both had extraordinary mothers who expected their daughters to excel. But as Jean explains today, none of the women in Cabot Hall were "expected to go to graduate school the way our daughters did." So performers like Anne struggled to find acceptable outlets for their energy and ideas.

Some of her energy continued to be directed toward public singing performances while she was on dates. Jean Davis introduced her to some men from MIT; Jean and Anne double-dated occasionally, and Jean had a serious boyfriend (Bob Bigelow, whom she later married). Anne danced with Bob Ennis, who was six feet four inches, and Austin Fish, who was putting himself through college by being an instructor at Arthur Murray Dancing School. Anne and her friends were somewhat wild, and they considered themselves adventurous. Jean's boyfriend and his MIT buddies frequented a bar/strip joint, Jack's Lighthouse, in a shady part of Boston known as Scollay Square. After Jean and Bob's wedding in May 1948, a whole group of their friends went back to Jack's Lighthouse, and Anne got up on stage and belted out a tune, to the delight of her friends and the rest of the audience.

While she was at Radcliffe, she met her first serious boyfriend, Don Bassist. Don was a year behind her in his studies; he had been in the air force. She was attracted to him not only because of his war experience, but also because "he didn't drink as much as other fly-boys, and [he was] smart." Her father liked Don; Anne remembers, "My father found a kindred spirit in him." But Anne's girlfriends didn't think he was right for her. More important, she was troubled by his lack of vision: "He didn't seem to know what to do with his life after college was over." He had proposed to her, but they both realized that they were too young to marry. Anne did not attend Radcliffe to receive a "Mrs." degree. She had ambitions of her own. However, in post–World War II America, she would find it difficult to find a career suited to her talents. Her search for meaningful work would reappear in many of her novels, as female characters like Killashandra in the Crystal Singer series or the Talents in the Tower and Hive series wrestle with finding suitable jobs for their remarkable abilities.

By attending Radcliffe and graduating with honors, Anne followed in her father's footsteps. She would have liked, also, to follow him in finding work abroad. She had always been strongly interested in working outside the United States, as he had, and her pursuit of this goal is reflected many times in the file that the Radcliffe Appointments Bureau kept on her. But even with her father's name to assist her, she was not able to find a job in diplomatic service. Her difficulties in so doing may have been, in part, the result of gender discrimination, because her lively behavior defied the social norms of the day. The very first entry in her Radcliffe job file describes her as "an extremely articulate and buoyant person . . . she is noisy, energetic, and rather insensitive. Would make herself in any group conspicuous."

After graduation she did apply for a posting in the Foreign Service as well as a job with Aramco (Arabian American Oil

Company). During the war and immediate postwar period, it was considered patriotic to work for oil companies, as their importance to the nation and to military maneuvers was clear. She was accepted by Aramco, which was willing to let her return to the States if her father became seriously ill. (Already in 1947, Anne was concerned about his failing health.) Unfortunately, the happy arrangement fell through; the secretarial posting to Bahrain had to be canceled because there weren't quarters suitable for women. Once more she experienced firsthand the limitations placed on women, but she wasn't surprised. A note in the Radcliffe job file, written two years later, explains, "She seems more nearly able to take care of herself in a foreign country than most girls her age," and reports that she has "a very realistic view of the whole [job] situation, and knows that any job a woman gets is going to be below the salt."

On the other hand, Aramco did pay Anne some severance money, which she used to take some time off to visit her college friend Pota Lewis in West Palm Beach. She worked as a waitress when she returned, then held secretarial jobs for the International Council of Nurses and for World Trade Intelligence, a company that she described as "ahead of its time" in establishing relationships between American and similar business interests abroad. Working various jobs in New York City, Anne first lived at home because city rents were so expensive. Finally, she found a job she enjoyed. She was hired as an advertising copy layout artist at Liberty Music Shops. She was, to an extent, following her mother's footsteps; her mother had worked for many years in advertising, an industry more open to women than most. Liberty Music Shops had a number of famous customers, including Rita Hayworth, Raymond Massey, Merle Oberon, and Tallulah Bankhead. New York City was an exciting place to work and live for a young single woman, and rubbing shoulders with the famous gave glamour to her position.

She was also fortunate in her roommate, Betty Wragge; she was a radio actress who wrote commercials. They had an apartment diagonally across from Carnegie Hall. Betty was a helpful roommate. She had a long-term contract with *Pepper Young's Family*, a radio soap opera, but more important, she knew Lila Schaefer, who was an editor for Ziff-Davis, a publishing firm specializing in science fiction. Lila, who was to become Betty's roommate later on, had lunch with Anne several times, reading her fiction and offering suggestions and encouragement. Anne remains grateful today for Lila's help, though she never sold Ziff-Davis a story. "Her discussions gave me parameters even for a fiction that has none." It was important, too, that when she left Liberty Music for a better paying job at Helena Rubenstein, Anne met a woman who read *Galaxy* magazine. Because she had written her thesis on a Russian science fiction writer, her coworker shared her copies of the magazine. It was a thrill for Anne when she "actually found someone who enjoyed the stories and s-f as much as [she] did."

She also dated a concert pianist named Ronnie Hughes. "But I knew even then that concert performers led difficult lives, and I like regular paychecks," she says, explaining that it was this practical streak that kept her from pursuing the advantage of knowing Wilbur Evans and Susannah Foster, though in the summer of 1949, she "helped them and played some minor roles in the Lambertsville Musical Circus." In addition to assisting Evans and Foster, Anne played the role of Margot, a tavern and brothel keeper in *The Vagabond King*. Anne enjoyed the thrill of performing in musical theater and the fact that her powerful voice earned her a place in such a fun and glamorous activity. She was active in church choirs, where her voice was strong enough to surmount even the church organ at full strength. She joined the Breck Mills Cronies, a group that produced operetta and opera.

In 1949, when friends of a friend arranged a blind date for Anne with Wright Johnson, it would be a joint love of music that drew them together. At this time, in the postwar world, there was tremendous pressure on American women to marry and have children, and Anne certainly felt it. She says, "I was nervous that I wouldn't get a chance to marry, as children had always been a part of my future." She says, "I got a little nervous about my lack of choices until I met Wright. We had a lot in common, our love of music, theater and ballet." Meeting Wright was a relief for her; she had "met a lot of guys with common interests but no passion."

Until she was introduced to Wright, Anne had decided that she "was crazy or far too picky." Wright offered common interests and passion. He courted her with songs from the *Beggar's Opera.*

Photographs of Horace Wright Johnson (he went by his middle name) capture a thin, handsome young man with an eager expression. The youngest of four children, Wright's background was quite different from Anne's. Her Irish people were city folk from Boston, while his father had grown up on a farm in Oklahoma and, ingeniously, started a business selling offal (butcher's waste) in New York City. Then, in 1936, Wright's mother inherited a small farm in Kissimmee, Florida. The farm had a small orange grove and chickens, and "Mother Johnson raised florist quality roses," which she sold. While the McCaffreys were having garden parties and distributing a dozen tulips to their guests, the Johnsons were raising roses to make a living. Still, in spite of the urban-rural split, differences in financial circumstances, and apparent disparity of class, there were important similarities in the ways the McCaffreys and Johnsons raised their children. Just as Anne's parents had introduced their children to literature, so Wright's mother subscribed to editions of the classics, had read them to her children and encouraged them to read. Further, Anne remembers Wright's father with special fondness, noting, "I did not meet them in person until I went down to Florida to recover from Dad's death, we were on very good terms, especially Dad Johnson who was a hearty optimist and a very warm, caring person." Wright's father worked in an airplane factory as a storage manager, and Anne remembers him as a man "who could turn his hand to about everything." A man of such resourcefulness evoked for Anne her own father.

Wright knew early on that his life would have to take him away from Kissimmee, which at the time was a rural backwater. (It is perhaps significant that Anne's brother Kevin remembered that when Wright was living on "Normal Street," he so disliked the name that he would not give people his street address.) As it turned out for him and his brother Phil, as for many others of his generation, the war and the GI Bill provided a way out. His brother Phil was a bombardier who attended the University of Illinois, earning a law degree. As for Wright, it was the savings bequeathed to him by his oldest brother, Dick, who had been a pilot in the Pacific, that along with the GI Bill enabled him to go to college. (It was a sad story. On his way home Dick's plane was lost at sea.) Wright had been thinking of attending Yale University when Van Varner, an army buddy who had attended Princeton, encouraged him to apply there. Wright did and was accepted, but he was so ignorant of university life that he arrived weeks early and had to find a job in New York City operating a drill press until classes began at Princeton.

These were tumultuous times at Ivy League campuses, which had to adjust to a new type of student—older, wiser, and often from backgrounds less comfortable than those of their usual students. Wright Johnson was one of these pioneering students who found many faculty biased against them. "Robert Goheen, Dean at the time, last year disclosed that he found great faculty resistance and contempt for G.I. Bill students." Yet unlike the men Anne says would have done better at local universities than Harvard, Wright throve on the challenge of Princeton, an institution with traditions and requirements very like those of Harvard. He did well, finding it difficult but managing, with summer classes, to graduate in three calendar years. That three years included the time applied to writing the thesis required of students majoring in the humanities. Wright's thesis runs 234 pages (Anne's was 58 pages) and reads more like a dissertation than an undergraduate work. Unlike Anne's thesis, Wright's has no acknowledgments page, perhaps revealing something about his character, or class—he typed the manuscript himself while she had her father's secretary type hers. Entitled *Harley Granville-Barker 1877–1946: A Critical Biography*, the work focuses on the English playwright, actor, and producer who is best known for his innovative staging of Shakespeare and his support of George Bernard Shaw and other modern dramatists. Wright's prose is polished and confident and his careful and persuasive analysis of Granville-Barker's plays holds up to scrutiny, even after more than fifty years. His sense of humor appears in the thesis in numerous witty phrasings. For example, he wrote, "Granville-Barker was never an extremely facile writer; the large waste-basket was a prominent piece of his equipment throughout." Wright obviously admired Granville-Barker and, like Anne in her thesis, used his to champion a man's art that he thought had been unfairly neglected. Still, his treatment of Granville-Barker's marriages and divorce merits a mention, as he scathingly denounces the second wife's novel writing, seeing it as inferior to Granville-Barker's plays. Wright's attitude hints at misogyny in the assumption which was then widespread, that great art is produced by men, not women.

Wright had a passionate and personal interest in theater. He belonged to "a small group that revived the Theatre Intime with Ibsen and Shakespeare—the administration never acknowledged us; I doubt we figure in Princeton history." He also recalls that he "shook up the English Dep't with a paper, drawing on her [Dorothy Wordsworth's] diary, positing that Wordsworth & his sister were lovers, now accepted as factual." His description of his time at Princeton suggests a nonconformist streak something like Anne's. Wright also had a keen interest in music; he sang in the choir at Princeton and at church. Anne continued the singing that she had done at Radcliffe, working with the Lambertville Music Theatre in summers. Wright had courted her by singing to her, and they enjoyed singing duets, Anne's soprano to Wright's bass. Like Anne, Wright had a flare for the dramatic. He eventually wrote a musical.

Wright and Anne shared an interest not only in music and theater, but also in literature, and she still recalls an anecdote about Wright's thesis research that reveals something of his character and influenced her own behavior as an author. Pursuing his study of Granville-Barker, Johnson drew on his subject's correspondence with George Bernard Shaw. Johnson also wrote to Shaw. When he received no reply, he wrote again, taking the Great Man to task for not responding to the first letter; this time, Shaw replied with a helpful letter. Anne seems to share her former husband's long-ago indignation that a writer (even an elderly, extremely famous writer) should ignore an inquiry. While it is true that science fiction writers are famous for being responsive to their readers, this exchange between Johnson and Shaw, remembered and retold over fifty years later, appears to be something of a touchstone for Anne, who goes to extreme lengths to be available to her fans.

While she undoubtedly felt the pressure to marry that was a central feature of the postwar years, Anne also experienced a strong attraction to Wright Johnson. He was a journalist for *Women's Wear Daily*, the standard industry journal for fashion, and like her, he loved the arts, especially opera, ballet, and music. She remembers him as "good looking, self-assured . . . [and] there was a definite sexual attraction." He was sophisticated, "hav[ing] martini lunches because he couldn't afford a Martini AND lunch" and insisting on designer colors for his apartment. After several months of dating, he proposed to Anne in September 1949; they married on January 14, 1950. Anne was twenty-three and Wright was twenty-five.

The wedding posed a bit of difficulty. Because Anne was no longer affiliated with the Catholic Church, she had to find a minister. Because Wright had been raised Presbyterian, a Presbyterian minister was the logical choice, especially as her brother Hugh had married in the Presbyterian Church two years earlier. The wedding service was held at Montclair Women's Club, with about a hundred guests in attendance. She had chosen the Montclair Women's Club for convenience, because the reception as well as the service could be held there. Betty Wragge was her maid of honor and her college friends Pota Lewis Meier and Jean Bigelow were her bridesmaids. Anne wore a silk dress made from fabric that she bought from Pongee Corporation, the Swiss textile company where she worked in 1949. She designed the dress, which was simple and elegant. It had long fitted sleeves and a scoop neck; her veil of net was hip length, held in place with a band of silk. Pota and Jean wore maroon velvet gowns with bustles, and the men wore morning suits. In short, it was a traditional formal wedding. Anne's mother ran the show. In Anne's words, "Mother had the ideas. I agreed or disagreed." Her in-laws did not attend, citing the cold weather and the expense of the trip. Instead, they sent a generous wedding gift of one hundred dollars. Anne recalls that she understood and "felt no hurt or rejection" in their absence. Wright's brother Phil, the lawyer, did, however, come to meet her. The McCaffrey family played bridge with him, and they passed what Anne felt had been an inspection. Her mother-in-law later admitted to her that she was afraid that Anne would have "one of those Bronx or Brooklyn accents." This anxiety, which is about class, is mirrored in Wright's anxiety about living on "Normal Street."

One of her friends remembered Wright as the opposite of Anne, who was always very warm and trusting. Wright, this friend says, was very cynical and critical of other people, whereas she says of Anne, "I never heard her bad-mouth anybody." Hypercriticalness and sensitivity, not to mention a sense of elitism, are qualities that would eventually lead to the breakdown of Anne and Wright's marriage. There were, however, a number of busy, happy years first.

Curiously, it was in 1950, only a few months after her wedding, that Anne discovered the lasting interest that eventually would come to fill her life. Sick with her usual spring attack of bronchitis, she turned to the stacks of pulp science fiction magazines that a previous tenant had left in the Johnson apartment. She picked up *The Star Kings* by Edmund Hamilton and "got so involved in the yarn that [she] even forgot to cough." She read copies of *Amazing, Fantastic, Galaxy,* and *Fantastic S-F.* "I couldn't read fast enough or get enough of this marvelous reading," Anne says, "and I was hooked."

In the late 1940s, New York City was an exciting place to be. World-class theater and art events abounded, and while Anne and Wright didn't have a great deal of extra money, they saw all the important and influential plays of that time. Because Wright had interviewed such celebrated actors as Laurence Olivier and Jessica Tandy for his thesis, he knew his way around city stages. Since Anne's former roommate was an actress and both Anne and Wright participated in musical and theatrical circles, they knew insider's ways to see great art at no cost. For example, they would "second act," which meant that they would mingle with the crowds at intermission and take empty seats. Wright recalled with a chuckle seeing Balanchine in a "second act" when the famous dancer performed. Wright and Anne knew how to have fun in the city, and surely seeing a great swath of America's greatest theater, ballet, and opera inspired Anne in many ways. And through it all, even after seeing the enchanting *Kiss Me Kate*, their favorite show remained John Gay's *Beggar's Opera*, the one whose music Wright used to woo Anne. Not only did Wright sing from the opera when they were courting, but a couple of years after they married, the two of them performed *Beggar's Opera* in their home to an audience of friends and neighbors. This performance, in fact, marks a great change in their lives. Anne became pregnant in 1951. She says, "I wouldn't have a baby in NY City," and the couple moved to the New Jersey suburbs.

Undoubtedly, 1950s ideas about mothering played a large role in this move, and Wright remembers the move to Montclair somewhat bitterly, seeing it as a move away from a life of independence to one under his mother-in-law's sway. At any rate, the home production marked the beginning of a new life: if they weren't going out to shows, they could presumably entertain themselves. They could sing and perform. For Anne and Wright, as for most couples, the arrival of children heralded a new way of life. In their case, it eventually meant increasing separation and alienation.

Once Anne recovered from morning sickness, the commuting was fine, but the summer of 1952 was exceptionally hot, and pregnant Anne felt it intensely. She once asked the local movie theater manager if she could stay in the building between shows because it felt so good to be cool! In her fifth month of pregnancy, she had some spotting. So, at the advice of her doctor, she quit her job and stayed home. Actually, she was relieved to have a good reason to leave her job because office politics had taken a turn for the worse: the outspoken Anne had inadvertently gotten herself in the middle of a fight between two of the bosses. So when her doctor advised her to quit her job, she left gladly. Then for three weeks she was on bed rest, lying with her legs elevated.

Wright had taken a new job at the Wool Bureau. Both there and at *Women's Wear Daily* his work was primarily writing, often under very tight deadlines. He had regular raises, but Anne had planned to keep working because with New York's high rents they had needed her salary to manage. Now, however, moving to her mother's building on Valley Road in Montclair meant they would have a reasonable rent. Wright and Anne had the second floor of an old Victorian house, with much more room than they had in New York. Their previous apartment, in fact, had been a small coldwater flat sublet from a conductor, and Anne and Wright had to vacate when he returned to New York.

In contrast, in New Jersey, they had two bedrooms and a nice, wide living room. Anne's favorite brother, Kevin, and his wife lived upstairs, and the downstairs apartment was occupied by a family friend, Mae Pangborn, recently widowed. (Anne had gone to high school with Mae's son Jerry, who had been killed in World War II.)

Not only was Anne living in her mother's rental house, but she also kept very much in mind her mother's precepts. Like many daughters, she says, "[I] did what I had seen my mother do—although I hated housework as much as she did, but basically it involved appreciating the guy who had to continue working with a good dinner, clean clothes when he needed [them], a neat house and friends for drinks and dinner which was something we always did. I was a good and clever cook so there was always more in the Friday and Saturday pots so we could have people in to eat—and drink." Without much money to decorate, she did the best she could to settle into the apartment, using the sewing and cooking skills she had learned from her mother.

Though she wanted to be a good wife, Anne knew that brains didn't end when motherhood began. Her mother's constant question, "You'll go to college, marry, have children, but what will you do with the rest of your life?" remained in her mind. After her hectic life in the city, living in Montclair again was a change. She doesn't remember being bored, but acknowledges feeling "alone, and perhaps lonely after having had so many people around me at work." Anne describes the situation, so powerfully criticized by Betty Friedan in *The Feminine Mystique*, of "a strange stirring, a sense of dissatisfaction, a yearning" by the suburban wife, "afraid to ask even of herself the silent question—'Is this all?'" Like

Anne, Friedan was the graduate of a prestigious Seven Sisters college (Smith) and a suburban mother. Not surprisingly, considering their proximity and similar background, the two met when Anne attended one of Friedan's weekend cocktail parties. While Anne didn't particularly care for Friedan, she did see the relevance of her message, agreeing that feminism explained why women did not get full credit for their work. Anne, however, had an equally feminist but perhaps more pragmatic view of the world. "I knew perfectly well that I wrote all the radio commercials and did all the copy for the Liberty Music Shop advertising which my boss got credit for."

Anne was encouraged to continue to look for a career by her mother's example of working and by her close friend Jean Gebrowski. Jean, the mother of two children, had continued to work at her job in fashion publicity in New York City. Anne explains, "She encouraged me all the time just by her own activity." Jean was her first friend who had a career and who was also a mother. Anne remembers admiring Jean tremendously: "She was all I would have liked to have been—suave, clever, and managing the volatility of Gebb [her husband] deftly. She was also friends with his two former wives . . . She was all a feminist should be." Both Anne and Betty Friedan went on to have successful writing careers, each exemplifying their feminist beliefs in their writing—Friedan in nonfiction and Anne in fiction. For Friedan and Anne, and for many educated women, writing has been the obvious choice of a career. While Anne demonstrated the compulsion to write even as a young girl, she also found a calling that could fit with being a wife and mother. In Anne's words, "I was going to give it [writing] a good try because writing was something I could do anytime I had a free moment." As any mother knows, with children, those moments occur infrequently. Here Anne's determination and even stubbornness served her well.

Ever the brave nonconformist, Anne had decided to have natural childbirth, which was quite uncommon at the time, and she had done it when her mother, half a world away in Japan, sent loving and encouraging letters. Then, when the time came, August 29, a week after the due date, she went into labor just as

Wright was leaving to catch his train to the city. Forsaking their 1937 Chrysler, they took a taxi to the hospital. It saved time and Wright could attend to Anne. He rubbed her aching back until she went into the delivery room. Because no fathers were allowed in delivery rooms in 1952, and she was not anaesthetized, she was able to yell the news to him. They had a son! The birth went smoothly, but when Anne was taken to her room, there was a feather pillow on her bed. She is allergic to feathers and started sneezing violently, in her words, "a very painful thing to do when you have just delivered." She alerted a nurse, was given antihistamines, and all was well.

A devoted and loving mother, Anne always wanted children, but she certainly acknowledges their effect on romance: "Having Alec sort of brought us both down to a level of reality with scant romance. But then, it can. Having babies is a messy, tiring, and repetitive business but now that I'm on the other side of it, [I am] glad I did." In 1956 Todd arrived a month late, and his was a meconium birth, where the fetus has already had a bowel movement in the womb. Because such children sometimes have lung difficulty, Anne was drugged—or, as she describes it, "knocked out." She actually woke up with a bruised eyebrow, from the anesthesiologist's forcefully checking of her eye. Then, in 1959, Anne had her last baby. Convinced that he was going to have a third son, Wright fell asleep in the waiting room, but Anne's second sight had come to the fore. She had intuited that she was going to have a daughter from the peculiar hot flashes she'd had all summer. While seven-year-old Todd wasn't happy that his sister's arrival caused his mother to miss his birthday party, Gigi was "a beautiful baby from the moment of her birth . . . pink and blond, and very dainty."

Nor was biology quite the whole story when it came to kids and the Johnson family. There was also the foster child, Josef Kaldi, a teenage Hungarian refugee, who at fifteen had swum across the Danube River to freedom, one of thousands who fled after the failed revolt against Communist rule in 1956. Josef's adventure may have inspired the flights of some of Anne's characters, such as Menolly's running away from her Hold in *Dragonsong*.) Anne says, "Clearly, I knew I couldn't cope with another baby. So we ended up with Josef as the fourth child." She also says that her relationship with Josef "had hiccups—mainly because he didn't trust anything a woman said." When he arrived and joined their family, he spoke no English, so that meant Anne had to learn enough Hungarian to teach him English. She was thankful for her Radcliffe training in languages. The family called the boy "Joe," and he called Anne and Wright "Mother" and "Father." Joe got along well with Alec and Todd, and although he wanted the new baby to be a boy, he adored Gigi when she joined the family. He lived with them until he joined the U.S. army in 1962.

The fascination with fostering in Anne's novels must have started with Joe. From Lessa to the Rowan and Cita, she depicts orphans who struggle but who eventually form new families. Despite her own positive and very close ties with her children and her own parents, Anne repeatedly valorizes families of choice, as, for example, when the psychic Talents in the Tower and Hive series bond with other Talents when their own biological families reject them or are dead. Similarly, in the Brain Ship series, the "Brains," deformed humans who are abandoned by their biological families, must find new families with their "Brawns," normally bodied humans, or other Brain Ships. In every instance, the new families of choice are presented as positive alternatives to the biological family. Anne admits, "I try to [depict fostering positively] mainly because I think 'fostering' is generally a good idea, especially if the birth parents are antagonistic to the personality of their child." At any rate, with four children to manage, suburban Mrs. Johnson had to work very, very hard to be a good mother and a writer as well. By all accounts she managed, but she did so by going without enough sleep for years.

Her music helped keep her occupied; she had a very positive experience with Frederic Robinson, with whom she studied opera direction and singing. According to Michael Hargreaves, he was the model for Masterharper Robinton in the Dragonriders of Pern series. Anne's musical career and her writing overlapped, but as her writing career blossomed she began to have to make choices. After 1965, her musical activities subsided to singing occasionally. Yet she remained proud of her many responsibilities in musical theater, as stage director for *The Devil and Daniel Webster* and *Kiss Me Kate* and as costume designer for *Guys and Dolls*. She played a number of character roles, including that of the Queen in *Once upon a Mattress*, a loud and talkative character who really rules the kingdom, and the Old Lady, who sings a duet with another female character, "We Are Women," in Leonard Bernstein's *Candide*. She considered her biggest success that of the Witch in a Christmas play, Carl Orff's *Ludus De Nato Infante Mirificus* in its American premiere. Anne's role as a character actress in musical theater and a stage director provided an outlet for her desire to perform and create. But Michael Hargreaves explains that Anne eventually "found she was fed up with amateur personalities, temperaments, and backstage antics." It was easier to direct characters in fiction than on stage. Yet Anne always retained her love of music, singing whenever she could and also giving music a prominent place not only in her Dragonriders of Pern series, but also, most notably, in the Crystal Singer series.

Anne saw herself as a bit of an orphan as a writer, needing to be fostered and encouraged. In her first published story, "Freedom of the Race," in 1953, Anne drew on her own experience with pregnancy with her first child, Alec, to craft a story about aliens using human females as reproductive surrogates. She continued to write but had difficulty placing another manuscript. The rejections were discouraging, but she kept writing, despite the arrival of her second child, Todd, in 1956. Busy with her children, it wasn't until 1959 that her second story, "Lady in a Tower," appeared. Throughout the 1950s and early 1960s, Anne struggled with doubt about her ability. She wanted to write, but lacked the self-confidence and knowledge about how to polish her writing and how and where to send it to editors. In 1961, her breakthrough story, "The Ship Who Sang," was published, but even after the influential editor Judy Merril chose it for a "Year's Best Science Fiction" anthology, Anne still doubted herself.

Finally, Anne was invited by Judith Merril to attend a weekend science fiction writers' conference in Milford, Pennsylvania. These were invitation-only conferences that drew many writers who became leaders in the field. There she met many of the writers who became her friends: James Blish, Ted Cogswell, Damon Knight, Gordon Dickson, and Avram Davidson. There she also met Virginia Kidd, who would become her agent, though that relationship was still years away. The conference opened up a community to Anne of like-minded individuals, writers who loved and believed in science fiction as she did. While, like most writers, Anne was independent, also, like most beginning writers, she needed encouragement and support. A second pivotal event was her attendance at Worldcon '63, in Washington, D.C. Already acquainted with many of the writers from the Milford conference, at Worldcon she met Isaac Asimov, Randall Garrett, and H. Beam Piper. Evvy Del Rey, at that time the wife of Lester Del Rey, an important editor and publisher, was at the bar, and she invited Anne over to sit by her. James Blish was sitting there drinking, too, and he said to her, "Anne, what has happened? You've published two lovely stories—what's happened? Why haven't you written anymore?" She replied, "Well, I'm *trying* to," and he insisted, "Well, you should continue." Inspired, on the long drive back to Delaware she kept thinking to herself, "Jim Blish says I can write. Jim *Blish* says I can write. Jim Blish says *I* can write."

Anxious and insecure, running a full household, it was a struggle for her to write. As she says, "I never let anyone read my stuff because I couldn't have stood the ridicule—especially once I started writing s-f." She says today, "I don't know as I asked for much encouragement—just to be let alone at the typewriter." Writing provided a perfect complement to being a mother. But to write Anne had to have, as most working mothers do, a split existence. She was "'just mommy' for a little while and [then] someone grown-up doing Other things." Writing allowed Anne to have another identity, another self; it provided an answer to her internalization of her mother's question, "What else will you be?" She was working to be a writer and that would fulfill one of her mother's ambitions. While Anne would eventually become well known for her writing for young adults as well as her adult science fiction, when she began to write seriously, her children were too young and "wriggly" to provide an audience. Unlike her brothers, her children would not sit or lie still long enough to be read even Kipling's short *Jungle Tales*, the stories she loved that her father had read to his children. Todd loved a story called "Crunch, Crunch, What's for Lunch?" which Anne would read to him while feeding him, but this was a far cry from the intense, complicated, and very adult fictional worlds she was creating.

Todd remembers very fondly vacations they took. They were family vacations, and Anne wasn't able to get much work done. On the other hand, she was at least able to socialize with Virginia Kidd and other writers. In the summers of 1964 and 1966, Anne and Wright, with Wright's colleague Jack Isbell and his wife, Peggy, rented the main building of what had been a boys' summer camp in Twin Lakes in the Pocono Mountains in Pennsylvania. Anne recalls that "the facility slept nine and had a good kitchen." She did the shopping and the cooking for the evening meal. The Isbells and Johnsons got along very well, leading to their home-sharing later when the men were transferred to the New York area. Todd McCaffrey remembers those summers fondly, especially the lake, which on their side was for non-motor boats only, and the abundance of blueberries, with which Anne used to make delicious pies. What she liked best was the cool weather and the parties she was able to throw, inviting her friends from New York and Virginia Kidd from Milford. Before her death, Virginia told of many wonderful evenings marked by Anne's wonderful cooking and camaraderie. Wright helped make one evening magical by placing candles in a number of small boats, lighting the candles, and then "sending the little boats out into the lake. Then they sailed and shone all night. It was a pretty sight to see, the lake bespangled with what he called Viking funeral ships." Wright's sense of the dramatic and love of words could have made him a helpful reader of his wife's work.

Wright could have been an appropriate reader, an English major who himself wrote professionally (though nonfiction), but, unfortunately, Wright's response to Anne's writing drove them apart. He remembers reading "The Ship Who Sang," the moving account of a Brain Ship who mourns the loss of her partner in a tragic adventure, and describing it to her as "perfect." He admits, however, that he found the science fiction setting and vocabulary off-putting. He did not read science fiction and had no appreciation for the genre. When she showed Wright other stories from what would eventually become the collection, *The Ship Who Sang*, she found his criticisms unhelpful. Like many readers, he had ideas for another story that should be told. Anne felt he was trying to control her writing, as he controlled so many other aspects of their lives. "'That's not the story I wanted to tell,'" she remembers telling him, surely a classic feminist response. While Wright's response to her writing was not supportive, his criticism may very well have helped her develop her own voice. She looked to see more clearly what *she* had to say. His wanting to control her showed her how important it was for her to speak strongly and to write her own vision. In a sense, her extraordinary career may be due in part to proving Wright Johnson wrong. In a number of letters to her agent, Virginia Kidd, Anne expressed the desire to prove Wright's assessment of her writing wrong. After describing Wright's hounding her about housekeeping, she writes, "How I would love to dangle a signed advance check in that bastard's face. He was singularly unimpressed by the Galaxy sale, . . . Whatinell [*sic*] does the man want?" The contumaciousness that runs in the McCaffrey family was here put to very good use.

There was a way, though, in which Wright did support Anne's writing. He provided the income and space that enabled her to write. It was, after all, while she was married to him that she began writing professionally. One summer, she hired a babysitter, Annie Phillips, to take care of the children for three hours a day. Anne acknowledges Wright's financial support of her—but this support came with the idea that she should write as he thought she should: "something 'significant' and 'meaningful.' Time has kindly proved that I was, if not on the level he hoped for." That so accomplished, feted, and successful a writer as Anne McCaffrey can still write such words, three decades after her marriage to Wright ended, provides testimony to his impact upon her as a person and as a writer. Her contrariness not only helped her withstand a hostile husband, but is also very evident in her literary taste and the genre in which she chose to write. In the 1950s and 1960s, women were not supposed to read science fiction, let alone write it. Most women writing science fiction, such as Andre Norton or C. L. Moore, hid their gender behind pseudonyms and initials. This practice continues in the twenty-first century: J. K. Rowling, the author of the Harry Potter books, became "J. K." at the insistence of her publisher, who said, "Boys don't read books written by women."

As a child, Anne had loved reading fantasy and science fiction, so when she rediscovered the genre in *Galaxy* magazine in the 1950s, she was hooked. She especially enjoyed reading Andre Norton, Isaac Asimov, Murray Leinster, Gordon Dickson, and Jim Blish. She enjoyed science fiction for the breadth of it away from the standard literary classics that she was supposed to read. "I thought I could write sf, too," she says. Anne, after all, was not an English major. Her major was in Slavic languages, and her thesis had been written on the Russian science fiction classic *WE*. But perhaps most important to her attraction to science fiction was the context of World War II and the emerging Cold War: she found optimism in science fiction and the hope of escaping from the world she knew. "We would get off our own planet," she hoped, "and away from poor war-torn Earth." In her thesis, a few years earlier, Anne had put it more histrionically, but it is worth quoting for its passion: "With the disruption of the world's order, first by war and then by the dreadful realization of the results of atomic energy, Fate has indeed conspired to shatter the existing scheme of things."

Anne's college classmate Freddie Brennerman says that Radcliffe students of that era showed "a strong undercurrent in our thinking of social responsibility, the desire to become better informed . . . and then to go out and *do* something about it." Like Alice Adams, another writer from the class of 1947, Anne "wish[ed] that the world were a better place." In Montclair, with

Mae Pangburn, bereft of her son through war, living down-stairs, Anne had a daily reminder of pain and suffering in the real world. Being trapped herself in a suffocating marriage reinforced her desire to travel to other worlds and to create other, better societies.

CHAPTER 4

Annie and Virginia

Hell, my association with Virginia lasted
a whole lot longer than my marriage did.
—Anne McCaffrey, e-mail

LIKE MOST WRITERS, ANNE has been a writer since she was a
child, but she became not just a successful writer, but a *good* writer
through her long relationship with her agent and editor, Virginia
Kidd. Their relationship began when a mutual friend, writer
and editor Judith Merril, suggested that Virginia consider being
Anne's agent. (Judith had included Anne's story, "The Ship Who
Sang," in a collection of the year's best science fiction.) Judith and
Virginia were close friends who had been roommates in New York
City during the 1940s, and in 1961 in Milford, while Judith and
Anne were in a grocery store, they ran into Virginia. Anne immediately liked Virginia's friendly and open nature and thought she
was very pretty. Anne recalls that Virginia "had much the same
sense of humor" as she did. Virginia also had a lovely speaking
voice that impressed Anne, who remembers, "She could use [her
voice] most effectively, from a purr of approval to a near-snarl of
dislike." In 1961, both Virginia and Anne had a few professional
sales, but neither could imagine the heights to which their relationship would take them. While other colleagues and friends
would be critical to Anne's success (especially Betty Ballantine
of Ballantine Books), Virginia was the one who really made it all
possible. Anne grew as a writer from having a demanding reader
who not only asked but *insisted* that she write her best; her unwavering belief sustained Anne.

While she might criticize aspects of Anne's writing, Virginia never deviated from her consistent praise of Anne as a powerful and effective writer. Virginia provided Anne with emotional support, practical advice, and unwavering acceptance. Anne's gratitude was unbounded; she responded (as one of her college supervisors described her) like a giant St. Bernard puppy. Where she found love, she gave love in return, and her relationship with Virginia stood the test of time and physical separation. Significantly, both Anne and Virginia referred to their long-standing personal and professional relationship as a marriage. These two women, whose own marriages had ended unhappily, found in each other the emotional support that their husbands had failed to provide. Anne and Virginia both entertained male lovers and other significant relationships, but for more than a decade, they were each other's emotional bedrock. Though Virginia Kidd would also work with a number of other important writers, including Ursula K. Le Guin, Gene Wolfe, and Alan Dean Foster, Virginia had her greatest impact on the career (and life) of Anne McCaffrey. This chapter covers a critical five years for Anne, 1965–1970, during which her life and work were influenced by her relationship with Virginia.

Nineteen sixty-five through 1970 were also critical years for the genre of science fiction, as it continued the transition from cheap magazines to the more respectable (and expensive) paperback and hardcover book format (that had begun in the 1950s). As science fiction began taking itself seriously, its writers met in organized workshops and formed a writers' association, Science Fiction Writers of America. Anne participated in one of the most famous workshops, the Milford conference, and became an officer in the national science fiction writers' group. One sign of the genre's increased respectability was the emergence of science fiction courses at universities. Anne's strengths in characterization and prose fit in well with science fiction's new, more ambitious, artistic posture. Through their respective roles as writer and agent, Anne and Virginia helped define and shape the development of American science fiction.

Five years older than Anne, Virginia was born in 1921, the

youngest of three children. Virginia contracted polio when she was two and a half, and was crippled until she had major corrective surgery at fourteen. Like Anne, Virginia was smart and precocious; popular and a leader, she recalls, "Boys walked me home from school . . . and I did much of their homework. I learned to read at four, and have never taken a writing class. I just wrote, every time I got a chance." At age nine she became a science fiction fan when her older brother gave her his science fiction magazines to read. She married James Blish, a well-known and respected science fiction writer, in 1947, the day her divorce from her first husband, Jacob Emden, was official. Like Anne, Virginia had three children, and also like Anne, Virginia divorced her husband after almost two decades of marriage and had to find a means of supporting herself and her children.

Virginia's science fiction credentials were impeccable. She had originally wanted to be "a famous writer" herself and was one of the founding members of the Futurians, a seminal science fiction society that included (before they became famous) writers and editors such as Isaac Asimov, Judith Merril, Frederick Pohl, Damon Knight, and Donald Wollheim. While Virginia sold a few stories and poems, she eventually discovered her true calling as an agent. Virginia was already informally acting as an agent to her many writer friends when Judith Merril told her she should *be* a professional agent and make her living at it. Being a successful agent, however, is as difficult as being a successful writer. Many of the same skills are required: you have to have talent, be hard working, persistent, have a tough skin, and be able to negotiate. Virginia's rare ability, however, was not only to recognize writing talent, but also to nurture it. In this regard, especially, Anne was very fortunate because Virginia really cared about the quality of a writer's work. When she saw potential, as she did in Anne's writing, she could be very supportive or critical, as the case required. Anne never took creative writing classes, but reading Virginia and Anne's correspondence reveals that Anne received graduate-level training in writing from Virginia Kidd. Anne recalls that Virginia was "a purely golden instructor of young and outrageous writers (which I was then—though others are [now] the genre's new outrageous ones)." While much of their exchanges took place on paper, they had frequent phone calls, too. Anne explains that she called Virginia "especially when I needed direction for some of my notions." Once, they were on a shared phone line, and as Anne was explaining about the Pern dragons, an exasperated male voice cut in, "What are you two dames talking about?" Anne responded that it was none of his business, but Virginia never wasted an opportunity to promote Anne, telling their listener to read the book when it was published.

Virginia lived at the center of science fiction's critical development, Milford, Pennsylvania. Conveniently near New York City, the town drew many famous science fiction writers to its summer conferences. A beautiful and historic place, Milford's attractions persuaded some of those writers to settle there, most notably Judith Merril. Anne's positive experience at her first Milford writers' workshop in 1959 inclined her toward Virginia. The Milford Science Fiction Conference was a prestigious gathering of science fiction veterans and beginning writers; it began in 1956. It was an honor to be invited to participate by the conference directors, and its sessions involved sharing unpublished work and receiving comments from the other writers. The participants were generally envied because they not only received help with their writing, but were also able to meet editors of important anthology series. Attending a Milford conference meant that publishers would pay more attention to your submissions. This favoritism was occasionally resented, leading to participants being called the "Milford Mafia." The group's esprit de corps led to the founding of the Science Fiction Writers of America, the important writers' group that bestows the prestigious Nebula Awards, and Anne's involvement in Milford conferences led to her two-year position as secretary-treasurer of the group in 1968.

While Anne benefited from a couple of Milford workshops, the decades of attention she and her writing received from Virginia were even more critical to her continued development as a writer. Their relationship bears some resemblance to the agent-writer relationship of Maxwell Perkins and Ernest Hemingway, a type of relationship heralded as part of literature's past, in which the editor molds the writer, becoming more of a collaborator than business agent. And perhaps in the twenty-first century, such relationships are even rarer than they were then. But Virginia and Anne's relationship provides compelling testimony that even the best writers need and require constructive criticism and scrupulous editing. What is especially encouraging about this relationship is that it provides vindication of Virginia's philosophy of aiming for quality, believing that financial reward would then follow. Perhaps because they were women, they understood that the boundaries between the professional and the personal could not and should not be maintained. In a way, their relationship embodied that 1960s feminist motto, "The Personal Is Political." Virginia not only was deeply involved with Anne's writing but also was her confidante. Their gender is essential to understanding their relationship. Virginia was a bit older, but she shared with Anne the experience of being a mother and a writer and having a difficult marriage with an alcoholic husband (in Virginia's case, it was her second husband who had a drinking problem). Like Anne's husband, Virginia's first husband was not supportive of her writing. In addition, Virginia had already experienced the difficulty of juggling writing and motherhood. As her roommate in the mid 1940s, Judith Merril explains, "Virginia not only understood but shared . . . all the dilemmas posed by our commitment to being both good mothers and great writers." Virginia's and Anne's frank letters reveal that they shared details about home life, financial problems, cooking, weight, and appearance, along with the main emphasis on writing and business matters. In some ways, Virginia became the older sister Anne never had. She advised Anne on how to deal with friends, children, and husband in the same letters that she discussed publishers, fan letters, and other writers.

Both women were well aware of the difficulties they faced in science fiction. Most of the genre's writers and editors were men who operated under the assumption that the readership was male. Women writers faced the derisive dismissal of their work as "diaper copy." The all-important Milford workshop included few women, and Virginia had trouble being admitted because Damon

Knight considered her collaborative work with her husband, Jim Blish, to have been written all by Blish. While Virginia recounted stories of discrimination, she rejected any identification of herself as feminist, a label the younger Anne accepted more readily. Yet even this significant distinction did not cause trouble between the two women. Virginia praised and admired Anne's feminist heroines and lobbied hard for Anne's work. Their first real bonding took place when Virginia made a trip to Anne's home in Delaware in early 1963. Virginia remembers being struck by Anne's Irish appearance and her adorable daughter, Gigi. Wright, she says, was polite, but she really had very little conversation with him. Anne enjoyed Virginia's weekend visit, and she recalls, "We drank a lot of white wine I had inadvertently made . . . a rough white but you could drink a lot of it without a hangover. . . . She was very kind to me. . . . She pointed the way and I followed." But due to their busy lives and straitened finances, the women communicated most often by letter. Anne has long acknowledged her debt to Virginia, explaining, "My relationship with Virginia was unusual because it was so rewarding for me . . . and I matured in my skills under her guidance. I was exceedingly lucky because Virginia has a very deft touch in bringing promising writers on and ensuring their maturity." Anne and Virginia's correspondence corroborates Anne's assessment, though in typical fashion Anne minimizes what she brought to the relationship. Anne had a backlog of fiction that she was eager to rework for publication, and she listened attentively to Virginia's every suggestion. And Virginia had suggestions, pages and pages, sometimes, of constructive criticism. In their exchanges, we can see a writer emerging.

At first, much of Virginia's advice, repeated over and over, is practical: how to prepare a manuscript, the importance of keeping a copy, proofreading. It is clear that Anne is delighted to have found a sympathetic reader, and she is rushing her work out. Repeatedly, Virginia cautioned Anne against haste and listed a number of common grammatical errors. She asked Anne to "post a little list of pitfalls somewhere near your typewriter, just to keep my proofreader's brow from wrinkling? Here are several candidates for the list, and to engrave the distinctions in your mind, you ought to look them up for yourself: dis*p*arate-desp*e*rate." She continued somewhat pedantically, "I think once you really notice the difference, you will probably use them with respect for their entymological [*sic*] differences." Many of Virginia's letters to Anne contain mini-grammar lessons, all of which Anne appears to have followed.

Virginia's comments went well beyond the importance of clean and accurate presentation of the manuscript. In letter after letter, she criticized not only word choice, but plot, characterization, and even concepts. She continually challenged Anne to produce good work, and chastened her when the writing seemed sloppy. Virginia didn't hesitate to edit when it seemed necessary to her, though she always let Anne know. For example, "Horse from a Different Sea" prompted Virginia to do some serious editing. She referred to "the blanket permission you [Anne] gave me a while back to meddle" and announced, "I rewrote the beginning entire, and retyped the last page to out some of the verbiage and to include my one (ineffably gruesome) new idea. I have sent it out, so changed, but if you are outraged I can always yank it and restore it to the version you wrote. The thing is, it was too good, to have such weak spots left intact! Possibly you'll like the changes?" The changes stayed; Anne respected Virginia's extensive editing and readily conceded that Virginia improved her writing. This extension of editing into rewriting was unusual, but the fact that Virginia would make an addition and Anne would accept it shows the degree to which they trusted each other. This practice reflects a feminist form of collaboration, rather than a masculinist model of individual achievement. To this day, Anne continues to work with other women writers in "shared universe" books, a practice that has its antecedents in her early collaboration with Virginia. One or two other times, usually with short stories, Virginia made similar interpolations, but as Anne's writing skills developed, Virginia restricted her editing to making suggestions rather than making changes.

In their exchanges, Virginia and Anne revealed their dedication to the work of writing and editing. Virginia explained her standard for being an editor/agent: "I decided when I first started out in this business that one reason Ken White was as respected and trusted on *both* sides of the desk was because he NEVER let anything go out of his office unread, no matter how good the author or how big a name. The one day to one week delay this normally entails is (in the long run) well worth it to the client as it is to the editors." Virginia's commitment and passion for meticulous editing is equaled by Anne's devotion to her writing. Anne described her transformation in 1965, facilitated by Gigi's entering first grade: "It was like 'who pulled out the plug' for novel-writing." Describing her passion for writing, Anne wrote, commenting on "that old saw so-and-so wishes to *'devote'* more time to writing. Devotion is not quite the word. Obsession, I believe, is better. Because I have been like one obsessed, sitting down at this hot typewriter hour after hour and even sleeping with the mss clutched in my hot little ink-splattered hand. . . . It has become increasingly difficult to leave Lothar [setting of her first novel, *Restoree*] and trek all the way back to earth, dinners to be got and kids to be shoved schoolwards et al." Anne writes of her "Muse" "driving, driving, DRIVING me." In Virginia, Anne found someone who appreciated and understood her intense desire to write science fiction. Their passion for the work was powerful, and each thrived on the work produced by the other.

In the very first exchanges, Anne seemed tentative, asking Virginia not to be her agent, but to collaborate with her. Virginia, after all, is already a respected and published writer, both as a poet and as a fiction writer with her husband, Jim Blish, while Anne lacked complete confidence in her own writing. But Virginia's enthusiastic responses soon had Anne feeling good about her skills. Virginia did not try to impose a certain style of writing or type of idea on Anne's fiction. Unlike the famous editor John Campbell, who directed writers to rewrite according to his ideas, Virginia tried to help writers do their own best work. For this reason, she was a successful editor not only with Anne, but also with a number of the genre's other famous writers. Despite her own strong opinions, Virginia never took advantage of Anne's insecurity. Virginia's response to early versions of "The Ship Who Wept" and "The Lady" demonstrated Virginia's confidence in

Anne's writing ability. "My dear girl! You don't need a collaborator! A poke here, a prod there, maybe. But your talent is your own. Let us (and I am serious) nourish it." Virginia described herself crying over these stories, moved by their characters' situations: "Imagine yourself a lifesize picture of me in tears, three times, and entitle it the Agent That Wept. Hardened Old Me!" Virginia presented herself as older and wiser, as an older sister, perhaps, but also as a dear friend and a professional advisor.

While Virginia was extremely supportive and doled out praise generously, she was also frequently blunt and always honest. If Virginia believed the premise or articulation of an idea was weak, she said so. Virginia's literary standards were exacting; she disliked pedestrian or pulp fiction, written without care for language. In March 1967, for example, she sent Anne a letter that begins, "THE GOLD RULING just isn't up to my standards, and I'd rather not market it. . . . It covers a wide range of too crude and obvious—the names are too obvious, and the style is your worst." She continued in this vein with quite specifically damning analysis and concluded: "I guess that's enough flaying. But in short I think your version of the Goldin' Rule stinks. In spades and ofays [*sic*]." And Virginia, despite her words, was *not* through. She elaborated, "The style is that of a drunken Sybil, . . . a hophead fortune teller." With some balm, Virginia told Anne, "Pick yourself up and dust yourself off. You are not the first (nor will you be the last) to whom a manuscript has been returned as unsaleable by his/her agent."

Over the years, Virginia continued to operate as Anne's conscience, warning her to slow down, to work more carefully, and to consider the aesthetics involved. She told Anne to burn the first version of *Dragonquest*, and, agreeing with Virginia's trenchant critique, Anne did. In a second version of the novel, Virginia complained about "innumerable carelessnesses" and warned her, "YOU REALLY MUST HAVE PEACE AND FREEDOM OF MIND ENOUGH TO DO YOUR BEST ON A MANUSCRIPT IF YOUR REPUTATION IS NOT TO SLIP, MY DEAR GIRL." The caps suggest that Virginia is yelling at Anne, but she softened the adjuration with the reminder, "I do not say that condescendingly, but with much love and concern."

In an earlier letter, Virginia admonished Anne again, "When you are *too* prolific, you get prolix and that means much re-writing, so better go a little slower." To a second version of *Dragonquest,* Virginia wrote a twelve-page, single-spaced, closely argued response. A letter such as that reveals a dedication and commitment to Anne's work that is quite remarkable, but quite characteristic of Virginia's attention to detail and her willingness to express her opinions bluntly. For a version of *The Rowan,* for example, she analyzed the story under headings, including "Art," "Craft," and "Clinically." Virginia's reading in this case was characteristically sympathetic and perceptive, revealing that the job of a good editor is to be part coach, part teacher, part literary critic, and even a bit of a psychologist. Under "Art" she cited James Joyce and praised Anne's creation of "a valid basic situation, some very good writing." Under the heading of "Craft," Virginia pointed to some problems created by the need to convey information. In this version, Anne had the protagonist, the Rowan, provide crucial facts, but Virginia argued that this was "out of character" and proposed remedies. She suggested that Anne was writing out some episodes in her own life: "Anne has a clash or clashes with own children, also with her own mother. . . . Anne is a romantic, troubled obscurely by who knows what." Most significantly, in terms of their relationship, Virginia experienced a shock of recognition that she argued is a part of all great art: "An artist who elicits a real twang in his reader is likely to have reached someone who shares his preconceptions, in some part." She acknowledged, "This story hit me so hard, because this is where some part of my own experience matches some part of yours, if only vaguely."

This resonance and the ability to convey deep emotion is one of Anne McCaffrey's signal achievements as a writer. Part of Anne's power as a writer stems from her ability to make the reader feel as if she is experiencing the character's feelings. Virginia's understanding that this skill was Anne's greatest strength as a writer made Virginia the perfect agent/editor for Anne's work. Virginia's ability to resonate, just as later Killashandra would resonate with crystal in *The Crystal Singer,* is what made their relationship so powerful and successful. As Killashandra can separate crystal from surrounding rock, so Virginia could sense the rare and beautiful in Anne's writing and separate it from the mundane and everyday. Killashandra almost becomes one with the crystal; so too did Virginia seem to become Anne as she was editing.

At first the salutations in their letters were formal, but as the writers' honesty and trust grew over time, the headings changed. From "Dear Anne" and "Dear Virginia," the openings shifted to "Anne, dear," "Dear, dear Virginia," and to "Dearest Annie," "Dearest Virginia dear," and even "Annie-panny pudding and pie." (In the mid-1960s Anne began to be known to all her friends as "Annie," the name she stills uses.) The shifts to endearments reflected a growing bond between the two women, as they shared everyday annoyances, financial worries, and intimate details of personal relationships. Since both women are accomplished writers, their correspondence is rich and lively, reflecting each woman's strong and vibrant personality. As might be expected, the older and wiser woman, Virginia is more often in the position of giving Anne advice than vice versa. Anne acknowledges this aspect of their relationship when she writes, "I tried to find a card entitled 'YOU ARE MY SHOT IN THE ARM' or considering all the Nun pictures lately 'YOU ARE MY MOTHER CONFESSOR' but none presented themselves. However, you are performing such functions, above and beyond, I am sure, the duties of an agent . . . long-suffering, etc." A few months later, Anne reiterated her appreciation of Virginia in these words, "Have I told you recently, in so many words, how much I appreciate you? How invaluable you are to me? A sustaining comfort . . . And one day, I sincerely hope, a source of income." Anne's wit and humor helped keep the intersection of business and friendship from being a source of trouble. Many of her letters to Virginia contained humorous asides about their business dealings. Anne's opinion of Virginia's place in her life is revealed in her reply to Virginia's thank you for a gift of stationary, an appropriate present when so much of their relationship took place via letters. Anne wrote, "I, too, rarely give outside the family. But what else are you, spiritually?"

Virginia's sympathies with Anne were direct and concrete. Because they share intimate details of everyday life, Virginia can understand why Anne's writing is often imperfect and rushed. She wrote, "I have never known anybody with as many outside interests (the drayma [*sic*] and all those charitable activities), as heavy a family burden (your well-cared for kids, your beautiful house that you paint miles and miles of wall of, the various personality problems with Wright and Alec & Todd & Gigi with which you cope instead of just saying 'Mama's writing, go away, dear!'), the shared household [with Jack and Peg Isbell] (which inevitably means you are nurse when Peg's sick and have more coffee breaks than not). *I* don't see how you get anything at all written, and yet you write fast, and good." The "drayma" Virginia referred to was Anne's active musical career, which by 1965 was winding down. Occasionally, Anne would write with pleasure of a production she was working on, but after 1966, the letters focus primarily on Anne's pleasure in writing fiction. Virginia insisted on, and Anne wanted, more time devoted to Anne's writing. Because both women write repeatedly about difficult finances, overdrafts, cars that break down, and children's medical expenses, the gift of stationery must be considered generous, and symbolic—a nice way of Anne saying to Virginia, "Keep writing me!" In the same letter, Anne confessed, "We have just trudged upward from the valley of payment to bare solvency . . . thanks to RESTOREE [her first novel], I might add." Despite her straitened circumstances, Anne is repeatedly generous in her business dealings with Virginia. For example, she insisted Virginia take 50 percent of one payment of fourteen dollars, instead of the customary 10 percent. In this letter, Anne revealed her growing confidence in her writing due to her tax status: "I discovered, after sweating the evening out with the tax man, that Anne McCaffrey is a business. This also restores my spirits. No news to you but fun for me."

Some of Anne's concern about money and independence appear in her interest, first expressed in a letter to Virginia dated August 13, 1965, about getting a degree in library science. The American Library Association, which awarded Anne the Margaret A. Edwards Award for Literary Lifetime Achievement, would probably be pleased to know that their honoree once considered their line of work. Of course, Anne would have been following the example of another famous science fiction writer she greatly admired, Andre Norton, who worked as a librarian for years. Ironically, it seems to have been the cost of tuition for one course, $132, as much as Virginia's discouragement, that kept Anne from a degree in library science. Her friend Peg Isbell, with whom the McCaffreys shared a Long Island mansion, also discouraged graduate school. Peg also was an aspiring writer, and, in Anne's words (in a letter to Virginia), "Peg insists I *devote* myself to the Muse for a while and if all else falls through and I cannot sell (I do not sell, rather) then try for other means of putting the family rocking finances back on their feet." Virginia was quite relieved by Anne's decision, writing, "Peg said what I felt," adding that since she made money from Anne's writing, she did not feel free to be as blunt as Peg. But with the decision made, she concurred with Peg and added, "But I hope you will be making good money writing, not too long from now," a prescient, if not timely prediction. It would be at least three years before Anne would see substantial income from her writing, and she herself feels that she was not financially stable "until the mid 70s when [her] books began to earn their advance and bring in royalties." In those lean years, Virginia provided vitally needed encouragement, practical support, and, perhaps most importantly, an unshakeable belief in Anne's writing ability.

Virginia's support and encouragement were backed up not only by Peg, but also by Anne's favorite aunt, Gladys. Anne described Aunt Gladys as "my biggest rooter and staunchest ally," and the effect of her visits as "extremely drunk-making as well as ego-inflating." Significantly, Anne compared Aunt Gladys and Virginia, explaining to Virginia, "Until I met you, she was the only one who had complete faith in my ability to be a writer. She is outrageously enthusiastic and approving to the point of red-faced embarrassment." Anne is grateful for "her apt remarks and direct analysis," comments which would certainly apply to Virginia, as well. Anne later wrote to Virginia about her aunt's "conversion" to science fiction, a conversion that she no doubt wished Wright would make: "My aunt, for whom RESTOREE was dedicated, wrote to say she's been hooked on s-f, . . . having read the Dragon stories and loved them." Her aunt's conversion foreshadowed that of many, many other readers whom Anne has similarly converted through the Dragonriders of Pern series. But it was to Virginia, not to her aunt, that Anne turned for advice on the worries and domestic difficulties that inhibited her writing, as well as her marital problems. The biggest obstacle to Anne's work, repeatedly mentioned in her correspondence with Virginia, was her husband. Initially, called "Wright" in the correspondence, he quickly became "Johnson." Virginia provided Anne with the support that she did not receive from her husband, but Anne also craved her husband's support and approval. She is delighted when she can write Virginia with the name of an editor at McGraw-Hill, courtesy of Wright. She crowed over not only the coup of the contact, but also how she got the name—her husband mentioned that his wife wrote science fiction to a friend of his college roommate, Van Varner. When Wright told Anne that "The Ship Who Sang," "was perfect," Anne was pleased.

As her letters to Virginia document, Wright's praise for "The Ship Who Sang" was a rare exception in a long list of sorry incidents, in which he was unable to give Anne the support she wanted and deserved. Now, three decades later, he can grudgingly acknowledge her excellence as a writer, but in the 1960s he could not or would not. In a way, Wright probably influenced Anne's growing feminism because his complaints to her are the stuff of classic feminist narrative. In Matthew Hargreaves's annotated bibliography of McCaffrey, he reproduces an article published about Anne's first story. The local reporter explained, "Being a Princeton man, Mr. Johnson takes a somewhat dim view of his wife's flights into outer space." In Anne's words to Virginia, "Johnson informed me that I am the world's filthiest, dirtiest, lousiest housekeeper, that he gives me all his money (implying I spend it all on *me*) and that he simply isn't getting his money's worth. And he isn't the least bit interested, pleased, etc. about my writing which he doesn't consider of moment at all anyway." Anne's anger was clear, and she responded by calculating the worth of her labor: "I have also been totaling up the hours I put in at the local rate of $1.25 per hr for housework and $5.00 non union rates for painting and the amount of money I could make in the market for the amount of work I do around this house makes it almost practical for me to take a lousy housekeeper's job and the hell with him." Anne vividly painted a picture of a home-maker trying futilely to keep a place clean with a husband and three children: "If all of them did not tend to leave peanut butter and jelly smears on the kitchen table and mop up juice from refrig and floor when spilled and not leave sugar underfoot when Johnson comes up early for breakfast. And/or mess up HIS room when watching tv . . ." Surely this description reveals in part how Anne was able to write convincingly about her heroines Sara (*Restoree*) and Lessa (*Dragonflight*) having to clean up after brothers and other men. Lessa is literally a servant, a "drudge," ignored and unappreciated except by the Hold Watchdragon. Her "ship who sang," Helva, with her tremendous powers, was a vicarious fantasy for Anne. As Anne later acknowledged, "Helva was my alter ego in the days when I suspected my marriage was failing. It would be easy to see that parallel in 'The Ship Who Disappeared' (which was written in 1968) with Helva's high decibel ousting of an unsatisfactory brawn. I did enjoy writing that scene!"

After venting, Anne thanked Virginia for her support and concluded, "I'm going to have to wait Johnson out on this house-keeping binge which cuts seriously into my writing time, unfortunately. However, I will persevere . . . as if my inner compulsion gave me any other choice in this matter." This account appears again and again: Wright's lack of emotional support, which eventually becomes verbal abuse, and Anne's determination to survive and to write in spite of his efforts to sabotage her. As Anne's confidence in writing emerged, she was able to write more cheerfully: "Johnson's been making neglected noises: screamed at me for running such a pig-pen. . . . Actually he has not been as neglected as he thinks he is! What's been neglected has been Pern #2." To Anne's description of her husband's complaints, Virginia immediately wrote back a long letter of encouragement, including practical as well as emotional advice. She joked, "It's a pity Wright could not spend a week or two in the domestic, if not the connubial situation with me! THEN he would see what Bad Housekeeping consists of." She addressed Anne as "Sister Anne" and explained (years before John Gray's and Deborah Tannen's scholarship that reached the same conclusion) that men and women speak two different languages. She commiserated, explaining that her husband also complained about her housekeeping when, of course, "a good three-quarters of the always current clutter was his projects, rather than mine." She responded to the economics of the situation by asserting that "IF he were buying you, he has the world's Best Bargain, dear girl—who else would put up with him?" Virginia's support for Anne as a person and a writer helped her continue, despite the incessant belittling she received from Wright.

The summer of 1968, with the country in an unacknowledged war in Vietnam and internally convulsed with students' antiwar protests, proved epochal for Anne. That summer she took two important trips, one with her Aunt Gladys to the country that would become her home, Ireland, and another to the World Science Fiction Convention in Berkeley, California. The letters reveal that Anne concentrated her energy on her fictional worlds, showing little trace in her correspondence of the Vietnam War, student protests, or changing social mores. Aware of Anne's marital troubles, Aunt Gladys took Anne on a trip with her to Scotland, Ireland, and England. With Peggy Isbell and Wright taking care of the children, Anne was able to travel abroad with her aunt for eighteen days. Because Aunt Gladys was older, she welcomed Anne's assistance in making such a long trip, and Aunt Gladys also wanted to show Anne her family homeland. Anne had always been proud of being Irish, even presciently signing a letter to Virginia in green ink, "Irish Annie." Anne and her aunt began in Roseneath, the town from which Gladys's grandparents had emigrated to America. Then they visited Glasgow, Edinburgh, and London, before journeying to Ireland for a coastal tour of Waterford, Cork, Limerick, and Shannon. They stayed at Dromoland Castle their last night in Ireland. Anne had particularly enjoyed the Dublin Horse Show (with the exception of a tragic accident that resulted in a horse being put down). Anne remembers being sorry to leave Ireland because she "loved Ireland and the easy way of the Irish folk to tourists and the weather, which is much cooler in the summer than NY." She had no idea then that she would be able to return, to live in Ireland permanently in just two years, but she knew that in returning to Long Island that she "was going back to trouble." The glow of that magical visit would linger, calling to her when she divorced and wanted to start a new life. Then Ireland would seem a logical choice for a new home.

While traveling to Ireland introduced Anne to the country that would become her new home, the 1968 World Science Fiction Convention (held over Labor Day weekend at the end of that summer) provided both inspiration and confirmation of Anne's choice to focus on her writing. She had just been elected secretary-treasurer of the Science Fiction Writers of America "and wanted to meet the other officers." Her decision to attend was propitious because an address by Ray Bradbury gave her the idea for one of her most-praised stories (and popular series), "The Ship Who Sang." Bradbury explained that he had written his story "The Snows of Kilimanjaro" in response to Hemingway's suicide. Unable to accept his hero's death, he rewrote the story to have his hero killed by a tiger. Anne admiringly described Bradbury's revision as "wishful thinking" and began to do some thinking about her father's death. She wrote "The Ship Who Sang" as "a therapeutic way to cure the shock" she had at her father's death. This revelation by Anne explains how some writers get their ideas—from conventions, from other writers—and also how they apply ideas and transform them into art. But this World Con did more than provide Anne with a concept she could rework. "Weyr Search," the first story in what would become Anne's most successful series, the Dragonriders of Pern, had been nominated for a Hugo, the award bestowed annually at the world convention. Anne became the first woman to win the Hugo. She was elated and said of the trip home, "I don't think I needed the plane's wings to get me home." The publishers, Ian and Betty Ballantine, were so pleased for Anne that they paid for her upgrade to first class, so that she could fly with them. The trip was a foretaste of the good things that would eventually come from Anne's writing. But in 1968, she was still struggling financially.

Anne McCaffrey's statement of earnings for 1968 reveals just how successful she had become—almost enough to support herself and her three children. While Anne's earnings were impressive, they still amounted to less than her parents' income in 1944 (as reported in a financial statement to Radcliffe College). In 1968 she earned almost six thousand dollars from her writing, of which Virginia received 10 percent (5 percent on two United Kingdom sales). In a note Virginia writes, "You're still my top money-maker, and I'm proud of you." Significantly, she adds parenthetically, "(what hath God wrought, Wright?)" Her career was firmly established as "Anne McCaffrey" because Johnson didn't want his name associated with science fiction. In this earnings statement, "Johnson" appears as an afterthought, in parenthesis. At this time, Wright was spending more and more time in New York City, with the excuse that he was working so hard that he didn't have time to commute home to Long Island. At the end of 1968, Anne told Virginia that she had announced to her oldest son, Alec, "that his father and I are estranged. . . . I even went so far as to check into a divorce [in] NY state and, while it's possible, it is also one of the dirtiest states in which to get a divorce." This is one of the first letters Anne writes with her new stationary, headed with her name, "Anne McCaffrey," and underneath, "Member SFWA" (Science Fiction Writers of America). Anne's new, independent identity now appears not only on her publications, but also on her personal stationary.

But Anne was still not completely separated from Wright. Despite Wright's heavy drinking and criticism of her, Anne still continued to want his approval. As her son Todd's account of the relationship reveals, Wright could be physically abusive not only to Anne but to Todd as well. "*I* remember," Todd writes, "one night when we were all at the kitchen table after dinner, drinking coffee. Dad and Mum were bickering back and forth. . . . Wright threw the empty cup at her face. . . . It was Alec who told Dad he had better leave." Anne worried about the effect of Wright's abuse on the children. She remembers, "It got so bad that none of the children would dare talk at dinner and that annoyed Wright even more. A no-win situation. But Todd took the worst of these encounters. The day that Todd told me that he knew why his daddy had to beat him, because he left marks on Gigi's face and Alec was too big. That's when I realized I had to tell my husband I wanted a divorce." Understandably, Anne's brother Kevin and other family members have little positive to say about Wright. But their negative comments pale in comparison to Virginia's. Anne can hardly say a negative word about anyone, but Virginia, her friend, was as harsh about Wright as she was about Anne's less-than-standard writing. "Wright," Virginia told me bluntly, "was a monster." Vaughne Hansen, who had worked for Virginia Kidd for twelve years, corroborates Virginia's dislike of Wright, telling me that when she first came to work for Virginia, almost the first story she heard was "the Wright Johnson story" of his abuse.

At age nine, Gigi, of course, didn't understand the situation, but she suggested to her mother that if she would give up writing, things would be okay. Anne knew that it wasn't that simple—not only could she not give up her writing, but that would not solve their marital problems. Anne saw another source of Wright's difficulties, "the corporate mind." She further explained, "Wright was forced to expedients which went against his upbringing and his own ethical code: firing an associate who was also a close personal friend and other corporate exigencies. He was also away a good deal, covering the fashion scene in Europe. I was no match for the elegant folk he met there, nor could I compete with such luminaries. I didn't try. In 1960, seeing how such corporate necessities were altering the man I had married, I begged him to leave and find another job that was not so stressful or demanding. But he really did enjoy the fashion work he was doing. . . . He also liked the salary and prestige of being with a major U.S. firm. He wouldn't even consider resigning." Years of living with an abusive man had deepened Anne's feelings of insecurity. She blamed herself for the change in their relationship: "I tried harder to salvage our earlier rapport but I wasn't clever enough." Anne even began to doubt her capability to be a good mother and imagined leaving the children, too: "I had come to see myself as an ineffective mother and began to believe that the children would be better off with their father. I'd just leave and go someplace I wasn't known and start over. I could find a job as a cook, or a waitress or a typist. I wouldn't be fussy." Despite her burgeoning career as a writer, Anne was demoralized and devastated by her marriage. She could not see beyond the divorce as a failure and herself as worthless. That is what years of verbal abuse had done to her.

As Anne's independent identity emerged and her marriage deteriorated, she turned to someone who was also experiencing the end of a marriage, the well-known science fiction writer Isaac Asimov. Anne and Isaac had met in 1963 at a science fiction conference in Washington, D.C., and they had remained friends. Anne liked his writing and told him so, a compliment every writer likes to hear, especially from another writer. She remembers him as "good company and his puns were fabulous." As Todd, Anne's son, recounts, it was to Isaac that Anne turned when she needed to find someone to present her with her first major award, the Nebula that Anne received from the Science Fiction Writers of America. Usually the secretary-treasurer presented the awards, but in 1968 Anne was the secretary-treasurer, and she could hardly present the award to herself. In a long and humorous speech, Isaac picked many science fiction writers' names and put them to popular songs. He concluded by belting out a version of "San Francisco" to these lyrics: "Anne Mc-Caf-frey / Open your golden gates! / I can no longer wait!" Anne joked in response, "Never trust a tenor," and promised to pay him back for the joke. They met a few weeks later at Boskone, the Boston science fiction convention. Isaac had been asked to present the E. E. Doc Smith Award. Somewhat maudlin, he addressed the crowd, saying, "Right now, among all my societies, it is you—and science fiction—whose good opinion I require. I want you to love me, love me, love me, or I will die." Loudly, from the back of the room, Anne yelled, "Live, Tinker Bell!" to the crowd's laughter. To even more laughter, Isaac replied, "Five minutes alone with you and I'll prove that I'm no Tinker Bell!" Their rather public flirtation, did, however, have a basis in reality. It was at this Boskone that Isaac got his rather more than five minutes and satisfactorily proved himself to be "no Tinker Bell."

Like Anne, Isaac had a keen sense of humor; and, despite his writing success, he, too, wrestled with feelings of insecurity intensified by his troubled marriage. They also shared a talent for singing, livening many a convention with their duet of "When Irish Eyes Are Smiling." While their relationship provided consolation in difficult emotional times, neither felt that they wanted or were able to consider a permanent tie. This attitude disappointed the editor Judy Lynn Del Rey, who tried to encourage both of them to make a permanent relationship of their affair. But as Anne explains, "He was going through a messy divorce and needed someone sympathetic to talk to. Me." While Anne provided Isaac with support, he also made her feel wanted and appreciated, something she had not felt for a long time. Professionally, Anne felt appreciated: her work had been recognized both by the fans, with the Hugo Award, and her peers, with the Nebula. She had achieved three firsts, being the first woman to win each award and the first woman to win both. And her relationship with Isaac made her realize that she needed and wanted a drastic change in her life. This time, however, she did not confide in Virginia.

Anne and Wright's divorce plans became firmer when Wright moved out completely in the spring of 1970. By this time, his departure was a relief for Anne. Unfortunately, as often is the case, the divorce also cost Anne a dear friend, Peggy Isbell, who ordered Anne out of her half of the large mansion the two families had shared. Her friend Peggy's dismissal of her, however, was unexpected and painful. They had been close friends for years, sharing writing ambitions, gossip, child-rearing ideas. Many afternoons they took a martini break, and Anne nursed Peggy through a number of minor illnesses. But after Wright moved out and the divorce was final, Peggy dumped her. A heartbroken Anne wrote to Virginia, "Peggy socked me into Coventry about three weeks ago which makes the atmosphere of this house *dismal* if not downright godawful." Virginia called later that summer, on the afternoon when Anne and Peggy parted for the last time. From the Toronto science fiction convention, Anne wrote to Virginia to explain that she couldn't do "much thinking when you called me that afternoon. I went and took two stiff drinks and still had a tremendous reaction to the 'Scene'—there are disadvantages to being an empath. . . . Fortunately she got out of the house Wednesday, leaving a message with Todd 'that I was to leave all keys to the house on the hall table'—*my* table says she with an amused chuckle. So I did!" Anne further related the unusual behavior of Peggy's cats, who uncharacteristically rubbed up against her, as though they were saying that they would miss her. Anne confessed that she would miss the cats, but surely between these lines is the palpable regret for her lost friendship with Peggy. Alec was about to start college in New York, so Anne took only Todd and Gigi to the North American Science Fiction convention in Toronto. There she and Isaac Asimov, who were co-guests of honor, "had a roaringly funny time but no big sense of separation. I knew we'd meet again. . . . No heartbreak." After the convention, Anne flew with the children from Toronto directly to Ireland.

Poignantly, Anne had earlier written to Virginia about Todd's desire to run away, a common childhood fantasy. Facing a bully at school, Todd told his mother he wanted to run away. Anne told him they would run away together. And after Todd was tested and found to have a genius-level intellect, Anne says she told him, "Maybe we better not run away quite yet." Four years later, Anne found that it *was* time. She felt that "it was going to be an adventure but I was sure I would manage . . . though part of me wondered how." She explains, "Like many of my heroines, I was nervous, but it was a step that had to be taken to break a pattern."

Anne had not wanted to get divorced, but not because of religious reasons; in fact, when her brother Kevin had divorced before 1970, she tried to talk him out of it. Their parents had raised them to follow through on their commitments, and no one in their parents' generation had been divorced. But undoubtedly Kevin's divorce, the first in their family, made it easier for Anne herself to end her marriage. In her letters to Virginia, Anne discussed the difficult nature of New York State divorce laws. At first it seemed that Wright's employer, Dupont, would send Wright to Mexico on business and that, while there, he would file for the divorce. Finally, Anne had to make the trip herself in August 1970. Although every divorce is a lonely, unique experience, Anne and

Wright were part of a trend in American culture. In 1970, divorces increased 13 percent from the previous year, to an all-time high of 715,000.

Of Anne's move to Ireland, Virginia says, "It surprised me tremendously, but it was the best thing she could do [to get] far away from Wright." She remembers Wright as "handsome, talented, and nasty." Her interpretation of their difficulties is that Wright thought he was a better writer and that he was jealous of Anne's success. The letters corroborate Virginia's understanding of the situation, for a couple of times Anne mentions that Wright had submitted a manuscript to a publisher, but the outcome is never mentioned; Anne never explained what happened, but presumably the manuscripts were rejected. Like Anne's mother, Wright wrote but never published any of his creative writing. While Wright's jealousy of Anne's success undoubtedly contributed to the demise of their marriage, Anne's sudden move across an ocean suggested something more ominous in Wright's behavior. Yet, even after the move to Ireland, Anne still expressed concern for Wright in her letters to Virginia, even going so far as to dedicate one of her novels to him. But once in Ireland, Anne became a free woman, reveling in horseback-riding, fulfilling relationships with men, and, most importantly, her writing.

CHAPTER 5

Emigration and a Best-Seller

It was her father who betrayed her ambition to be a Harper,
who thwarted her love of music. Menolly had no choice but
to run away. She came upon a group of fire lizards . . . [and]
her music swirled about them; she taught nine to sing,
suddenly Menolly was no longer alone.
—Anne McCaffrey, *Dragonsinger*

Now we were back! Reverse immigration. . . .
And thus began the Irish adventure.
—Anne McCaffrey, letter to Virginia Kidd

ALTHOUGH IT CERTAINLY surprised her family and friends, Anne
McCaffrey's sudden removal to Ireland heralded her new life.
Eight years after her emigration she would appear on the best-
seller's list. Her immigration to her great-grandparents' home
country led to the pinnacle of Anne's writing career. Matching moves as bold as those of her heroines—from Menolly to
Killashandra to Nimisha—Anne boldly relocated, taking herself
away from the people who emotionally supported her, especially Virginia Kidd. Betrayed by a male figure (her husband)
who thwarted her love of writing, Anne felt like Menolly, that
she had no choice but to run away, even with few resources. Divorced with two children dependent on her, no money, and an uncertain financial future, Anne landed in Ireland at age forty-two.
Her migration and her transformation into a world-renowned
author is the focus of this chapter, which connects her independence and her fictional and real-life romances to her development as a writer.

Confronted with the many difficulties of adapting to a new
country, Anne threw her frustrations and worries into her fictions. Her adjustment to Ireland took creative shape in the books

she wrote during this decade, reflecting her desire for romance, her passion for animals, and her rage against injustice in many forms. Already an award-wining author when she relocated her family to Ireland in August 1970, Anne gained much more freedom to write, but also felt much more financial pressure to do so. For the first time in twenty years, Anne McCaffrey was the main breadwinner for her family, which included her mother. Even with her mother's contributions and her former husband's occasional child-support checks, this role meant she had to make the transition from being a respected part-time writer to a full-time writer. Now, she had to consider not only what she wanted to write, but also what would sell. This pressure seemed a positive catalyst for her productivity: she published thirteen books, including her highly acclaimed Harper Hall Trilogy—*Dragonsong, Dragonsinger,* and *Dragondrums*—and *The White Dragon.* She also garnered many awards, becoming, in 1978, the first science fiction writer to appear on the *New York Times Bestseller List* (for *The White Dragon*). Most importantly, however, she began earning a substantial income.

Anne not only created imaginary worlds, but also saw herself in them, too. Her imagination proved an advantage as she struggled to cope with emigration. Her editor, Shelly Shapiro, suggests, "The fact that Anne McCaffrey lived in Pern helped her make the transition to living in another country. It's hard to take on another culture, but she'd practiced." The Dragonriders of Pern, the series that Anne began developing in the 1970s, owes a great deal to her residence in Ireland. Her agent, Virginia Kidd, claimed that Pern changed after Anne moved to Ireland, that the move "deepened" Anne's writing and that "Pern became a real country after Anne moved there." She has written eighteen novels (and two with her son, Todd) set on Pern; this world and series are her most thoroughly developed and most popular.

In their first three years, the family lived in three different homes and had to adjust to Irish accommodations and also had to navigate a new cultural system. For example, Anne was shocked to discover that in Ireland you had to own property to have a library card. Like the rest of Europe, Ireland featured much smaller, older houses with what, to American tastes, seemed like impossibly tiny kitchens. The change was all the more dramatic to Anne because her last home in Sea Cliff, New Jersey, had been half of an enormous mansion (with ten bathrooms). It wasn't until 1973 that Anne settled in a larger home with a long-term lease of six years.

Moving across an ocean and thousands of miles from what had always been home, Anne had to create a new identity for herself. Part of this self-creation meant becoming "Anne" instead of Mrs. Johnson, and in doing so she was letting go of Wright. As was true in America also, in Ireland a woman without a husband faced prejudice and obstacles to her independence; Anne had to cope with these sexist attitudes. Getting her name put on her bank (credit) card proved difficult; she had to insist that she had no husband and that she was the only person who would use the bank account. Anne's eventual success in obtaining a card in her own name was a tribute to her dogged persistence, a quality that sustained her writing. Antoinette O'Connell, a family friend, remembers with awe what an impact Anne's independence had on her as a young girl. Anne was a role model for Antoinette, who admired her as "the first divorced, independent woman [she] met." The relatively backward position of women in Ireland at the time steeled Anne's feminism, making her all the more determined to be recognized as a breadwinner and head of her household. The adversities she faced as a woman appear in her fiction, as her characters face down sexist male characters and societies.

While she and Wright had always had money problems, now Anne was on her own financially. One incentive for moving to Ireland had been the Haughey's Artists Exemption Act, which exempted creative artists, such as writers, from paying tax on their earnings. This financial recognition of her position as writer was important to Anne, who wrote, "On the strength of four published novels, contracts for four more, I was accepted as a resident under the Artists' Exemption, promulgated by Charles Haughey." But exemption from taxes alone would not pay bills, so, not surprisingly, McCaffrey's letters to her agent contained a new urgency and a frantic tone about payments due to her from publishers. It wasn't until months after her move that she received payment from her work as editor of a collection of short stories, *Alchemy and Academe*; only then was she able to retrieve her family's belongings from the sea-freight storage in Dublin. Anne's motivation for writing short fiction was in part financial; she needed money, and short stories provided the quickest payments. The immense financial pressure Anne experienced actually created a writing process that has stood the test of three decades: she tries out ideas and characters in short fiction, and then later (often decades later) develops the short stories into a series of novels. Not having had the time to write in the 1940s, 1950s, and 1960s meant, too, that Anne had "a backlog of ideas and notions." It was only after her move that she would have the time to develop them.

Financial problems and worries continued throughout 1972, and it is no accident that 1972 was the only year that Anne failed to publish any books. Another Gothic novel, *The Year of the Lucy*, had been rejected by an editor at Dell. This slowdown in publication affected Anne's finances, and the problem was exacerbated by the disappearance of Wright's child-support checks. For example, Anne and Wright fought a battle over orthodontia for Todd and Gigi. Wright expected Anne to foot the bill alone— over $500. But while he claimed he had no money, he and his new wife, Annett, took a three-week tour of France. Anne found Wright's trip upsetting because she could not afford to travel, even for professional conferences. Invited to the Los Angeles Science Fiction Convention, she had to decline. Wright's check for $500 finally arrived, but Anne had to borrow 126 punts (about $100) from an Irish friend to get her car running.

Compounding the financial woes was the separation from a supportive network of family and old friends. Anne's separation from her agent and confidante, Virginia Kidd, was harder on Anne than on Virginia. Anne very obviously missed Virginia, as Anne's repeated, often plaintive, invitations for Virginia to visit her reveal. Although she was thousands of miles away, Anne kept in regular touch with Virginia. The time it took for mail to travel

Anne McCaffrey's grandfather in military uniform. Grandfather McCaffrey began a family tradition of military service.

Anne McCaffrey's parents. Horseback riding provides an important source for Anne's dragons.

Anne McCaffrey's mother, grandmother McElroy, and the three siblings.

Anne McCaffrey's grandfather McCaffrey, the three siblings, and their cousin Joe Gibney.

Cousin Joe Gibney and the three McCaffrey children in a lifeboat on the ferry on which their grandfather worked.

Anne McCaffrey's mother and the siblings.

Anne McCaffrey's father and the siblings.

Anne McCaffrey with her brother and the horse Chief. One of young Anne's first stories was about a horse.

Anne McCaffrey's mother in Egypt.

Anne McCaffrey and her two brothers during World War II.

Anne McCaffrey's parents and brothers during World War II; Kevin was fighting a serious disease and is in his robe for that reason.

Anne McCaffrey on her wedding day with her husband Wright Johnson and her parents.

Anne McCaffrey, her foster child Joseph Kaldi, his wife, and Wright Johnson.

Anne McCaffrey in the early 1960s.

Anne McCaffrey and Isaac Asimov at a convention.

Anne McCaffrey and Issac Asimov singing at a convention.

Virginia Kidd, Anne's agent and friend.

Derval Diamond, close family friend and manager of Dragonhold Stables.

Anne McCaffrey and her beloved horse, Mr. Ed.

Autographing.

John Greene, Anne McCaffrey's friend, in his Foreign Legion uniform.

Anne McCaffrey and Todd McCaffrey in her study in Dragonhold-Underhill.

An aerial view of Dragonhold-Underhill.

Anne McCaffrey's friend Richard Woods in Dragonhold-Underhill.

Elizabeth Anne Scarborough and Anne McCaffrey.

Anne McCaffrey's sister-in-law Sis.

Gigi and Geoff Kennedy at their wedding.

Anne McCaffrey and her three children: Alec Johnson, Todd McCaffrey, and Gigi Kennedy.

Astronaut Pamela A. Melroy in space, with a copy of Anne McCaffrey's *Crystal Singer*.
Photograph courtesy of Anne McCaffrey.

Anne McCaffrey with friends Marilyn and Harry Alm (standing to Anne's right) at
the 2005 Science Fiction and Fantasy Writers of America (SFWA) award ceremony
in Chicago, where Anne was the recipient of the 22nd SFWA Grand Master Award.
Photograph courtesy of Keith Stokes.

from Ireland to the United States meant that the response time between letters was much longer, so their communication lost some of its immediacy. Both missed the intimacy and impact of their previous relationship. Her plaintive appeals for Virginia to visit reveal Anne's need of her friend. In December 1970, four months after she moved to Ireland, Anne wrote, "In case I haven't mentioned it recently, I love you, dearest Virginia dear, and I am always deeply sensible of how skillfully you have steered the bark of my ambition. One of these here now days, you'll come to Ireland . . . and never leave it." In February 1971, she insisted, "You MUST come to see me in Ireland." But because of a disinclination to fly, lack of money, and her business, Virginia never made the trip. Fortunately, both women enjoyed writing letters, and their business relationship meant that they would still need to write each other frequently. Their letters consistently combine business and highly revealing personal information. While Anne always showed her determination and strength to other people, with Virginia she could display her emotional vulnerability, and, in the first few years in Ireland, her always pressing anxiety about money.

Difficulties with the mail and banks made Anne's life as a professional writer more difficult. Postal delays added to her financial woes, because checks mailed from the States would often take weeks to reach her. Anne found the banking system in Ireland both frustrating and (occasionally) helpful to her in her impecunious state. The bank manager would provide overdrafts, but then the bank would refuse to cash a check if it was not certified, or take a long time to credit the funds to her account. Anne used letters from Virginia and publishers to assure the bank manager that funds would soon be deposited, but until the mid 1970s, Anne worried constantly about how she would pay her bills. As she acknowledged to Virginia, "I do seem to keep harping on money." A ledger of Anne's earnings reveals that from 1969 to September 1971, she made $9,750, hardly a princely sum, especially considering that these payments were for six novels and an edited book. She wrote to Virginia, "the [publishers'] delays have been excessive and beginning with [her husband] John-son's delinquency last June, my financial position has been pre-carious indeed, despite the prospect of improvement which never arrives."

Establishing herself as a writer took most of the 1970s. A dis-couraged Anne wrote somewhat bitterly to Virginia, "Mucking out Edward's [her horse's] stall this morning, I was of a mind to chuck writing completely and take the job of a stable manager. I am very good at mucking out horses, cleaning tack and groom-ing coats. It takes little brain, only physical effort, and one gets paid on time." While her rant may be mere venting, the family's financial hardships were real; Anne even had to sell all the family furniture and belongings she had left in storage on Long Island, as she didn't have the funds to pay for their continued storage. Despite financial pressures, however, when one of her stories was rejected by a magazine, Anne held firm, refusing to change her narrative. She explained to Virginia, "In my financial position, I shouldn't let any opportunity to make money slip me by, but damnit, I write the story I'm telling and if it doesn't fit maga-zines, well, tant pis!!!! [too bad] again!!!!"

Despite her willingness to separate from Wright geographically, Anne had trouble completely separating from her ex-husband emotionally. Although Wright had been abusive, and they now lived thousands of miles apart, Anne still worried about him, as her letters to Virginia reveal. She clearly felt responsible for him, referring to a suicidal depression of his and his failed attempts at non-business writing. Angered by his unreliable payment of child support, she nevertheless dedicated a book to him. While Anne was ready to move on to other relationships, she still sought Wright's approval, as her dedication of the 1971 novel, *The Mark of Merlin*, to him showed. Significantly, this novel is one of a hand-ful of Anne's novels that are not science fiction, the genre that Wright despised. The dedication (written before they were di-vorced) reads, "To my husband, who is more often Wright than rong [*sic*]." Poignantly, the dedication suggests not only Anne's desire to placate Wright, but also a playful sense of fun that char-acterized their happier days.

His remarriage (ironically, to a woman named Annett, who was also a writer/editor) allowed Anne to detach further. She wrote the news twice to Virginia within a few weeks. In the first letter, she discussed reassuring her son Alec about the new wife, telling him that "he was a stepson most women would be proud of," but she revealed in the second missive her own reaction: "I am deeply relieved that Wright is remarrying , , , [sic] particularly someone in his own field [writing and editing] who, presumably, understands his drives and talents. I've been asked recently if I weren't still in love with him, and the answer is emphatically NO. I've felt a responsibility for him because he seemed so close to suicide again this summer and THAT would be hard to adjust to for me. But 'love'—no, no, no." Anne found, however, that breaking free of a twenty-year marriage was not quick or painless. Similarly, her characters find they must make radical breaks—run away or move to another Hold or planet—to escape confining relationships.

In May 1971, Wright made a brief trip to Ireland to see his children; though he would be there only four days, the prospect of seeing him troubled Anne. She wrote Virginia, "I'll show him the book dedicated to him and see what happens. Maybe it's as well he has another woman now. I met him with Gigi and Todd at the airport today and he was reasonably mild. It might continue in that vein, I hope . . . because I am rather fragile otherwise." Her vulnerability, painful though it was, allowed her to see and create characters who suffered, but coped. Many of her characters, like Menolly, struggle for the approval of a male figure; but, like Anne herself, these characters usually have to find validation from new sources. Her comment also shows the strain of relocating to a new country and beginning a new life as a single woman. New companions in Ireland helped her to rediscover a stronger, fun-loving side of herself shortly after relocating. Of that time, she acknowledges, "I developed a disastrous tendency to meet charming men and fall under their spell." She met one such man, Michael O'Shea, in a furniture store; and when the six-foot, red-haired, handsome man promptly invited her for a drink, Anne said, "Yes." She recalls, "Through him, I met other charming men and learned about the sanctity of the Irish pub. That is to say, if I had a problem and didn't know the answer, if I went to my local pub and chatted up the publican, I'd very soon have others listening in—attracted by the Yank accent—and then there'd be a discussion as to how I could solve my problem. . . . It was a great way to learn the customs of the country I was living in." At the pub, Anne found another version of the support and encouragement she experienced at the Milford writers' workshops and science fiction conventions.

Her son Todd describes her friends in Ireland as a "wild gang" and recalls his mother, as was the custom in Ireland, going over to a pub to socialize with Bernard Shattuck (an Irish sea captain), O'Shea's girlfriend, and O'Shea, described by her oldest son Alec as "a real Irish character, a teller (and embellisher) of tales." As her fiction suggests, Anne had a healthy sexual appetite, and once freed from her marriage she was ready to enjoy life and all its pleasures. After being unappreciated by Wright, Anne told Virginia, "It is so reassuring to be considered bright, intelligent, fascinating, stimulating and all that jazz." A single mother, Anne faced the difficulties of juggling children and lovers. She learned that the Irish word for hangover is "'fluttered.'" In December 1970, Anne wrote to Virginia describing the Thanksgiving feast she threw to the appreciation of several Irishmen, but she complained, "If Todd doesn't stop chaperoning me . . . I am going to beat his ears in." As a divorced mother, Virginia empathized and responded, "Do I ever understand what you mean about Todd's chaperoning you!!! Ben [her son] too—when I *know* he has other things he has to do, wants to do, but NO. If I have male company, he sacrifices ALL." Despite her son's shadowing her, Anne found time for lovers. Her very human need for love appears in her books as characters like the young woman Lessa in *Dragonflight* or the older woman Clodagh in the Powers series; these characters and others find love even in inhospitable circumstances.

In February 1971, Anne described to Virginia another beau, Bernard Shattuck, whom she said looked exactly like the portrait of F'nor on the cover of *Dragonquest*. She mentioned both the resemblance and Bernard in a number of letters. The reader can judge for herself the degree to which Bernard resembled F'nor by examining Bernard Shattuck's photo in Todd McCaffrey's memoir, *Dragonholder*. Eventually, she reveals that she and the young Englishman, twenty-two, have become lovers. A fisherman, a first mate, Anne described him as "true to type," and exclaimed, "Gawd, it's awful to see a facsimile of a character *you* invented alive and well in Dun Laoghaire." This inversion reflects a power reversal in their relationship. Anne created a character, but now he is alive and out of her control. The relationship was a pleasurable one, however, and Anne confided in Virginia, "I shall enjoy the experience while I can." Bernard took Anne's oldest son, Alec, under his wing, getting him a job on a fishing vessel. By May, however, their affair ended, leaving Anne poignantly regretful. She wrote admiringly of Bernard, how he had managed to change their relationship—"without leaving me bitter or us unfriendly." But she complained to Virginia how difficult it was, especially because "Alec keeps trying to get me and Bernard out on dates with him. Bernard merely grins and asks me if I want to go and we go. Crazeee world." Bernard remained a family friend, helping Anne with what little money he had. Anne writes, "I got over the mad-pash for him, but I still love him muchly."

Anne would also find another character-image come to life in Jan Regan, who appeared to Anne as "Jan-who-is-Lessa." Jan Regan was David Gerrold's landlady, and, according to Todd, Gerrold phoned Anne with the news that "Lessa is my landlord." Married to an abusive husband, Jan turned to Anne for help. Anne offered Jan a place to stay; Jan stayed with Anne, nursing her through a virus and taking care of the kids. Eventually, when Anne founded Dragonhold Stables, Jan managed them for her. In 1971, Anne wrote to Virginia, "My Jan-Lessa descended on me Sunday after her husband beat her up seriously (my gowd [*sic*] the bruises on her and she's no flesh to speak spare)." Domestic violence was much in the news just then, in both America and Ireland, and Anne knew a woman named Mary Banotti "who helped abused women." Anne would later draw on both women's lives for aspects of characters in a Gothic novel (discussed in greater detail later in this chapter). Anne clearly likes the fictional characters she creates. Seeing her characters in real people she met in Ireland was one way she could explain her attraction to new people and make Ireland more familiar. Implicitly, she put herself in a superior position by being, even imaginatively, their creator. This relationship provides another clue to the imaginary or dreamworld character of Anne's life in Ireland. Because of her strong connection to her fictional worlds, she saw connections between characters she loved and people she loved. The parallels between fictional and real people enabled her both to feel a stronger connection to people and to make her characters more believable, three-dimensional. She imagined them before they ever knew her. A few years later, she would meet and befriend Derval Diamond, "who is the epitome of Menolly [protagonist of the Harper Hall Trilogy], in looks and manner." In the cases of Bernard, Jan, and Derval, these people who seemed to parallel her characters developed into life-long friends.

By November 1971, she had fallen in love again, this time more seriously. The object of her affection was Derek Waters, a forty-two-year-old Irishman and successful television producer in Canada and America. Derek had moved home to Ireland with his sons, and he was in the process of getting a divorce from his wife of fourteen years, Mabel. Derek couldn't have appeared at a better time because Anne was at a low spot in her life. Short of funds, she was waiting to hear from Dell about publishing *The Year of the Lucy* when the clutch on her car seized up and she didn't have the money to replace it. Although her story "Dramatic Mission" had been nominated for a Hugo, she had to decline the offer to be toast-mistress at the Los Angeles Worldcon because she couldn't afford the trip. Nevertheless, she still enjoyed the prestige of being a professional writer, and she picked Derek Waters up "in a pub just after my first PEN Writers Club meeting."

Despite her financial woes, Anne raved to Virginia that her "excellent frame of mind [was] due to having met a cookie." Less than two weeks later, she wrote, "My new boyfriend continues attentive." Anne was truly in love, and in December 1971 she wrote to Virginia to announce her engagement: "You may have heard me mention that I'd never marry an Irishman? Well, I'm going to . . . unfortunately not until his divorce comes through from Canada and we haven't a clue when that will be." Derek was fighting for the custody of his two sons, ages eleven and eight, who were living with him. His boys liked her, and Anne described them as "considerably better behaved than mine ever were at that age," and they "seem to get along well with me." Her children liked Derek, too, and Anne hoped that they could find "a big roomy house similar to this one in which our combined families can spread out." She wrote a glowing description of Derek's physical appearance: "I call him my Jewish Leprechaun because, although he is pure Irish, he has that black Irish look (with silver sideburns) and a slightly semitic nose." Anne gushed, "I've never gotten along so well with another human being in my life." She explained, "We've been trying out the living together bit to see how we would get on. He admires my brains and beauty, and I find his shrewdness and leprechaunishness a decided relief." They planned a future together in Ireland, for neither wanted to leave. Derek worked a few projects for RTE, the Irish national radio and television service, and he had dozens of aunts, uncles, and cousins nearby. Looking back on the past year, Anne told Virginia she was sorry that she had not been more productive as a writer, and she promised Virginia she would be so in the future. She explained that she and Derek were "setting up a strict schedule to DO WORK IN and still have time for play." She reported to Virginia that Derek had lost his job with RTE for not being Catholic. Anne began to write a movie scenario featuring horses, and she planned for Derek to direct it.

Anne included Derek in her science fiction life when, flush with funds from the sales of short stories that would later become the novel *Crystal Singer*, she traveled to Chesmacon, the science fiction convention in Chester, England, with Derek, his two sons, and Todd and Gigi. Derek's sons were thrilled by the science fiction movie screenings. Anne was pleased that "everyone seemed to like Derek and Derek really enjoyed himself." She exclaimed, "I do adore that man so much." Anne was also rather pleased to find Harry Harrison, a popular science fiction writer, jealous. She wrote to Virginia that he "was annoyed to find [she] had an escort—tough titty!" But in her customary good-natured form, Anne also told Virginia, "He was in rare form with his new book, however." A gregarious and social woman, Anne enjoyed the attention and the new version of herself as a woman with a lover. In love herself, Anne was generous and interested in the love affairs of others, especially her good friend Virginia. Being in love fit her need of male approval and validation. Both the strength and the weakness of Anne's fiction is their great emotionality and an emphasis on romance—the same can also be said of Anne's own life.

When Virginia wrote to Anne that she and Roger Elwood, who had been publishing Anne's work, had become lovers, Anne responded by congratulating her. Anne seemed to have been interested in Roger, too, for she wrote, "I shall miss the challenges of his letters, and bank down the fires of anticipation of his arrival [in Ireland]. . . . But I am pleased about the Roger Lovinman arrangement. Jealous, too. . . . I am very pleased that he took the road to you. . . . enjoy! ENJOY!" She described with measured tones her relationship with Derek and the comfort and support he provided: "I do believe I am very helpful to Derek and *I* need to be helpful. There is much in the Derek-Anne relationship which is very good and worthwhile—not the least of which is the security I give his eldest son—and no relationship is without some defects. I have a lot to give Derek and he gives me much in return. We shall see how the whole matter resolves itself once he is, indeed, free to remarry—if remarriage is in his mind at that time." In October of that year she wrote about a misunderstanding that she and Derek had, but she said that it "has made for more deeper understanding. Despite his flaws, I really want that guy and no one else. In fact, we are probably going to combine households in the *very* near future." Anne's need to be helpful came at a time when she could not help her aging mother cope with tinnitus and aging, and later in her life Anne would channel her need to be helpful to a large, extended family and community. Her heroines, too, are self-sacrificing, one Moreta, Dragonlady of Pern, to the point of death. In this character, whose death caused even the somewhat cynical Virginia Kidd to cry, Anne put all her longings and struggles and exhaustion. Significantly, it is when she goes *between*, too tired from flying life-saving vaccine across Pern, that Moreta dies. So Anne could depict the dangers of being needed and giving too much, but at the same time she romanticized and validated such extreme self-sacrifice.

Anne's relationship was adversely affected by Derek's estranged wife's presence in Ireland. Presciently, in her response to Anne's letters, Virginia worried that Mabel would harass Annie and Derek. Indeed, in early 1973, Mabel acted up when she returned the boys to Derek, refusing to leave. The police had to be called, for Mabel threw the phone at Derek and broke the front hall window. Derek's father had to chastise her in front of the police before she left, threatening to offer assault charges against Derek because he grabbed her arm. Despite the unpleasantness with Mabel, Anne and Derek continued to have fun together, one time even getting involved in an attempt to expose an international drug conspiracy. She wrote to Virginia that she and Derek "gave Interpol the information that led them to crack a L2 million pound [*sic*] drug smuggling chain. If I *wrote* it, no one would believe me! We still don't. What a fluke!" In her files, Anne still has the article from the *Irish Times*, with the headline, "DRUG HAUL MAY HAVE BEEN WEEKS AT AIRPORT." Derek had hired an Australian girl to look after his two boys, and, unfortunately, she turned out to be a drug courier. Because of his difficulties with his soon-to-be ex-wife, Derek could not have the babysitter's drug connection made public. Mabel would have used the fact to try to wrest custody from him. So Derek fired her, after informing Interpol, who then followed the girl. She escaped their surveillance, however, and nothing more came of it. But the excitement and turmoil of Mabel as villain, added to a case of smuggling, rather appealed to Anne's sense of adventure. In addition, she was determined not to be run off by Mabel's crazy actions. In her fictions, characters always persist when they know they are right, especially in the Gothic novels, where Anne seems to write through the experience with Mabel.

Derek's estranged wife continued to cause trouble, however. Her appeal that Derek should have to pay her support was denied, and she had to pay her own court costs. She pitched a fit in the court, calling the judge a liar, and was removed by two police officers. Anne wrote to Virginia that Mabel "mentioned my name in an uncomplimentary fashion in Court and I am asking for an injunction to stop her talking about me, I am *not* a floozie and I have not been posing as Mrs. Waters and I was not living with Derek in Courtown. No one would believe what that one has tried!" When Anne moved, she had to have an unlisted phone number because "Mabel started another of her phoning campaigns." In December 1973, Anne made an appearance on behalf of Derek in his custody suit. A notebook from the 1974 English Milford Workshop reveals that Anne's focus was not entirely on the proceedings; she headed a list, "Nov 1971–Oct 1974," apparently a list of her own good qualities and a chronicling or justification of her relationship with Derek, perhaps in response to Mabel's accusations. The list reads thus:

1. raised 4 children, fostered 2 one summer
2. 3 years of Cub Scouts
3. Headstart Program
4. functioning children
5. lock on room door [justification of her spending the night?]
6. legitimate reasons for being there
   babysitting
   film production [she and Derek formed a film corporation that never produced any films]
   business
   black ice [a dangerous road condition, common in Ireland]
   child illness
   car malfunction

The focus on Anne's excellence as a mother reveals what Anne thought was important in justifying her relationship with a man who had two sons. It also reveals a side of Anne conspicuously absent from the novels: she does not write about mothering. Even in the Tower and Hive series, which is about generations of a family, Anne's fictional children require little assistance from their parents. This entry is followed by one that details Mabel's failings and explanations of why and how Anne and Derek spent time together:

1. *her* immorality in deserting the children with no
   justification [and then it returns to Anne and Derek]
2. met through mutual friends, David Gerrold
   in tv film industry Dec 15—Todd was sick
   Aug 13 Todd with me
   caravan instability
   April Derek detained
   I had key because of business. He kept change and
   stocks in the house.

These notes suggest how the ups and downs of the relationship with Derek affected Anne and how she justified their relationship to herself and others. Her letters to Virginia show how much Derek meant to her at the time. The trouble with Mabel, though, weakened Anne and Derek's relationship. Their difficulties were exacerbated by her children's attitude. Faced with the prospect of their mother remarrying, her children, Todd and Gigi, rebelled, both telling their mother they would never accept the marriage. Todd remembers telling his mother she could marry Derek and he hoped she'd be happy, but he would leave home as soon as he turned sixteen.

The year 1974 saw the end of Anne's relationship with Derek. Anne recalls their breakup with candor, remembering that she "had always said he'd go after a younger woman." After he began a relationship with a younger woman, however, he called Anne up, invited her out for a drink, and propositioned her. A sadder and wiser Anne turned him down, and Derek moved back shortly thereafter to Canada. Although she remembers it now with equanimity, at the time, the end of her relationship with Derek was traumatic for Anne. She now says of that time, "I didn't socialize a lot. I had very little confidence in myself . . . [and] my energy and emotion went into my books." The role of men in Anne's life, at least those with whom she had physical relationships, appears to have been a negative defining force that turned her toward fiction. Recently, Anne reminisced about Derek, recalling that he had asked her to marry him, "but that I realized I couldn't marry because I needed to devote more time to my work." She recalls Derek as "another Aries," fundamentally incompatible with her, and remembers that he was "occasionally macho" and unable to understand her perspective. As an example, she cites his finding a house for her to rent, and at a good price, but he was angry when she refused to sign the lease. "He didn't understand I couldn't live there," she said. "All the houses exactly alike—I need to be different." Anne's mother, whose health was failing, followed her own mother's judgmental streak, disapproving of Derek because she thought Anne could do better. Anne remembers that although "Derek was gone by the time mother died. I could have used his comfort." Both losses affected Anne deeply, but neither stopped her from writing.

Throughout her relationship with Derek, Anne kept writing at a furious pace. Her busy life coincided with her final revision of *Dragonquest*, an earlier draft of which Virginia had told Anne to burn. Published in 1971, the revised novel represented an important turning point in Anne's career. In radically revising this text, Anne would demonstrate again her ability to respond positively to criticism, this time from her publisher Betty Ballantine. Anne had gotten bogged down in writing the novel, until Betty invited her and the children to visit over the 1970 New Year's holiday. She and Betty went over the draft together, and, telling Anne she was emphasizing the wrong plot, Betty pointed out to Anne that "'this story isn't about F'lar and Lessa [the protagonists of *Dragonflight*, Anne's first Pern novel]: it has more to do with F'nor and Jaxom.'" Betty's analysis freed Anne to write the rest of the novel quickly. Anne described Betty fondly in a letter to Virginia: "She is such a magnificent person, . . . she reminds me that you can be tempered to a warm, giving person by frustrations and disappointments: you don't have to be cynical or bitter." This was an example that Anne and her characters would follow.

Unlike Virginia, Betty did come to visit, stopping in Ireland twice on the way to visit her brother on the Isle of Jersey. Like Virginia Kidd, Betty was an early and voracious reader of science fiction. She and her husband, Ian, founded an important publishing firm in 1952, Ballantine Books, and soon became known for the quality of their writers, including Arthur C. Clarke, Ray Bradbury, and Theodore Sturgeon, among many others. Like Virginia, Betty had the attitude that an editor's first "job is to help the author say what he wants to say in the way he wants to say it" and that "the second editorial role is that of psychologist." She describes Anne as "a feminist—very obvious from her spunky heroine, and several later works—in fact, all later works." Of working with Anne, Betty writes: "I loved working on her stuff. Its quality was always very personal (the best kind to grab reader interest and identification), exciting action, memorable characters—the stuff of bestsellers as the Dragon series proved. Her interest in opera (she has a marvelous singing voice) evidenced itself in her stories about the singing ship—in fact, a lot of Annie is in her work and since she herself is a lively, courageous and interesting person, so are her books."

Betty Ballantine's description of Anne reveals her admiration for her Pern series. *Dragonquest* (1974), the second in her Dragonriders of Pern series, put Anne on the path to becoming a world-famous author. It is significant, surely, that this second novel was so difficult to write. But Anne persevered, demonstrating a determination that would see her through similar writing blocks later in her career. Because she was able to re-write *Dragonquest* successfully, even in her darkest moments, Anne knew that if she shared her work with others and continued to write, she would eventually find a way to finish her novels. *Dragonquest*'s success set the stage for all the other Pern novels, turning one successful book into a prize-winning series. In addition, Anne taught herself how to expand a concept beyond one book into several. Developing and re-articulating the characters and setting from one novel became a pattern that Anne would use not only in Dragonriders of

Pern, but also in her other series. In part, Anne's confidence in her writing grew because it had to—she was far away from Virginia and other writer friends. She had escaped the negative influence of Wright, who had belittled her writing and her choice of genre. One sign of the change in her status was her key role in the creation of "English Milford" in 1971, a science fiction writers' workshop comparable to the Milford conferences that Anne, then a novice writer, had attended in the 1960s. Anne was the co-founder (with Judy Lawrence Blish) of the English conference. There was a familial connection of sorts with Judy since she was Jim Blish's second wife and Virginia had been his first wife.

Re-creating Milford in England re-created the heady excitement of the first Milford conferences. She described Milford as "a state of mind," one conducive to writing, networking, and critiquing by peers. In the English Milfords, the writers work-shopped five stories a day. In fall 1972, Anne's Killashandra stories were rigorously critiqued, but she seems to have enjoyed the process and found the response of other professional writers stimulating and encouraging. Other writers in attendance included Brian Aldiss, Jim Blish, John Brunner, Josephine Saxton, Samuel Delany, and Christopher Priest. Anne not only was running the show, but also found her writing had improved so much that "everyone liked and approved of [her writing] so that I felt I could rest on my laurels after that." Her success at the English Milfords demonstrated her achievement and provided her with confidence in her talent. At the same time, Anne was also developing increased confidence in herself as an independent woman and as a lover. It was in this guise that she turned to writing Gothic romances.

In the 1970s, Anne experimented with the romance genre, what she calls "her Gothics," novels that are part mystery, part realist, part romance. In contrast to the science fiction settings of her other novels, these Gothics contain realistic settings. Because the realistic novels' settings and characters draw more directly on Anne's own experiences, these books contain a wealth of biographical details. Her son Todd describes one of her Gothics, *The Kilternan Legacy*, as "an autobiography" and explains, "A lot of what occurred in that story had definite shadows in the real world." Moreover, her realistic novels provide confirmation of Anne's feminism and her interest in art as a means of fulfillment and escape, especially for women. Her Gothic characters' abilities to read and interpret correctly are key to their survival and happiness. The emphasis on reading in these books valorizes the act of interpretation—it literally saves her characters' lives, as reading metaphorically saved Anne's. Anne's Gothic novels acknowledge the importance of women as readers of culture. Here Anne put her own experience of self-discovery and knowledge into her writing. At the same time that the novels point toward the female characters' salvation, through "reading," the suspenseful aspects of the novels indirectly reflect the ups and downs and anxieties of Anne's everyday life, especially financial troubles.

A self-described "voracious reader," Anne has always "liked historicals [and she] still rereads Georgette Heyer with delight for her inimitable style." Heyer was and is one of the biggest names in the field of historical romance, just as Anne became one of the biggest names in science fiction. But she and Heyer shared many other qualities, in addition to the success that made Anne identify with Heyer. Heyer had to deal with a "ravening fan public," in her biographer's words, including fan clubs and fans who dressed up and acted out scenes from her novels. Like Anne's father, Heyer's father was away fighting a war (World War I) during her adolescence. Like Anne, Heyer wrote "not only because she was a compulsive writer, but because she needed money." Like Anne, in both real life and in her novels, and according to her biographer Hodge, for Heyer, "religion, as a mainspring of human behavior, simply did not exist." Like Anne, Heyer enjoyed cooking meals in her home for others and, most saliently, according to Hodge, Heyer "created her private world, perhaps, because she needed something nearer to her heart's desire, and because of this it provides an escape for her readers, too."

In the 1970s, the Gothic field was a larger one than science fiction (and, indeed, romance is still the best-selling fiction genre). The Gothic novel, popular at the end of the eighteenth century, featured a medieval-like setting (such as a castle), a plot of mystery, fear for a female protagonist, and often language that is inflated and melodramatic. Anne admits, "The gothics were quasi-mystery which was also the rule while I was writing them." But like many other writers, Anne wrote beyond the formula, stretching and developing the eighteenth-century romance plot. Her Gothics provide an example of what Rachel Blau DuPlessis describes as "the project of twentieth-century women writers to solve the contradiction between love and quest . . . by offering a different set of choices" than those allowed by male-dominated culture. Here, then, is a description of what Anne contributed to the genre, and to her readers. Jane Donawerth suggests that Anne's dragons and Dragonriders offer a compelling alternative to traditional masochistic heterosexual relationships based on male dominance; in her Gothics, too, Anne created supportive, egalitarian relationships. She wrestled with being an over-forty female writer with children and a lover. In her novels, the heroines find resolutions that are difficult to achieve in the real world. In her Gothics, as in her science fiction novels, Anne creates likeable young female heroines who narrate their own tales of adventure and romance. While Anne did not make her reputation writing Gothic romances, it was a genre she admired. More practically, the Gothics sold well, especially in France. In the 1970s, particularly, they created much-needed income. These novels deserve attention not only for what they might show about her life, but also about the real-life issues that concern her.

Whereas Anne can only put touches of her knowledge of the Irish and horses in her science fiction (such as the character Niall in *The Ship Who Sang*, for example), the Gothic novels draw directly on these experiences. While Anne depicts intimate relationships between people and dragons in the Dragonriders of Pern series, in her realistic fiction, she creates special and believable relationships between a woman and her horses and her cat in *Ring of Fear* and between a woman and her dog in *The Mark of Merlin*. In her Gothic novels, Anne develops themes that also appear in her science fiction, but the realistic settings limit the optimism that characterizes her science fiction. The Gothic novels reveal that her dragons and other science fiction creations are based on relationships with actual animals. Anne's depiction of animals can be described as ecofeminist; that is, she draws on the premise that women and nature "share a subordinate and instrumental relationship to men; both are subject to patterns, attitudes, and institutions of male domination and control; both are gendered as 'feminine' as one means of control." Anne's Gothics resist the reduction of the heroine to an object. In addition, Anne's Gothics reflect a nascent ecofeminist rejection of animals being treated as objects. In this way, her Gothics make explicit the lifelong love and commitment to animals that lead Anne to adopt her own horse, work at a horse stable, and, as soon as she could afford it, own a stable herself.

In her science fiction, Anne's devotion to animals appears in her portrait of dragons and other alien beings; but in her realistic fiction, she depicts relationships to animals that parallel her own life. Anne has always lived in a full and lively household, and her households have always contained cats, dogs, and, in Ireland, horses. Her current study has a large picture window that looks out on a horse pasture, so that even when she is writing, Anne can be surrounded by her beloved horses. The room is so designed that, sitting at her computer, Anne can almost feel she is outdoors. Her cats, too, have a proprietary interest in her study; large and imposing Maine Coons, they exude personality. One named Echo sat on her printer as she gave me a tour. Anne's animal companions expect attention and respect. She has strong ties with her pets, and she believes that animals and humans can have sympathetic, even telepathic relationships, explaining, "Ed [her first horse] and I had a terrific rapport. . . . [H]e used to let me cry on his broad shoulders when things went wrong—that is, if he didn't step on my toes." In a biography of his mother, *Dragonholder*, Todd details their family love of animals; his family history is at least partially a history of their pets.

Anne's interest, work, and knowledge of horse shows appears in *Ring of Fear*. The novel's heroine, Nialla, has formidable riding skills and a special relationship with one extraordinary horse. Anne detested the exploitation of animals, and in *Ring of Fear* she criticizes the exploitation of horses and the emphasis on commercialism, implicitly paralleling it to the exploitation of women.

Like sex, jumping horses is supposed to be a pleasure and a joy, rather than an event undertaken to assert dominance and control. Anne asserts that animals should be respected and treated as companions rather than as property. The novel is remarkable also for its sensitive and believable depiction of rape, years before feminist critics such as Susan Brownmiller documented women's unfair treatment in law and culture. Nialla, the protagonist, had been sexually exploited and raped by her father's employer; and as she begins a new relationship, Nialla worries about how she will feel about sex and how to tell her new boyfriend what happened to her. Anne's description of the rape is vivid, and she makes the protagonist's recovery believable by providing insights into her feelings of mistrust and gradual recovery from the trauma of rape. Like a horse that has been physically abused, a rape survivor must and can learn to trust again.

The depiction of horse shows and jumping draws on Anne's love for these activities from childhood, and they point to her adult participation in the horse world, first as a worker and later as an owner/manager. Today she explains that she wrote the novel before she had the extensive experience in Ireland with horses, commenting that it was a "cart before the horse thing." One of Anne's most serious relationships, mentioned in many interviews and all biographical material, is her relationship with Mr. Ed, whom she acquired in February 1971. Ed's owner, Hilda Whitton (to whom Anne dedicated *The Kilternan Legacy*), raised him, but after a fall, she realized he needed a younger rider. She and Anne came to an arrangement where Anne could pay for the horse in installments, and Ed, a dapple-gray over sixteen hands, went home with Anne. He had to be stabled elsewhere, and Anne worked at the stable until 1976 to help pay for his upkeep there. While Anne only hunted with Ed four times, she rode him almost every day. Ed provided much needed comfort and stress release for Anne. An accomplished and enthusiastic rider herself, Anne drew on personal experience to depict the horse world in *Ring of Fear*.

Anne actually owned a German shepherd dog, called Merlin, who turns up as the title character in *The Mark of Merlin* (1971).

The novel's autobiographical elements include a protagonist who is the daughter of an army colonel in the years after World War II. But while in real life Anne worshiped her father, in the novel, the military father is killed off, leaving the young woman to find her way in the world by herself. Orphaned by her father's death, the heroine uncovers a smuggling plot (as Anne would in real life, a couple of years later) and exposes the military's paternalism and ineptitude exclaiming, "Ha! Have you men done so well with the world?" The backdrop of World War II and the issue of smuggling valuables out of conquered and allied countries emphasizes that, despite male heroism, male dominance has not resulted in an ideal world. War and smuggling activities are contrasted to the heroine's idyllic relationship with her dog.

The early 1970s were a very productive time for Anne. In 1973, Anne wrote a number of short stories for Roger Elwood, the editor who was romantically involved with Virginia Kidd. Through these short fictions, Anne laid the groundwork for many of her later series. They include the Pern stories "Dull Drums," "The Greatest Love," "Milekey Mountain," "A Proper Santa Claus," "The Rescued Girls of Refugee," and "Rabble-Dowser"; three stories that would later become part of *Crystal Singer*, "Killashandra-Coda and Finale," "Killashandra-Crystal Singer," "Prelude to a Crystal Song"; and "The Smallest Dragonboy." This last story, Anne's most reprinted, is based on her brother Kevin's battle with osteomyelitis in his legs. In "The Smallest Dragonboy," the protagonist, Keevan, overcomes a leg injury and the taunts of bullies to drag himself to the dragon-hatching ground to Impress a dragon. The story appeared in 1973, and in August of that year, Anne's beloved brother Kevin visited her, bringing his wife, Marcia. Also in 1973, *To Ride Pegasus* and the long-overdue cookbook, *Cooking out of This World*, appeared. In contrast to the other-world settings of the Pern novels, *To Ride Pegasus* is set on a near-future Earth in which human beings begin to develop their psychic powers. The setting draws on Anne's own family history of precognition as well as on her sense of animals' empathic abilities. Mary Brizzi analyses this book at some length, suggesting that the psychic abilities can also be read as metaphors for artistic ability.

The cookbook had been designed in 1970 by Anne's good friend and editor, Betty Ballantine, as a going-away present for Anne— a contract with an advance to help her out of her financial difficulties. Unfortunately, the book ended up costing Anne a great deal of time and effort, as edited works often do, and it took two years to finish.

While Anne kept busy writing, she also suffered family problems typical of women her age. Many women in their forties and fifties find they must take responsibility for two generations— their children and their aging parents. Anne worried about her children's adolescence and her oldest son's need to find a career, for in 1970 Alec was eighteen. But in addition to caring for her children, Anne was concerned about her mother's unreasonable behavior and health. Always a loving woman, her mother became irascible, yelling at Todd and Gigi. Anne's mother had tinnitus, or ringing in her ears, and she was "no longer competent enough, memory-wise, to be on her own." Anne insisted, "Mother or no, she is NOT interfering in my life or with my friends." Nevertheless, caring for her mother did affect Anne's life and her friends. In December 1970, Anne's friend David Gerrold, also a science fiction writer, came to visit when he was considering moving to Ireland permanently. Anne's mother, who had become increasingly difficult to live with, took an instant dislike to David; and Anne, greatly embarrassed, had to find another place for David to stay. Anne had a close relationship with her mother throughout her life, and she dedicated her second Pern novel, *Dragonquest*, to her. In June 1971, Anne's mother was diagnosed with arteriosclerosis (hardening of the arteries), but she had manifested some of the symptoms before the diagnosis. Anne wrote to Virginia about the time it took to drive her mother to the doctors, the library, the store: "Mother has taken quite a toll on my nerves already acerbated and roughened by the onset of menopause . . . I think."

Anne and her mother's relationship improved after her mother moved to a nearby apartment. As Anne described it, "Between the noise my kids made (mostly normal) and the traffic on the main road in front of the house, Mother was terribly uncomfortable. . . . [T]he generation gap showed badly, with me caught in the middle. . . . Having taken the children from their own friends and homeland, the least I could do was allow them friends and certain freedoms in Ireland that were inconsistent with my mother's requirements. She decided to move out. And, God love her, she decided it was all her own idea. I, however, have never forgiven myself." With her characteristic sense of responsibility, Anne was, indeed, caught in the middle between her children and mother and unable to express her needs or feelings in such a situation. In April 1974, Anne wrote to Virginia that her mother had read the draft of what would become *The Kilternan Legacy*, Anne's third Gothic novel, and approved of the book. In June 1974, Anne's mother suffered a catastrophic stroke. Anne was devastated and stayed by her mother's bedside. She described her mother's condition: "The woman in that bed was not the vibrant, humorous, steadfast person I had known for forty-eight years but a motionless hulk." Anne's mother had a second stroke July 12 and died. Like many middle-aged adults, Anne found herself orphaned emotionally when her mother died, leaving her on her own. She found she couldn't cry until she called the Samaritans (a counseling group in the United Kingdom). Her mother had wanted to be buried with her husband, so when Anne received the burial urn with her mother's ashes, she placed it on a shelf with her father's PhD thesis until she could travel to the United States, to her father's grave.

Gigi had been ill after a vacation that same summer to France, and Anne ascribed the illness to the stress of losing her grandmother and traveling. However, as Gigi's symptoms continued, Anne realized that Gigi had a serious illness, which was eventually diagnosed as Crohn's disease. Gigi was only fourteen when the symptoms first appeared, and Anne took her to specialists in London and the United States, but to no avail. An incurable inflammation of the intestines, Crohn's disease can be quite debilitating and very painful. Anne had experienced what seemed to be incurable disease before, and when her brother Kevin was then almost miraculously cured by the then-experimental drug penicillin, she retained her faith in medicine. Like her mother with Kevin, Anne persisted in trying new doctors and treatments, fighting for Gigi's health. Gigi tried a number of new drugs, none of which worked, and had to endure several exploratory surgeries. Anne spent time with Gigi whenever she was in the hospital, and took her to doctors, but this illness provided even more impetus for Anne to keep writing. She wanted the best medical treatment for her daughter, and that was expensive. The system of Irish socialized medicine meant basics like medicine and bandages were free. But Gigi's travel to see specialists was not covered, and Anne had to borrow money from her friends Harry and Joan Harrison to pay one of Gigi's first hospital bills. Wright's second wife, Annett, included Gigi in her health insurance plan, but there were still many uncovered expenses. But more than the additional financial stress, Gigi and Anne just had to accept the illness. Anne wondered, "[Why] my own child, my own very pretty daughter?" Anne blamed herself, as mothers of very ill children often do, irrationally thinking the illness was the result of "something [she'd] omitted doing at a crucial time—Gigi was not breastfed as her brothers were." As it did after her father's and mother's deaths, writing provided an escape for Anne from the grim realities of death and illness. Anne explains that Gigi is "somewhat Moreta in her indomitable approach to her personal problem," but "I didn't write in the illness, only the character." *Moreta* didn't appear until 1983; it took Anne that long to process Gigi's illness. Much more quickly, however, Anne drew on her romance with Derek to write another Gothic novel.

The last of Anne's realistic novels in this decade appeared in 1975. In her last Gothic set in Ireland, the plot is a thinly veiled autobiography. Ironically, or perhaps significantly, Anne says that *The Kilternan Legacy* "is probably the least autobiographical of my books." But she goes on to acknowledge that "some of the shenanigans were based on the antics of a friend of mine whose estranged wife was trying to make him look so bad to the Irish courts that they'd give custody of the sons to her." Elsewhere she comments, "Such antics were much too good to waste. You will note that my hero vaguely resembles Michael O'Shea but his character was far more ethical. The novel also uses some of my early experiences in Irish family homes as well as the differences in culture." The heroine of *The Kilternan Legacy*, an American, moves to Ireland after inheriting money and an estate from a great-aunt. The heroine struggles to adapt to Irish culture but eventually finds a new identity there as a "queen," establishing an estate where she supports other women who live in cottages on her holding. While Rene, the fictional character, creates her queendom through inheritance, Anne would create her fiefdom through her writing. The idea of a "queendom" certainly owes something to Pern's fictional Holds, communities that are ruled by a lord. When I wrote Anne to ask if she thought her estate, Dragonhold-Underhill, was like a Pern Hold, she replied, "I have created a hold of my own . . . though it's more like the 'queen-dom' in *Kilternan Legacy*." Anne's queendom, though, was not the result of an inheritance, but of her own very hard work and skill as a writer. And Anne's largesse extends not just to women, but to her two sons and male family friends—even to her ex-husband.

Anne wrote to Virginia that Gigi (aged sixteen), thinking the book *was* autobiography, had objected, saying, "I'm not at all like that. When did this happen to us?" Her brother Todd, older and wiser at nineteen, said patronizingly of Gigi that she "hasn't a clue [about fiction writing]," but he "didn't mind appearing as Simon." The parallels to Anne's own life are astonishing: the character of Simon is fourteen, as Todd was when they moved to Ireland; the protagonist, Rene, is recently divorced and falls in love, and she discovers that the laws in Ireland do not protect battered women. Rene describes the situation of a battered wife in Ireland as "in the Dark ages." Rene's ex-husband reflects Anne's descriptions of her own ex-husband, who was verbally abusive. As an American, protected by greater legal rights for women, Rene has a position of privilege that enables her to see the misogyny in Irish women's subordination. Anne wrote to Virginia, "I hope that KILTERNAN does get published over here, since it is so immediate to the problems under discussion." The book was sold in Ireland by a British publisher, Transworld, but it wasn't until 1995 that divorce was legalized in Ireland.

The Kilternan Legacy was to be Anne's last non–science fiction novel for nine years. She would turn from cathartically dealing with her relationship with Derek, and her adjustment to Ireland, to writing some of her most successful and critically acclaimed science fiction novels, beginning with *Dragonsong*, the first novel in the Harper Hall Trilogy. Anne wrote to Virginia about Todd, explaining "on the strength of [the contract] for DRAGONWINGS? SONG? SON he can go to college next year." These novels are sometimes classified as young adult novels because the protagonist is a pubescent girl named Menolly, but while the novels are shorter than some of Anne's other novels, they are also enjoyed by adults. As she had done earlier, Anne tapped not only into her own experiences as an adolescent, but also into her own emotional intensity, honed by her relationships with Bernard and Derek and her mother's death. The books expand our factual knowledge of Pern, introducing a new kind of dragon, the diminutive fire lizard. In this series, Anne further develops the world of Pern. A misunderstood and unappreciated child, the main character, Menolly, has musical gifts but is denied the opportunity to use them because she is a girl; and on Pern (at this time) only men can be Harpers, the planet's performing historians and educators. Ireland's own legacy of bards can be seen in the Harpers. Menolly has to run away from home and, in the process, Impresses nine fire lizards and, eventually, finds training and recognition for her work. Although Menolly is a much younger character, there are certainly parallels in Anne's own "running away" to Ireland, where she was able to develop her talent, writing, and eventually receive recognition and achieve independence.

Vaughne Hansen, who works with Virginia Kidd, says that "Annie *is* Menolly," meaning that this character contains Anne's personality. But the novel provides a good example of how an author works many elements of her life into her work. Anne recalled and represented her own adolescent angst and her sense of being an outsider. Menolly's musical gifts parallel Anne's own musical talents. Anne's father was not the tyrant poor Menolly's father is, but Anne has channeled into this patriarch her anger at the sexism she encountered, not only in jobs, but also in the science fiction world and as a single mother. Anne's bonds with animals—cats, dogs, and horses—appear in the relationship Menolly has with her fire lizards, who respond to her emotions and to whom she can cry, as Anne did with her horse Ed. The fire lizards and, indeed, even the larger dragon can be seen as stand-ins for children, for a Dragonrider or fire lizard owner must feed and care for the creatures as though they were infants. Even her son Alec's experience with fishing boats emerged in the book, since the fishing world that Menolly grows up in is depicted as harsh and dangerous. Throwing herself back into Pern proved salubrious for Anne. Menolly's problems were more solvable than Anne's own losses of her mother and her lover, and as the writer, in a science fiction world, Anne could create bonds with loveable fire lizards and full-size dragons that were more intimate and rewarding than those with real people. In the real world, your family, friends, and lovers could die or abandon you; fire lizards and dragons are telepathic and, in the case of dragons, when you die, they die, and vice versa. No nasty living on without your loved ones.

While Anne wrestled with loss in the first part of the 1970s, from 1975 on she began to realize more professional and personal triumphs. In March 1975, Anne received the prestigious E. E. Smith Memorial Award for Imaginative Fiction. As the guest of honor for the New England Science Fiction Association, she was invited to write a short novel, published in a limited edition of eight hundred, for the conference. Anne wrote *A Time When*, a novella that deals with the dragon that is featured in *The White Dragon*. The novella was well-received and, despite its limited printing, was nominated for a Nebula Award. Her writing continued to flourish at the end of the 1970s. In 1977, Anne followed *Dragonsong* with *Dragonsinger* and published a collection of stories, *Get Off the Unicorn*. The short-story collection has one of the most infamous typos in science fiction; it was to have been called *Get "of" the Unicorn* (the product of the unicorn, rather than a riding unicorn). Including stories from 1959 to 1977, the collection demonstrates Anne's status, since to sell a collection of your reprinted stories shows the power and appeal of your reputation as an author. Such a book demonstrates the power of her name to sell books.

In *Dragonsinger* Anne appears to have drawn on elements of her experience at Stuart Hall, the exclusive boarding school she had attended for one year. Anne, a northerner at a southern school, was as much out of place as Menolly, a Fishing Hold girl, is at the Harper Hall school. She endures taunts and feels very lonely and out of place. What saves Menolly is her music and her fire lizards. Of course, Anne uses creative license, in that she extrapolates, the classic science fiction quality of taking something that is real—relationships with pets, a difficult school experience—and developing and extending it logically beyond what is known. Anne's lesson in real life, to be flexible and to develop your Talent, worked for her as it does for her characters.

In 1978, *Dinosaur Planet* appeared, the first of a trilogy that deals with dinosaur life on another planet. The contract for these novels with a British publisher, Futura, had been sent Anne's way by Harry Harrison. The publisher had approached him to write the series, but he was too busy with other novels. Harrison, however, knew that Anne would appreciate the work and payment. Anne's flexibility in writing to a publisher's suggestion worked out well, for the series was a big success.

In the late 1970s, Anne's work continued to receive recognition, both financial and literary. In 1978 *The White Dragon*, the third in the Dragonriders of Pern series, appeared, and it immediately landed on the *New York Times* best-seller list. The other Dragonriders of Pern books had sold steadily and were out of print, and Ballantine re-issued *Dragonflight* and *Dragonquest*, with new covers by the renowned science fiction artist Michael Whelan. Anne received three prestigious awards for *The White Dragon*: the Ditmar Award (Australia), the Gandalf Award, and the Streza Award (Eurocon).

On April 2, 1976, Anne's friends in Dublin gave her a surprise birthday party. Her friend Joan Harrison tricked her into leaving her house and then brought her back. Anne wrote to Virginia, "I have never been more astonished in my life! I wept! No one has ever given me a surprise party and it was so nice of everyone—because I don't mind being 50 but sometimes it bothers—like at Texas A & M [convention where she felt old and undesirable and had trouble getting into a space ship cockpit]." The party revealed how much Ireland had become home to Anne—a home where she had close friends and a community.

Anne had had a wonderful time in Chicago, where Del Rey threw a big party for the launch of the hardback edition of *The White Dragon* in 1978. Her wild cousin Tony McElroy attended, and he made a big impression when he went around asking all the guests if they thought *The White Dragon* was any good at all. Flush with the success of the hardcover, Anne agreed to tour when the paperback was released. In spring 1979, Del Rey booked Anne on a whirlwind tour of the United States: twenty-two cities in thirty-two days. Excited as she was about her new status, Anne did not think about herself or her health—she let the publisher make the arrangements, and they were exhausting. She had two or three interviews for radio and television, as well as two book signings in most cities. The tour had begun with a science fiction convention in Antwerp, Belgium, and Anne flew directly from there to the United States. While Anne was treated like a star, with limousines and the best hotels, nothing could make up for the exhausting pace and emotional demands of such a tour. Traveling by herself, Anne was soon overwhelmed, a feeling that was compounded by worry over her son Todd. He was in the army and had told a friend he'd received a concussion. Ever the concerned mother, Anne tried to reach him repeatedly, but with no success. Finally, Anne's oldest son, Alec, called his U.S. Senator; and after days, Anne found out that his unit had been called out on maneuvers. In Anne's words, "The tour went on. And on, and on." Suffering badly from insomnia, Anne found a doctor through the hotel who prescribed Valium, but it did nothing to help her sleep. Her hands shook so badly that she spilled a glass of milk trying to drink it. At one book signing, she actually had to ask what city she was in, covering up the question with a laugh, as though she were joking. But at that moment, Anne was not sure where she was. In typical Anne fashion, she worried about her handler, realizing it was "not much fun for him shepherding someone on the brink of nervous collapse."

When she visited St. Louis, her brother Kevin was quite worried about the stress she was experiencing. It was a turning point for Anne, as she realized, "I had honestly thought myself able for most things—especially the hit of being so popular. But that sort of hit brings a downer all its own. I could then appreciate why rock'n'roll groups go for 'illegal substances.'" By the end of the tour, Anne had come to rely on Seconal and Serac. She got a prescription for these drugs in Minneapolis when she went to the hospital in the middle of the night. In a curtained alcove, she heard a nurse whisper to the doctor, "Don't you know who she is?" Anne commented wryly, "A fan when I needed one." After she showed them her schedule, she got the prescriptions, being warned she should only use the drugs for a short time. Of course, in between the exhaustion and tension, Anne had some pleasurable experiences. A handsome fan whisked her off to lunch, a man she described as "salvation . . . in the form of a tall, dark-haired man, mid to late twenties, in work shirt and jeans, wearing the heavy sort of boots outdoor men require. He wore a belt of tools around his waist with a Bell Telephone icon. He also carried the old-fashioned round-topped, black lunch pail." Anne also met her old friend Gordy Dickson in Minneapolis and was able to vent her frustration with the tour to him. She met George Takei, a treat because Anne had always enjoyed *Star Trek.* She even got to go a *YES* concert in Los Angeles in her limousine.

Anne concluded the decade with the publication of the last of the Harper Hall Trilogy, *Dragondrums.* In this novel, Anne drew on Todd's difficulties in elementary school with a bully. She also evoked her brother Kevin's and her daughter's experiences with serious illness, bravely confronted. By writing about Gigi's illness in a fictional setting, Anne was herself able to confront her pain at her daughter's suffering.

In the late 1970s, Anne's household began to resemble the Holds of her Pern novels. A variety of people came to stay and work for her, including Antoinette O'Connell, who took care of Gigi, and Mare Laban, who was studying for a British Horse Society instructorship and who also managed the household while Anne was on book tours or at conventions. With a string of triumphs, Anne entered the 1980s with a new sense of purpose and the awareness, wrought from the experience of that tour, that she would have to make decisions about what was best for her and not be quite so trusting of the publishers and others. She also had the raw material that she would later transform into her romance novel, *Stitch in Snow*. The 1970s saw her dramatic move across an ocean and new experiences with love. But the most dramatic transformation was from being a writer to becoming a world-famous writer.

CHAPTER 6

Struggling with Success

I dearly wish I could have been a mouse in the woodwork of the
bank manager's office when you marched in, clad in your manly
jeans and oldest sweater with a check for $50,000. I love it.
—Win Catherwood, letter to Anne McCaffrey

BECOMING THE FIRST SCIENCE FICTION writer to reach the *New
York Times* best-seller list and signing her first million-dollar contract undeniably marked Anne McCaffrey's success as a writer. As
award after award showered upon her in the 1980s, she also faced
the difficulties of success. Yes, it was wonderful to be appreciated
and to finally, *finally*, not have to worry about money. Yet the old
worries were replaced by new ones: the effect of money and fame
on relationships. She had the opportunity to rest on her professional laurels but continued instead to be driven to write. Even
when she experienced insomnia and depression, Anne wrote
through her pain. In the 1980s, Anne was in her fifties, confront-
ing a midlife crisis compounded by society's negative attitude toward aging women. A classic romantic, Anne faced the challenges
of love and romance as a middle-aged woman. With characteristic
verve and humor, she insisted on being in love, even if platoni-
cally, with a younger man. Now a successful writer, she wrestled
with fanships and friendships, worked to make her children independent, began adjusting to an empty nest. She developed
strength and wisdom; she built relationships that supported her
intellectual and emotional growth.

An intermittent physical problem became serious just as Anne
reached the point when she might relax and enjoy her achievements. Anne had dealt with insomnia off and on throughout her

life, but in the first few months of 1980, she had a case severe
enough to cause extreme exhaustion and depression. She attributes the illness in part to the effects of her demanding 1979 U.S.
book tour, compounded by jet lag. The depression forced her to
consult a psychiatrist, who prescribed anti-depressants that actually made her feel worse. After taking the pills, she felt "disconnected from her imagination" and even less able to write. Investi-
gating the medication, she discovered one woman had died from
the drug's side effects, so she promptly discontinued its use. She
decided to work through her depression on her own. On a trip
to London, she met a dietician who recommended Anne try B-
12 injections to restore her energy. At this point, willing to try
anything, and remembering that her mother had taken B-12,
Anne began taking vitamins. They restored her energy, stamina,
and health, leaving Anne with a lifelong faith in alternative thera-
pies. Her belief in alternative science, depicted in her fiction,
emerged as practice in her life. But it was not only vitamin therapy
that helped Anne; she also found great consolation in reading
science fiction. Unable to concentrate on writing because of her
insomnia, Anne continued to read science fiction; some nights
she could only manage a few pages, but she found that reading helped her, as it had so many years ago when, suffering from
bronchitis, she first turned to science fiction for solace.

Reading science fiction had helped Anne through many a difficult time; the book she turned to now was Robert Silverberg's
Lord Valentine's Castle, an ingenious series of connected tales by
one of Anne's contemporaries. The main character, Lord Valentine, is burdened with immense responsibility for an entire world
and various species. His trouble, like Anne's, is how to deal with
power and success. Lord Valentine suffers from amnesia and so
anonymously travels through his world. He is about to be ap-
pointed coronal, a potentate who rules over billions of people
and "keeps the world from collapsing into chaos." Valentine has
trouble sleeping, for he has disturbing dreams that he cannot
properly interpret. On his planet, the King of Dreams is feared as
a figure of terror—a folk rhyme declares, "He's never asleep." Valentine struggles on his journey, finding friends and love before he

discovers his identity. Valentine's powers, then, are like those of a science fiction novelist, who has the responsibility of maintaining a fictional world and of keeping thousands of its fans content. As Valentine finds comfort by traveling as a commoner instead of the royal personage he is, Anne found comfort in being a science fiction reader rather than a science fiction writer.

While Anne enjoyed aspects of her fame and, indeed, had always wanted to be famous, being rich and famous also brought burdens. Though Anne did not control the fate of billions of people, she had now created and ruled not only Pern but other fictional worlds. She felt a responsibility to her fans, who mobbed her at conventions. Anne enjoyed conventions or "cons," as they are called by participants, but they were also exhausting; for Anne, cons were performances. By 1983, two of Anne's closest fans who later became friends, Marilyn and Harry Alm, remember that she "had stage presence" at conventions and that "she had the theatre training for it." They report at conventions that Anne "said that she's scared out of her mind but she puts on her persona." A signal sign of her fame, success, and influence was the first Pern-based con, Istacon, held in Atlanta, Georgia, in April 1984. (The organizers chose that date to coincide with her birthday.) Some fans didn't seem to realize Anne was human, expecting, for example, that Anne would sign *all* their copies of her books, even though she had been signing books for hours. And some fans would come up to Anne and react emotionally, bursting into tears or becoming speechless. Anne felt her power acutely, and while she always behaved graciously and warmly to all her fans, she dreaded intense encounters. She worried that some of her fans lived too much in her fictional worlds and not enough in the real world. Like Valentine, she longed for an escape. Where Lord Valentine found escape in amnesia and traveling, Anne found respite in Ireland, with her family, friends, and animals, especially her horses. But in the 1980s, she still spent a tremendous amount of time at conventions, which compounded her sleep troubles.

Anne's continuing delight in reading science fiction provided not only knowledge of her field—she frequently advises aspiring writers to *read* science fiction so they know what is being done in the genre—but also common ground with her fans. That is to say, Anne knows what it is like to lose yourself in a book, to have favorite characters and authors. When she is feeling low, books provide comfort and an escape.

As if running a stable and writing at least two novels a year weren't enough, Anne also threw herself wholeheartedly back into touring by 1983. She has always believed that extensive touring is what lifted her out of the mid-list writers into best-seller status. Her list of con appearances and book tours is daunting; by 1985, she had traveled to all the United States except the Dakotas. An example of her travels in 1983 is typical of her frenetic pace in the 1980s. She flew to the United States to attend Lunacon in April 1983 and participated in Star Trek Con in Birmingham, England, in July 1983. At the end of 1983, she was back in the United States, with speaking engagements in Texas and New Mexico during November and December. As she did with so many activities, Anne threw herself into touring, not thinking about her own physical and emotional needs. That meant that when she encountered crises, she was already stretched thin.

In the world of Pern, Anne could create and end life, but in the real world, she had to confront unpredictable and inevitable loss through death. Nineteen eighty-one brought both great sadness and great joy. Ed, Anne's beloved horse, had been a part of her life since 1971. Although she no longer rode him much because he had become arthritic, Anne spent time with Ed every day. In their new home, Anne could step out the kitchen door and call "Horseface," and he would run over to greet her. Her lovers had left, her children had grown up and moved out, but Ed remained her faithful companion. Eventually, his arthritis became so bad that he had difficulty walking, and in September 1981, Anne had Ed put to sleep. It was a bitter loss, ameliorated when that same day Anne received a call from son Alec that Eliza Oriana, her first grandchild, had been born. The simultaneity of death and life appeared two years later in one of Anne's most powerful novels, *Moreta: Dragonlady of Pern*, in which the title character and her dragon die, just as another queen dragon, Moreta's dragon's daughter, hatches. The novel's dedication obliquely refers to Gigi's struggle with Crohn's disease: "This book is dedicated to my daughter Georgeanne Johnson with great affection and respect for her courage." Anne's characteristic sentimentality was affected by Gigi's devastating and apparently incurable disease. Moreta's extremely moving death comes at least in part from Anne's mourning for her daughter's lost health. The title character also reflects Anne herself. *Moreta: Dragonlady of Pern* is a powerful and compelling story of a strong-minded heroine who dies after saving Pern from an epidemic. The title character pushes herself and her dragon to exhaustion to get lifesaving vaccine to all the communities on Pern. Moreta's endless traveling surely owes something to Anne's own rigorous schedule of appearances. In the novel, Moreta succeeds in saving the population, but dies herself when her exhausted dragon goes "between" and they don't return. Set back in Pern's past, before the events of *Dragonflight*, the first Pern novel, *Moreta* demonstrates the use of a prequel setting that Anne would use to great advantage in later years—developing the history of Pern.

As Gigi and Anne dealt with Gigi's illness, Anne struggled, writing to her ex-husband, Wright, who returned her letters unopened. Wright was living with Alec and his family in Ohio. Yet in early 1985, after Annett divorced him in June 1984, Wright volunteered to move to Ireland to help Anne care for Gigi—or so Anne wrote to her friend Win Catherwood, who had always detested Wright. Anne's friend Win felt that Wright was a negative influence on Anne, telling her, "I always felt he was violently jealous of your smallest success in writing." Win thought the idea of Wright moving in with Anne was ludicrous: "W. [Wright] as a companion indeed! I'd prefer the plastic-bag-over-the head or the slit-wrists in the bathtub." Perhaps Anne in part agreed, for she wrote to Win: "Wright moved out of Alec's house just shortly before Kate was going to insist on his removing. He got drunk in front of [granddaughter] Eliza once too often. It's a shame because she adores him . . . and once suggested that I would like grandpa. I assured her that I did." Even though they had been divorced for fifteen years, Anne still felt a connection with Wright.

In part, this attachment reveals her capacity to feel. Once gained, Anne's love was hard to destroy. She kept many friends for years, even when she was separated by an ocean from them (her continuing devotion to Virginia was just one example of Anne's loyalty transcending distance).

Perhaps because of her daughter's illness and the feelings about Wright that it stirred up, Anne had some trouble with the manuscript of *Moreta*. The book was overdue, so she sent it directly to Judy-Lynn Del Rey, the editor at Del Rey Books, with some anxiety on her part. Anne was quite relieved when Judy-Lynn's response to the manuscript was enthusiastic. In reply to Judy, Anne wrote, "One never knows when one is bombing and I really sweat out these new books, fearing that somehow I will have lost the 'touch' between books." Originally annoyed that Anne had sent the manuscript directly to Judy-Lynn, her agent and friend Virginia Kidd nevertheless was moved by the novel. Discussing the death scene, Virginia wrote to Judy-Lynn, "I thought I was enough of an old hand so that I could read just about anything objectively, but by golly, by the time I finished page 2 of this there were tears standing in my eyes. Annie has surely not lost her touch!" Her ability to move even so experienced a reader as Virginia shows Anne's mastery of the art of transforming her own real-life pain at Gigi's ill health into powerful fiction. In part, too, however, Anne's novel reflects her own sense of depletion. Like Moreta, Anne had pushed herself past the point of exhaustion, not only on her 1979 book tour, but also in her search for a cure for Gigi's debilitating illness. No wonder Anne could write so movingly about exhaustion and loss, for she had experienced so much of these in her own life. A caretaker by nature, Anne gave and gave of herself—to her fans, her children, her friends—until she collapsed. It was easier for her to take care of others than to take care of herself. That energy seems to have been expended in heroines like Killashandra, who were the antithesis of Anne, around whom people congregated. Where the Crystal Singer lived alone with her art (until she found love), Anne lived in a Hold, in which she was the lord holder, responsible emotionally and financially for many others.

Not all of her books focused directly on her own and her family's pain; Anne also continued to write novels that were set on other worlds besides Pern, such as *The Coelura*. In *The Coelura* (published in 1983, the same year as *Moreta*), Anne deals with environmentalism, but she also criticizes Western culture's obsession with appearance, especially for women. A young woman crashes her space car and discovers the coelura, a life-form that spins beautiful rainbows that can be used to create spectacular clothing that beautifies whoever wears the material. The novel's heroine works with a young man to save the coelura from exploitation and threatened extinction. Reworking the idea of transformation that shaped her first novel, *Restoree*, Anne reiterates the theme of inner beauty, one she would repeat in a variety of settings and plots. The novel follows a basic romance plot, in that the heroine is aided by a young man with whom she falls in love. Through the couple's rejection of the beautifying power of the coelura, Anne wrestled with her own feelings of aging and appearance. In science fiction, at least, she could make the external less important.

Anne's success as a writer occurred at the same time as she had to cope with being an older woman in a society that overvalues youth. She stopped hormone replacement therapy and began gaining weight, an occurrence of some concern to her. "Fat and fifty has no chance of snagging a man, not that I've been *at* it, but as you well know," she writes to Joanne Forman, "hope glimmers occasionally even though I know no man who would put up with the life I lead." Anne's Gothic novels reveal her working out of her own issues about men and romance. In November 1987, she wrote to her dear friend Win, "I gave up on men for another reason. The ones my age were interested in my daughter and in no way [would I] be in competition with her generation. Still the romantic is very much a part of me." Anne's innate optimism and interest in romance were, in part, channeled into her fiction.

In a realistic novel, Anne deals very explicitly with personal issues of love and sex. In 1984 Anne published a Gothic novel (part mystery, part romance) entitled *Stitch in Snow*, which, like

The Kilternan Legacy, contains a character similar to Anne: a mature woman and a successful writer, with a son in college, who lives in Ireland but who travels to the States on book tours. She even meets with two friends in Boston, named Jean and Pota, the names of two of Anne's college friends. Anne admits that the book's title is based on a real encounter: trapped by a blizzard in an airport, she drops a ball of yarn that a handsome man picks up and returns to her. In the novel, the main character, Dana, does the same and so begins a love affair; in real life, Anne says she and the man both caught their separate planes shortly after the encounter. Nevertheless, the novel is quite revealing in other, less literal ways. Anne's deft and sensitive handling of an older woman's concerns as she has a sexual relationship separates this novel from a conventional formula. Dana, the novel's heroine, worries about her aging and her appearance, but resolves to enjoy life fully. The book's opening pages reveal that Dana has had an affair with a man younger than she, but that it wasn't a permanent solution for her. In the novel Anne rewrites her relationship with Bernard Shattuck so that it is the older woman who ends the relationship, rather than the younger man.

When Dana sends a sweater to Dan, with whom she has fallen in love, he correctly reads the significance of the sweater and follows her to ask her to marry him. *Stitch in Snow* suggests a parallel between knitting and writing and the feminine image of a woven, intertwined life. The main character's knitting provides a clue to her need for companionship, and it also functions as a sign of her affection for a lover. The similarity between their names, Dana and Dan, also suggests the romantic ideal figured in Plato's *Symposium*—that lovers are two halves who meet to form an androgynous whole. Anne's innate romanticism shines through in this lovely fantasy romance. In depicting an older woman as a romantic heroine, Anne challenges our culture's celebration of only youthful sexuality. Through Dana's passionate love affair, Anne reminds her readers that humans are sexual beings throughout our lives. Her portrait of a healthy and pleasurable sexual life for mature adults also appears in later novels, such as the *Powers* series. Like that series' heroine, Yanaba, Dana in *Stitch in Snow* demonstrates that older women have sexual desires and needs that can and should be met.

In addition to expressing liberating ideas about sexuality, *Stitch in Snow* also describes the delight and stress of book tours, which were beginning to dominate Anne's life. Dana's frustration with impossible questions and her delight in meeting her readers seems to reflect Anne's own experience. For example, at one book signing Dana has to deal with all sorts of bizarre questions from people. One reader even asks Dana whether her stories are drug-induced. She shudders at the thought of being asked to look at unedited manuscripts of aspiring writers. In a hotel, she must endure the unwanted advances of men who assume that, because she's dining alone, she's easy prey. Giving lectures, signing books, and traveling frenetically leaves Dana "utterly, completely and thoroughly drained," an experience Anne certainly shared.

While Anne did not have the fictional love affair depicted in *Stitch in Snow*, she did have a romantic flirtation with one of her son Todd's friends, John Greene. He became a family friend, particularly enjoying banter and surprises with Anne. Todd says, "I don't know why she didn't marry him," remembering "the things that they said to each other—they genuinely loved each other." He recalls that Johnny said, "If I could I would be in front of your mother's door and die to protect her." Gigi remembered, "Mum and Johnny often commented that they hadn't been born to the same generation but should have been; they seemed to spark well together, in my opinion." Anne said that she and Johnny had "great rapport." Handsome and jocular, he would surprise Anne by appearing at the store when he knew she would be shopping and carry her groceries home. Anne remembers that he was known as "the Fist of Bray [a nearby town]" because he delighted in punching out bullies. She admired his sense of justice and his bravado. John had no serious girlfriend, and Anne seems to have functioned as his confidante and closest female friend. In 1988, however, while serving with the French Foreign Legion in Orange, France, he was found shot in the head, and no murderer or motive was ever discovered. *Renegades of Pern*, published in 1989, is dedicated to John Greene, and the hero of that novel is based on him. Anne mourns John to this day; she has a large photo of him in her study, and she has placed a character based on John in every novel she has written since 1988—to give him the life he so tragically lost.

Anne also dealt with her former lover Derek in fiction, addressing a situation very like his marital disaster in *The Carradyne Touch*. In November 1986, Anne finished work on *The Carradyne Touch* (published in the United States as *The Lady*), an autobiographical romance set in Ireland in 1970. In this novel, Anne again tackles the oppression of women, but here it is the laws in Ireland that she exposes, along with the damaging and misogynistic attitudes promoted by the Catholic Church. While Anne's other Gothic novels are short (at or less than 250 pages), *The Carradyne Touch* weighs in with the heft of her science fiction novels. Over 450 pages, and a family saga, the novel evokes Anne's science fiction Tower and the Hive series with its development of a special family. Instead of psionic powers, however, the Carradyne family is special because of their gift for raising horses. The novel focuses on the youngest member of the family, a girl named Catriona. Like the Gothic *Ring of Fear*, *The Carradyne Touch* develops the importance of human-animal relationships. But the novel also explores Catriona's development into a woman and the negative example of her mother's sexual frigidity, caused by her unhealthy religious fervor. The issues of battering and the inadequacy of Irish law to protect women are developed through Catriona's sister, who is a feminist activist, and through the plight of a battered woman Catriona knows.

In her portrait of Catriona's mother, Isabel, Anne returns to the importance of a healthy sexual life to a woman's psyche. Isabel is the flip side of Dana—what an older woman could become if she represses her sexuality. Through Isabel, Anne shows how a denial of sexuality and physicality leads to unhappiness. Increasingly neurotic, Isabel is addicted to Valium and tries to dominate her daughter, squelching her interest in horses and art. Isabel also interferes in Catriona's relationship with her father, forbidding him to hug or kiss Catriona. Eventually, Isabel dies, her heart weakened by her addiction and presumably also by her unhappiness. In Isabel's death we may see Anne's fantasy wish for her former lover Derek's estranged wife, Mabel, to disappear, if not die. The novel also contains a real-life strategy that did work for Anne—throwing herself into her love for horses and developing female friendships.

A neighbor, Selina, also becomes important to Catriona, who learns from Selina's experience how few rights Irish women have under the law. As Selina examines her options to leave an abusive marriage, she is "appalled at how little protection she received under the law. In essence she was no more than a man's chattel." She complains to Michael, "You men really have it all your own way here in Ireland, a fact I never previously appreciated." Even after the beating, Selina must obtain three witnesses who saw her husband attack her—a requirement that helps the batterer get away with his crimes. As in *The Kilternan Legacy*, published a decade earlier, this novel exposes the differences not only between American and Irish law, but also between English and Irish law.

The subordinate position of women in Ireland is an issue close to Anne's heart, in part because of what she suffered in her marriage and also because of what she saw her friend Jan Regan endure. Happily, like Selina, Jan Regan escaped and leads a fulfilling life in Scotland. She is just one of many female friends whom Anne has helped over the years. The problems faced by battered women couldn't be explored in Anne's science fiction because, optimistically, she creates a future in which laws are far more just to women. But even the Gothics contain Anne's characteristic optimism, as Catriona's sister explains, "Some are going to find . . . that the worm is turning in Ireland." Anne didn't just write about the worm turning—she lived it. She directly challenged Irish ideas about the subordination of women. For example, in 1984, when Anne decided to purchase another bigger farm, Ballyvolan Farm, she had trouble getting an Irish banker to approve a mortgage for her. Even today she remembers with anger her difficulty in obtaining approval, for she had substantial and impressive earnings by then. The difficulty wasn't only that she earned money in an unorthodox way, as a writer, but that she was a single woman. Eventually, she had Seamus McGraw, a famous horsebreeder, sign on as a guarantor, but it irked Anne to no end to have to have a man vouch for her. She wrote to Win Catherwood about the situation, and he wrote back, "I dearly wish I could have been a mouse in the woodwork of the bank manager's office when you marched in, clad in your manly jeans and oldest sweater with a check for $50,000. I love it."

Win was just one of Anne's many friends who helped her develop tolerance and understanding of sexual orientation. Anne had real-life platonic relationships not only with female friends, but also with gay men. One especially fulfilling relationship for Anne was with her homosexual friend Win Catherwood. Win was devoted to Anne, often telling her she was the one woman he could imagine marrying. His letters are filled with admiration for her writing and her verve. In one letter, Win marvels at Anne's tremendous productivity as a writer: "How the hell can you work on three books at once?" Indeed, while there are other people and influences that explain Anne's sympathetic treatment of homosexuality in her fiction, Win was undoubtedly the largest factor. Anne herself credits Win with opening her eyes: "I understand the male version [of homosexuality] better because of Win." In one missive, Anne brags to Win about the response to her depiction of homosexual characters: "I'm sort of real chuffed [Irish expression meaning pleased or gratified] because I got a charming letter from a self-proclaimed gay, living in Georgia, thanking me for my treatment of green and blue riders in *Moreta*, and complimenting me on my portrayal of useful homosexuals with a valid status in a complex society. . . . It's nice to know that I've done it right in that quarter!" Anne insists that "young men and women who have not a sexual identity need to see good examples of sexuality." She notes wryly that she has received criticism for her openness from people who tell her they are never going to read another book of hers again. This kind of reaction is painful to Anne, but she takes great comfort in the support she receives from other fans and, even more importantly, from friends whose expertise she values.

Anne has often been commended for her depiction of male

homosexuality as an integral part of society, but she has done less with lesbians. Anne's homosexual friends have helped her understand male homosexuality, but she has no close lesbian friends. She also found herself upon occasion approached by lesbians, whose advances were unwelcome. With her generous nature, Anne found it unpleasant to rebuff these women, but lesbian sex held no interest for her. Some were even famous writers, such as Marion Zimmer Bradley. To Joanne Forman, Anne wrote, "She made a pass at me. . . . I sorted out the matter but I have great respect for her as a writer." Due in part to her still anomalous unmarried status and her frequent female visitors and house guests, Anne had to confront local rumors that she was a witch with a coven of lesbians. Characteristically defiant and humorous, Anne responded by conspicuously lining up a series of twig broomsticks outside Dragonhold. If the village wanted to say she was a witch, she would show them her collection of magical brooms! One of the brooms still has a place of honor in her living room. The rumors about Anne's sexuality and an association with witchcraft demonstrate one way societies try to control women who defy the limited roles available to them. Anne responded to this pressure not only by creating alternative worlds, but also through gestures, such as the brooms, that show her sense of humor and defiance. Anne's good friend Maureen Beirne showed how persistent and troubling such attempts at control are; when I interviewed her, practically the first words out of her mouth were, "Annie McCaffrey is NOT a lesbian."

Richard Woods, a Catholic priest who has extensive counseling experience and works with young people, is one person who supports and reinforces Anne's views on tolerance. Anne has a longstanding close relationship with Richard Woods, with whom she published *A Diversity of Dragons*, a large-format, illustrated book about dragons. Anne's family and friends see him as a very positive influence in her life. A critic of fantasy and science fiction, he met Anne in 1981 when he interviewed her, and then he visited her in Ireland. A Dominican, Richard teaches and works in counseling, so he has been able to support and encourage Anne in her fictional representation of outsiders, including homosexuals. Anne's and Richard's personalities resonated: they both loved horses and science fiction, and Richard provided a lively, supportive, and engaging male presence for Anne. They met when he was forty and she was fifty-five. Shelly Shapiro, Anne's friend and editor, says that "he has a sense of rightness in the world and he's a calming person. I'm sure that he's helping her." They shared a dream of creating a writer's community in Ireland, realized in part when Anne bought a cottage where writers and friends of hers and Richard's could go to have peace to be able to write. The cottage was completely renovated and called Dragonthorn. Unfortunately, due to financial reversals, Anne had to sell the cottage; but to her delight, Richard's family trust bought the property, meaning that Richard is often nearby. He reads her novels, occasionally makes suggestions, and helps with the editing of Anne's manuscripts. Richard is also the family chaplain, having officiated at the weddings of two of Anne's children. He embodies the tolerance that Anne values and is also a charming, handsome man who might feature in one of her romances.

Everyone I interviewed agrees about one aspect of Anne McCaffrey: she is extremely generous. She herself has described her tendency to be "a fairy godmother." Although she vehemently denies that any of her heroines are Cinderellas, in real life Anne has created many Cinderellas. In the 1980s, freed from her own formerly pressing poverty, Anne found herself able to help others. And she did, mostly with money, but also with an equally valuable commodity, her name and time. For example, Joanne Forman had written a number of Pern songs, an endeavor that Anne, so musical herself, endorsed. Her correspondence with Joanne reveals that they became friends, as occasionally happens with Anne's readers. In Joanne's case, Anne became involved in the marketing of Joanne's cassette tape, even selling it at some conventions. Selling the tapes was just one of the many ways that Anne has helped friends. Win Catherwood in 1983 was already a very ill man, and he was another of the uncounted dozens for whom Anne has been a lifesaver. Win came from an established society family and, under the pseudonym David Telfair, wrote a handful of arch English-style novels in a Georgette Heyer style.

Like many writers, Win had no health insurance. He suffered from a rare blood ailment, and Anne sent him several thousand dollars so he could get proper treatment, a wheelchair, and other necessities. He and Anne had been good friends since they met in Delaware, when both were aspiring novelists. His letters reveal Anne's extensive generosity to him at a time when he was quite desperate.

Anne could also be generous to people she did not know very well. She enjoyed playing hostess at cons—often to large groups. In 1983, for example, during the U.S. tour in support of *Moreta*, Anne enjoyed the company of Houston area fans and Texas A & M fans. A large group went out for dinner at a Chinese restaurant. It was a typically lively, raucous event, with much laughter and noise. At the end, Anne picked up the check, with the result that a bewildered waiter asked, "Are these all your children?" Anne replied, "Yes, but by different fathers," to a peal of laughter from the group. In at least one spectacular instance, in October 1984, she rushed in to save the day by paying a six-thousand-dollar dinner bill for a convention, Western Recon II, using her gold American Express card. After the salad had been served, the hotel was refusing to serve the meal unless the hotel fee was paid immediately. She was never reimbursed for the cost.

Anne also gives generously to people who help her. Fortunately, Anne's friendship with Marilyn and Harry Alm provided some comfort at cons; they traveled to be with her, and it was a relief to Anne to have friends there with whom she could relax and in whom she could trust. By the end of the decade, the Alms would assist Anne with the world of Pern, creating maps and checking facts for her. In their devotion to Pern, the Alms acquired a clearer sense of Pern's details and history than Anne herself. Parceling out some of the responsibility for Pern's continuity problems to the Alms gave Anne a measure of relief. Never a meticulous or obsessive fact-checker, Anne instead continued to develop Pern from her heart rather than from diagrams or timelines. For *Dragonsdawn*, Anne gave Marilyn and Harry 1 percent of her paperback royalties as an indication of her respect and appreciation for their work. Anne's editors said that such generosity was quite unprecedented, as map-makers or fact-checkers customarily receive a flat fee for their work. By creating their pay as a royalty, Anne was showing the Alms how much their dedication to Pern meant to her.

In her brother Hugh's oldest daughter, Karin, however, Anne acquired another dependent. Because Anne so loved her brother and because of her loyalty, caretaking propensities, and wealth, Karin became Anne's responsibility rather than anyone else's in the family. Karin herself had intuited this, for she gravitated to Anne in Ireland. Karin had visited Anne in the 1970s, and even then Anne commented on Karin's princess behavior—she expected to be waited on. Yet this might have been just typical youthful self-centeredness. Tragically, Karin developed a mental illness, schizophrenia. Suffering from such a life-shattering disease, Karin soon became a trial to Anne. At first, Anne blamed Karin's addiction to drugs for her mental illness, but Karin has been diagnosed with schizophrenia and committed to the local psychiatric hospital for treatment. Karin got marginally involved with the IRA, pretended to be Lady McHughes or Lady Sean McAvoy, and quickly ran through her inheritance of seventy-five thousand dollars from her mother's estate. Valerie, Karin's sister and Kitti Ping, Karin's stepmother, both tried to help Karin, but to no avail. She lived in Bray, a nearby village, and Anne paid half her rent. But even with money, Anne could not cure her niece's mental illness.

In one case Anne's generosity paid off when she gained a supportive companion. In 1985 Anne invited Sara Virginia Brooks, her former sister-in-law, to come visit. As she often did, Anne paid for her guest's trip. After a second visit, Anne invited Sara to move to Dragonhold to manage the house and gardens. In her brother Kevin's words, Anne lost the husband but kept the sister. Sis, as she was known, had had a difficult life. Anne first met Sis when she came north to help with Anne's firstborn, Alec. Sis already had a child, Dick, whom she brought with her, but more importantly, she brought emotional support and practical advice. Sis had been a nurse before her marriage and later worked in public relations. A beautiful woman with blond hair and striking features, Sis had trained as a nurse, worked as a floral judge, and done public relations work. Her adopted son, Dickie, never settled into a job and relied on her for funds until the day she died. He left his daughter, Melissa, for Sis to raise. Moreover, Sis's husband turned out to have been a bigamist. In the 1980s, Sis had been having a difficult time financially and emotionally. Like many women, Sis had devoted herself to her parents, nursing them through their final illnesses. She only had Social Security income, and that wasn't enough for her to maintain her parents' home. Anne suggested a way out: Sis could move to Ireland, and then she wouldn't have to worry about rent or other expenses. At the first Dragonhold, Anne generously turned two stables and a large spare room into an apartment for her. It was a good arrangement, since Sis felt useful running the house and specialized in creating beautiful gardens. The gardens that Sis created at Dragonhold-Underhill in the early 1990s are still magnificent. Anne, of course, paid for the gardeners. But while Anne loved beautiful gardens and they reminded her of the gardens her father had cultivated, she had no desire to work in or manage a garden.

The two got along famously, enjoying each other's company, and Anne found it "nice to have someone of [her] own generation, remembering the same things" she did. Like Anne, who was enjoying knitting, Sis was a handicraft person, but she exceeded Anne, "doing beautiful embroidery and sewing." Their friendship was a great comfort to Anne, who took Sis on several overseas trips with her, to Paris, to Madrid, even a cruise on the *Queen Elizabeth Two*. Anne remembers, "We had a grand time, spiffing it up on the QE-2." With Sis, Anne was able to share her worries and concerns about her children and her household. Sis would travel to Florida each year to visit friends. She would take an empty suitcase, filling it with the foods and delicacies that she couldn't find in Ireland: "She used to get by the airlines by affecting her Charleston accent and acting an ineffectual but charming southern lady. . . dithering." She was able to get all the cake mixes and spices she wanted into Ireland that way. Sis loved Mexican food and hot spices, which Anne's digestion wouldn't accommodate, but Sis and Derval, who ran the stables, would have an occasional Mexican meal while Anne had an egg. Unfortunately, Sis did bring an emotional problem with her—depression and a concomitant abuse of alcohol. She would binge and go on lost weekends. Sis's reaction to alcohol differed from Anne's. Anne preferred wine to hard liquor and would go to sleep when drunk. In fact, Sis's alcohol abuse was uncomfortably like her brother Wright's. Characteristically direct, Anne confronted Sis, explaining that Sis's behavior terrified her. Subsequently, Sis reduced her intake and there were no more binges. Sis, then, was an important addition to Anne's household, the sister she never had. While Sis read all of Anne's books as she wrote them, she never commented or made suggestions. Sis was supportive, but she helped Anne write by giving her emotional support and companionship. Sis provided much-needed breaks from writing rather than being a part of it, as Anne's good friend and agent Virginia Kidd had done. But Sis's gift was equally valuable; she freed Anne from the daily running of the household, allowing Anne to devote more energy to her writing.

People tended either to love or hate Sis, depending on her reaction to them. Anne's son Alec found her horribly self-centered, but Elizabeth Moon, a co-author of Anne's, thought Sis was wonderful and explained, "She reminded me of one of those small old-fashioned apples that is tart and juicy and crisp all at once." Sis's most important quality, at least in terms of her relationship with Anne, was her loyalty and protectiveness. Sis jealously defended Anne against those whom she saw as exploiting Anne's generosity. And, indeed, Anne finds it difficult to say no to people. Sis would be unpleasant to people—workers, family, fans, friends of Anne's—whom she thought were taking advantage of Anne. For example, if someone was taking money from Anne, Sis would be downright rude to them, making Dragonhold so unpleasant that they would leave without getting more money from Anne. She had no scruples about telling people who had overstayed their welcome to leave.

In addition to ridding Dragonhold of unwelcome hangers-on, Sis also ran the household, overseeing the purchase of groceries, the preparation of most meals, and the maintenance of the gardens. Richard Woods says Sis was "a keen and ruthless judge of character" who alleviated the responsibility of running the household for Anne. Of Sis, Derval Diamond, whom Anne has described as her "adopted daughter," says, "She was a wicked old bitch but I liked her. She really protected Anne. Nobody could pull a fast one on her. Sis could see them coming and she was nearly always right." Sis and Anne shopped together, which Anne says they both enjoyed. Sis "enjoyed playing lady of the manor," according to Anne, whose evaluation of Sis is appreciative: she "was a very valuable asset to the house. She sometimes agitated me which can be good." Sis also agitated others. Maureen Beirne, Anne's best friend, says that, unlike Anne, "Sis was always an American." Sis used to treat the Irish gardeners as if they were poor white trash; born and raised in Oklahoma, she was passionate about American Indian culture, and she would often rail at the Irish ignorance of Native American issues. Occasionally, she would pretend to outsiders that Dragonhold was *her* home, owned and maintained by her rather than Anne. But Anne didn't mind Sis's playacting and seemed flattered rather than aggravated by Sis's behavior. Anne knew Sis loved her and appreciated all she had done for her. Anne appreciated Sis's very dry sense of humor. Sis, Win, and Richard, as well as Derval and Maureen, provided important emotional support and relief for Anne as she continued her extensive writing schedule.

Anne also found a friend and confidante in Kitti Ping, her older brother Hugh's second wife. Somewhat enviously, Anne has remarked that both her brothers made good second marriages. But, of course, it is easier for men to remarry, and they do so at a higher rate than divorced or widowed women. Anne admired Kitti Ping and enjoyed her company, basing the character of a biogeneticist in *Dragonsdawn* on her. Anne was at NOLA Con when she received the news that her brother Mac had died of a heart attack. She immediately flew to Los Angeles, met Todd, and from there flew to Hawaii to attend her brother's funeral. She cried the whole way from LA to Hawaii. It consoled Anne that all the flags on the military base there flew at half-mast, to honor her brother. Anne was as proud of Mac's military and government service as she was of her father's. Since Mac's death, Anne and Kitti have remained in touch, with Kitti remembered at Dragonhold as lively and fun. Derval Diamond, Anne's friend and manager of Dragonhold Stables, recalled one evening when the whole entourage went out to a local Chinese restaurant, where Kitti encouraged Derval's daughter Jen-Jen to dance. Kitti spoke Chinese to the restaurant owners, getting the whole group a custom Chinese meal, the best Derval had ever had.

Anne's friends and family provide an important context in which to understand her work. We often think of writers as working in isolation, but, in fact, writers often depend on a network of family and friends to foster their writing. Famous and successful writers like Anne often have entourages (see Brian Herbert's biography of his father, Frank Herbert, for another example). At the beginning of the 1980s, Anne wrestled with fame and felt isolated, but by the end of the decade she had used her vision and money to create a version of a Pern Hold, a unit that provided support for many people. Yet a television documentary that aired in 1988, focusing on Anne, completely neglects them, fostering the illusion that a writer lives in isolation. Anne's art, in contrast, has always been created in the midst of a full life with family and friends. For example, in November 1988, Anne became a grandmother for the second time when Alec's daughter Amelia was born, an event that delighted her. But there is no sense of Anne as grandmother, mother, or friend in the 1988 television show on Anne (part of a series featuring women writers); they undoubtedly provided an important, if unseen, backdrop to her life in Ireland. The documentary, entitled *Women Writers: Anne McCaffrey*, is a vivid and engaging profile, featuring Anne in her Irish home and in the Irish countryside. The film shows Anne reading, somewhat stiffly, from her books. Her reading is illustrated by views of the Wicklow Mountains and some rather inadequate animated versions of dragons and their riders. From *Dragonflight*, Anne reads a lurid sex scene, when the dragons mate, and their riders feel and act on the dragons' passion with other humans. Anne obtained permission for the television crew to film her walking the

grounds of Spring Hill Farm, the farm she had tried unsuccessfully to buy. Although another couple outbid her, Anne set her
novel *The Carradyne Touch* on its grounds. Some of the documentary consists of Anne walking around the farm grounds, pointing
out settings for important events in that novel.

But the film's real charm comes when Anne speaks to the
camera about why she writes and when the filmmakers follow her
to the 1987 World Science Fiction Convention in Brighton, England. There we see some of her fans, one with a stuffed fire lizard perched on her shoulder. The fans ask questions and Anne
signs their copies of her books and laughs and jokes with them.
With her characteristic humor and charm, Anne entrances the
fans. Asked about why she uses music as a theme in her books,
she responds, "Because I am a failed singer," and then she breaks
into a ribald song, demonstrating her impressive vocal skills and
her ability to capture a crowd. The filmmakers asked Anne to explain in her own words her contributions to science fiction and
to describe her writing. Anne repeats themes she has iterated in
published interviews, but in this television documentary we can
see her vehemence, as when, for example, she declares, "There is
not a Cinderella theme. Cinderella was a wimp. My heroines are
victims—strong people—who become survivors." She explains,
"What I have achieved for women in science fiction is science
fiction that is women-oriented, that they can read with a great
deal of enjoyment because my viewpoint characters are women,
strong women–role models." Discussing her first novel, *Restoree*,
Anne describes it as a corrective to all the passive female characters in science fiction who sat by screaming when something bad
happened. "I wouldn't have been standing there in the corner
screaming," Anne reveals, "I'd be in there with something. . . .
[SF in the 1950s] was totally unrealistic as far as women were concerned." "I put romance in science fiction, put emotion in science
fiction and used it as a tool of the trade," she explains.

But the relationships that she depicts between human and
dragon are, she acknowledges, idealistic. In words that evoke Anne
herself as well as her fans, she describes the effect of dragons on
humans in her books. Using the pronoun "we," Anne shows that,

like her fans, she, too, would appreciate the kind of love that dragons offer: "If we had someone who knew exactly what we felt and who supported us even when we were wrong, if we had that kind of support, someone standing behind us, we'd be a lot happier, we'd feel a lot more adequate." At the end of the program, she comments again about romance, this time from her own perspective as a fifty-year-old woman, with a wry sense of humor and awareness of ageism and sexism: "I would like a tall handsome man to sweep me off my feet, except he's more likely to be looking at my daughter." "Romance is as much a part of the human condition as anything else," Anne says, somewhat defensively, "particularly for females." The concluding frames show Anne listening to music in her living room, her cats meandering to and fro, with Anne's final question, "Why write if you're not fulfilling some need or dream of your own?" Anne's question was rhetorical; in her writing she fulfilled many needs of her own, and in so doing fulfilled her many readers' needs as well.

In the 1980s, Anne learned to live with success. She found joy and comfort in creating an extended family around her with her Irish friends Maureen Beirne, Johnny Greene, the Callahan family, Derval Diamond, and her former sister-in-law, Sara Brooks. She turned fans like the Alms into friends and settled into the life of a successful author, writing and then traveling to cons. The challenge of the next decade would be how to continue to write and to find new challenges. In her development of relationships with younger writers, Anne would find the way to continue to write and expand her real and fictional worlds.

CHAPTER 7

Being a Fairy Godmother

A house that looks like the house in which an
internationally famous writer resides.
—Anne McCaffrey, letter to Annett Francis

Anne McCaffrey is bigger than the one person.
—Gigi Kennedy

Annie loves to believe the best of people.
—Richard Woods

HER REWARD FOR A DECADE of hard work writing, Anne's new
home would carry the name of her last, "Dragonhold," but she
would add "Underhill" to commemorate her determination in
building this house and its specific placement. While Anne was
pleased with the builder's progress, Sis often spoke harshly to the
builder, whom she mistrusted. Always more optimistic than Sis,
Anne was pleased with each step that brought the house nearer
to completion. As the weeks and months passed, the large white
stucco house gradually took shape, transforming what had been
an uneven field into a dramatic setting for Anne's dream house:
it was set down into the hillside, and another mountain loomed
behind, covered in iridescent green. After thirteen other relo-
cations, Anne knew she would not move again. With her 35-mm
camera, Anne smiled as she took another roll of photos to send
to Annett, her ex-husband's ex-wife and executive editor of *House
and Garden.* Five years ago, Anne had written Annett, humor-
ously claiming that after renovations she would have "a house that
looks like the house in which an internationally famous writer resides."

With the completion of Dragonhold-Underhill, Anne became her own fairy godmother, creating a beautiful home, built near her beloved stables, with a commodious study and plenty of room for the many guests who came to visit her. The house was quite modern in design and atmosphere. With its large windows, contemporary kitchen, a large Jacuzzi in her bathroom, open floor plan, oak cabinets, and furnishings, Anne added heraldic touches—three teak-wood medallions based on animals from the *Book of Kells* (the medieval illuminated book at Trinity College in Dublin) for the outside walls, and two beautiful bronze dragons, one for each of her black wrought-iron gates. In addition, Anne bought new furnishings: new beds, chests, blanket chests, tables. She spared no expense: a slate roof, maple flooring, a green-house section connecting the pool to the rest of the house. The extensive gardens all around the house were Sis's creation. The planning commission objected to a second kitchen because they worried she was building a hotel and not a single-family home. Nevertheless, Anne also had a small separate apartment created for Sis, including a tiny kitchen (to mollify the planning commission) and access to the outside. If the 1980s were marked by Anne's solidification of her success, she was able to rest on her laurels in the 1990s and begin to appreciate what it meant to be a well-established and highly regarded author.

The eleven years from 1990 to 2001 also saw additions and losses in her family. Her daughter Gigi married and adopted a son, her son Todd married and had a daughter, and her son Alec moved to Ireland and divorced. Anne not only gave two weddings, but also threw a huge party for her own seventy-fifth birthday, flying in family and friends from the United States, including her ex-husband, Wright. This triumph and reconciliation of sorts was, however, soon followed by the loss of her dear companion, Wright's sister, Sis. Throughout the decade, Anne wrestled with her own illnesses, having a knee replaced in 1991, then surgery in 1996, a mild heart attack in 2000, and a mild stroke in January 2001. Yet these setbacks had little perceptible effect on her writing, and she continued to publish at the rate of two books a year. At this point in her career, the awards rolled in. As the decade ended, Anne received news that she had won the prestigious Margaret A. Edwards Award, given by the American Library Association and presented for Lifetime Literary Achievement. (She was also the first science fiction writer to receive the award.) This time period, then, was marked by professional success and family milestones and tempered by health issues and family worries.

As an extremely successful author, Anne faced unique problems, compounded by her generosity. When I asked her how she rewarded herself, Anne replied, with a twinkle, "By playing fairy godmother." Then she said with a sigh, "It's very expensive." How much money her books made was an important index of achievement for Anne, who wrote to Virginia, "It is a point of pride in me that over the past fourteen years, every book I have written has paid back its original advance in the first six months." That Anne's first priority was not money, however, is revealed by the terms of her million-dollar contract, which specified that she would receive a $300,000 advance for a Pern book and only a $250,000 advance for other titles. An author motivated only by money would have only written Pern books, whereas Anne has steadily alternated between Pern and non-Pern titles. Finally wealthy (she received her first million-dollar contract in 1993), Anne was able to indulge herself by indulging others. Her editor Shelly Shapiro commented that "taking care of people is very important to her." Anne's collaborator, Elizabeth Ann Scarborough, dedicated her novel *The Godmother* to Anne with these words: "This is dedicated with admiration, gratitude and affection to Anne McCaffrey, who manages very nicely without the benefit of a wand." Felicity, the godmother of the title, is Irish, and *The Godmother's Apprentice*, the sequel, is based on people in Anne's household. Anne soon found that there was an endless line of people who wanted to be Cinderella to her fairy godmother. One fax to Virginia, her agent, is revealing, "Dearest Virginia dear, My Gawd, how the money rolls in. Thank Gawd the money rolls in!" Despite her large income, Anne indulged herself very little, buying semi-precious jewelry only occasionally, treating herself to clothes from Harrod's, having her books bound in leather, traveling first class. Her "adopted daughter" Derval said Anne never took a trip for sheer pleasure, and son Todd said that Anne's 2001 trip to Sicily was the first vacation she ever took. Building herself a deluxe home, however, was a large and public admission of how far she had come since her early poverty-stricken days in Ireland. Always a willing hostess, she became more so when she had the space to accommodate more people.

Her daughter, Gigi, described Anne's open-door policy: "Mum likes having a lot of people around. She enjoys the coming and going." When I commented on the commotion in the house, with at least eight people bustling in and out, Gigi said, "It's just been another Dragonhold day." Gigi described her mother as "a universal Mum" and explained, "She collects people or they gravitate to her." While she had become an Irish citizen in 1984, Anne's version of the ideal home was still decidedly American—so much so that the first plans were rejected by the planning commission for not fitting in with the land and the other Irish farmhouses. They stated that the two-story design with dormers "did not look like an Irish farmhouse." The planning commission asked Anne if she was going to start a bed-and-breakfast (four of the six bedrooms have their own bathrooms). Pithily, Anne explained to them that she and her sister-in-law "were elderly and needed access to a bathroom THEN, not when someone else had finished." The house design and the conflict with the planning commission revealed not only that Anne was still somewhat American in her outlook and values, but also that she was accustomed to having her own way. Anne was afraid that the planning commission would balk at her swimming pool, but other than requiring a certain kind of drainage, she had no problem with her enormous eighteen-by-thirty-foot indoor pool. The neighbors did, however, complain that she would take all their electricity to run her computer. This was in 1989, and there were not very many computers in rural Ireland. The complaint suggests something of Anne's relationship with her neighbors and the degree to which she was seen as different. The Hogans, owners of a nearby bed-and-breakfast, who house many of Anne's guests, hold her in high esteem, but they thought she was still an American citizen. One fellow in a pub described her as "horse-mad," and, indeed, building yourself a home only after you built beautiful stables, including a heated barn, might strike some people as unusual.

Irish planning commissions have power unimaginable in the United States, where simply owning property usually means you can develop it any way you choose. In Ireland, zoning laws are strictly enforced, and even in the twenty-first century, when land values have risen astronomically, landowners are forbidden to develop or subdivide, with the exception of building homes for family members. Even these houses (and Anne built one on her property for her oldest son, Alec) are subject to stringent oversight. After her first proposal for an American-style house with dormers was rejected, Anne modified her plans and agreed to nestle her house in the hillside, so it would be less obtrusive—hence Dragonhold's hyphenated suffix of "Underhill." Irish homes, even modest ones, have names, and Anne wanted to keep the name Dragonhold for its reference to the books that built the house. But she also wanted to distinguish her new home from the earlier, far more modest house she had inhabited for fifteen years. The tangible fruit of her labors, Dragonhold-Underhill represented Anne's settling into her success. With Anne's burgeoning income, investing money in a larger home seemed a good idea. Typically, though, Anne had first put her money into her stables, and her new home was to be situated on six of the less usable acres of the forty-seven that comprised Dragonhold Stables.

She and her entourage (Sis, various young people who stayed with her, workers, and many visitors) had long since outgrown Dragonhold-Kilquade, which had just one bathroom. Even with the apartment added on for Sis, and a kitchen expansion, the first Dragonhold was too small. Anne designed the floor plan to suit her needs, with her office next to her bedroom at the back of the house. The kitchen is the front room, an enormous nineteen by twenty-one feet, with a window seat, a fireplace, a large table for guests, bookshelves, and innumerable cabinets. Anne reports that the house is "as near to perfect (for me) as it could get." She is very pleased with her house (though she's still a bit miffed that when the finishing touches were being put in, the wrong tiles were put in one of the bathrooms). Each time I visited Anne at Dragonhold-Underhill, she pointed with pride to the house's unique features and its splendid gardens. Ironically, the child who deeply resented her father's devotion to his gardens and his conscription of his children to work in those gardens grew up to be an adult who cherishes her own beautiful formal gardens—on a site far larger than her father's. Sis handled much of the day-to-day work with the builder, who turned out to be something of a scoundrel. (He did some of the work with substitute materials and did not complete all the work as contracted, especially the heating elements.) She also supervised the laying out of the many gardens and elaborate beds. Sis bought a sign that Anne enjoyed and that may have typified their bantering relationship: "KWITCHURBELIAKIN!" Despite feeling overwhelmed Anne continued to write. She wrote to Virginia, "I doubt I could take a year off writing—I still can't not write—but a break is obviously now a necessity." With her talk of a break, Anne did not take one.

Success, it turned out, could be exhausting. Anne wrote to thank Virginia for having negotiated a good contract with Del Rey for a series of books. Anne was grateful for the advance, chortling, "What a marvelous contract you have managed to carve out of the collective Del Rey hyde [*sic*]!" Anne reported her pleasure in her series with Annie S. (Elizabeth Anne Scarborough). The Powers series reached several best-seller lists, the first collaborative effort of Anne's to do so well. Nevertheless, the rest of the letter is filled with less glee and a more plaintive tone. "Well, I always intended to spend the rest of my life writing so it looks as if I will. I wish I could honestly yell and cheer. I know I should. . . . It's just that I keep waiting for the next problems to develop (some are clearly in the offing) or maybe I'm just TIRED!" Anne acknowledged that "the writing of novels is now an unremitting exercise of discipline something I believe you mentioned not long ago but the total effect had not then caught up with me as it may well have done so now." Anne continued to write, creating a new series with *Pegasus in Flight* and *The Rowan*, the first volumes in what would later be called the Tower and the Hive series. This series demonstrated that Anne did not need co-authors; her fertile imagination took root in stories she had written decades earlier, and this new series, featuring psychically gifted humans, did very well. A family saga spanning three generations, the first novel, *The Rowan*, draws on the concepts she first developed in a short-story collection published the early 1970s, *To Ride Pegasus*. In this book a clairvoyant character suffers a head injury, and as the doctors examine him, they discover electrical impulses in his brain. McCaffrey thus cleverly skirts a classic division between fantasy and science fiction by making magical powers scientifically verifiable. While this first book deals with male characters, in her new series, Anne draws on her own life and matriarchal status. By now the head of a family that included not only her three children and grandchildren but also her former sister-in-law, staff who had been with her for years, young people who had grown up and were now in her employ, and numerous visitors, Anne depicts a character, the Rowan, who develops and cares for a large, extended family. The Rowan has the dramatic silver hair that is Anne's signature (like her mother, Anne had hair that turned silver before she was thirty). Orphaned, the Rowan has to start a new life alone on a new planet. All she has going for her is her "Talent," or psychic powers, rather parallel to Anne's emigration to Ireland, where she relied only on her "talent" of writing. In this series, Talents are ranked in order of their skills and success in psionics or mental powers, from a high of T-1 to T-10. The more adept Talents often work with lesser Talents, combining their powers. Writing about the possibilities of psychic collaboration presaged Anne's own real-world partnerships with other writers. Although she continued her prodigious solo writing, Anne developed a new outlet, co-authorship. Anne, a "T-1" in terms of her fictional universe, was a first-tier writer, and the authors she would help were analogous to lesser-ranked Talents in her series.

A well-established publishing convention, especially in science fiction, co-authorship can take many forms. Usually, the more famous co-author allows another lesser-known writer to create a novel based on the first author's world. The famous author may write none or only a little bit of the novel, but it will still blazon the more famous author's name on the cover. Anne had a number of reasons for considering co-authorship in the 1990s. Co-authorship provided Anne with a mini-version of the Milford conferences that had enriched her career. Always a reader as well as a writer, Anne enjoyed the intellectual exchange with other writers. In previous years, Anne had found this intellectual stimulation at conventions, where she would meet other authors and discuss literary issues with them. But as Anne's popularity grew, she was no longer just one author among others. As Guest of Honor at conventions, she had no time to herself, nor the time to be on panels with other writers. Instead, fans and the convention organizers monopolized her time, and when she spoke, it was usually by herself. The huge turnout for her book signings also exhausted her, so she had neither the energy nor time for intellectual exchanges. Todd continued to read and comment on his mother's work, but he was in the United States, and then he married and had a child. At the same time, Anne's trouble with jet lag and arthritis meant that she could travel less frequently. Ironically, at the height of her success, Anne found herself intellectually isolated and lonely. Having a writer come to live and write with her, in her new spacious home, seemed the perfect solution.

After she built her new home, there was an explosion of books Anne wrote with other authors. These "shared universe" books demonstrated the staying power of Anne's fictional worlds and the selling power of her name. Four books about Anne McCaffrey were published, another sign of her growing reputation. Anne had already co-authored two books, done primarily by mail and long-distance phone conversations. In 1990, she published two co-authored books: *The Death of Sleep*, with Jody Lynn Nye, and *Sassinak*, with Elizabeth Moon. These collaborations can be interpreted in two fashions, either as "shared universe," a positive term that gives credit to the original author's concepts that she "shares" with other authors, or, more negatively, as "share-cropping," the term Anne McCaffrey's agents use. Share-cropping obviously carries the connotations of exploitation that the original farm term does, one person working another person's land, but with the inversion here that the original author, the landowner, is the one being taken advantage of! To Anne's agents, these collaborations meant that the lesser-known authors were trading on the value of the name "Anne McCaffrey." In the agents' opinion, the collaborations also diluted the value of Anne's name.

Anne's tremendous success as a writer meant that she not only was a writer, but also had become a commodity. As a result, there were power struggles over who would control her output. Anne herself had already employed a divide-and-conquer strategy, finding a new publisher in Putnam for her Tower and Hive series. That meant no one publisher controlled her work. Fortunately for Anne, she had an editor at each firm who was willing to work cooperatively, Shelly Shapiro at Del Rey and Susan Allison at Putnam. Both editors, too, respected Anne and were committed to her best interests; for example, they carefully coordinated the publication of her books to make sure they did not release two books too close together.

The collaborations began after Anne had been cornered at a cocktail party back in 1988 by Bill Fawcett, an aggressive editor who happens to be married to Jody Lynn Nye, a writer with whom Anne had co-written a nonfiction guide to Pern. Bill told a sympathetic Anne how many mid-list writers were getting the short end of the shelf-space stick—that is, booksellers didn't want to give their books shelf space. If they co-authored a book with the famous Anne McCaffrey, however, these writers would have much better sales. Anne keenly remembered her own hard days as a writer, struggling financially, so when Bill suggested a way that Anne could help these writers, she readily agreed. But Fawcett was preempting Anne's agents and the publishers. Anne resented that "publishing had gotten very difficult because of bean counters and the bottom line." She remembered how much she had been helped by Virginia Kidd and Betty Ballantine but realized that those days of generosity were over. "Many of our editors are tied by merchandising considerations," she lamented. So in characteristic Anne fashion, she leapt in to help. "Taking advantage of Annie's niceness" is how Vaughne Hansen, who works for Virginia Kidd, saw it. Of course, the Virginia Kidd Agency was not a part of the negotiation, so the agents didn't receive any money, nor were they able to help Anne secure an advantageous contract. Anne explained that Bill Fawcett "suggested the names of published authors and I picked those whose books I already liked." Anne explained, "I got talked into writing outlines by Bill Fawcett, but it seemed a very logical thing to do at the time." Unfortunately, writing an outline that another author would then flesh out did not always work out well. Anne described the process as "forcing some poor person to write against their best inclinations and follow the damned outline." She soon found that this sort of collaboration was not emotionally or artistically successful.

Her collaborations with some writers were more successful aesthetically and commercially than others. Her series with Elizabeth Ann Scarborough, the Powers series and the Acorna series, have done better than her other collaborations. Anne said that "it's good to have another writer to lob ideas off to." Another older writer whom Anne had always admired, Andre Norton, had done a number of successful collaborations, and Anne explained that Andre had not run out of ideas, but out of energy. Ruefully, Anne said, "It takes an awful lot of energy to write a book." She was glad to have her energy sparked by other writers, and as Susan Allison, Anne's Putnam editor, explained, "It's flattering when people want to write in your universe." Unfortunately, despite Anne's best intentions, the collaborations were not always successful— in one case, it was singularly problematic. To her dismay, Anne found that she and Jody Lynn Nye were not "on the same wave length—the way Annie Scarborough and I fortunately are." One letter that Virginia had forwarded to Anne read, "Ms. Nye may be a capable writer in some ways, but she's fouling up the McCaffrey waters." To Virginia, Anne replied: "Well, honey, I got myself into this and I'll just hope I can weather the storm it's caused. You warned me and I had the gall to think I could 'fix' anything up to scratch. Would that I could unmuddy the waters! I haven't had that many really scathing letters but I've received a few [from editors] . . . mainly for collaborating with anyone. . . . I shan't work on anymore of these efforts—once I've finished the PTB trilogy [Powers That Be series, written with Elizabeth

Anne Scarborough]." Fortunately, Anne did not keep strictly to this resolution, co-writing Acorna books with Annie S. and later collaborating with two of her children, Gigi and Todd. It was the positive experiences with Annie S., and later with Elizabeth Moon, that kept Anne from totally abandoning co-authorship.

Anne had always admired the work of Elizabeth Ann Scarborough, winner of a Nebula award (a prestigious award, presented by the Science Fiction Writers of America, that Anne had won in 1967) for *The Healer's War*. Anne had spent a good deal of time with Annie S. when Anne was writer-in-residence in Alaska for ten days in April 1982 and Annie S. lived in Alaska. Annie S. took Anne to parties and to see the Aurora Borealis, a bear show, and dog-sledding. It was the last activity, which Anne truly enjoyed, that would years later turn into the inspiration for their Petaybee, the ice world that is the setting for their Powers That Be series. Though Anne only spent several weeks in Alaska, the two stayed in touch ever afterward. As Anne commented when I sent her a recent picture of Annie S., "That's a great photo of Annie, looking mischievous . . . which she often does. . . . She can also be quite wicked, when she wants to." Annie S. explains their friendship by pointing out how many similarities they share: Both have an odd connection to the military, in that they both love and hate the military. While Anne's fathers and brothers served in the army, Annie S. served in the army as a nurse (she drew on these experiences for her Nebula Award–winning book, *The Healer's War*). Both women are Aries, "much more independent and action-oriented than other women"; in addition to sharing a name, they both love music, and Rudyard Kipling was an important influence on both of them. Moreover, both are divorced writers who love science fiction. These similarities allowed them to work together effectively. Living in Alaska had given Anne the idea of writing about an ice world, and she liked the idea of developing a new series with Annie S. As usual, however, the impetus came from Anne's good nature. At that time, Annie S. was having difficulty with her publisher, Bantam, and when she called Anne up for advice, Anne immediately asked, "Why don't you come write a book with me?" When Annie S. asked what they would write about, Anne replied, "Dog-sleds and the Irish!" Anne went to the States for a convention, and in January 1991, Annie S. came back to Ireland with her. Anne even paid Annie S.'s airfare and she put in a modem and desk in the guest room. The first guest to the new Dragonhold, Annie S. stayed for almost five months. Anne remembers that "it was great having her there as lunches usually included plotting sessions." Both women would get up early, discuss ideas over breakfast, and then write the rest of the day in their respective studies. Each had favorite characters in the first book in the series, and they divided the work by writing the scenes that featured their favorite characters. Not surprisingly, Anne focused on Yana, the older heroine, and Annie S. focused on Clodagh and Cita, the latter a teenaged character. All three characters followed the writers' example of female solidarity, working and living together. Anne and Annie wrote separately in the morning, met for lunch, and then composed scenes together in the afternoon. In Anne's words, "It sort of grew from tossing the bull across the table to, 'OK, here's the disk, it's your turn. I can't go any further.' We both knew who the characters were and what we wanted to do." The schedule made for a busy but fulfilling time for both writers. Anne described it as "true collaboration."

Unfortunately, jealousy reared its ugly head, as Sis took a strong dislike to Annie S., which surprised Anne. Because both Sis and Annie S. had worked as nurses and did handicrafts, Anne imagined that they would get along. After all, Anne liked them both! With her characteristic optimism, Anne did not see that Sis felt displaced by Annie S., who literally moved into their new home, and did so before Sis herself did. Sis was not satisfied with some aspects of the building, so she refused to move in until the problems were fixed. It was not Anne, after all, who was nicknamed "Queen of Dragonhold," but Sis. The tension was palpable. Sis had always protected Anne from those who she thought were exploiting Anne, but Anne saw Annie S. as a dear friend. Annie S. reciprocated; she truly felt at home in Dragonhold-Underhill, and she would take a dish and leave it, dirty, in another room. Or she would drop her sweater on a sofa and leave it there. Sis followed around, resentfully picking up after Annie S. and glowering. At lunch Anne and Annie chattered away about what each character should do and what would happen next in their book. Sis sat listening, feeling left out. Finally Sis exploded, accusing Annie S. of being a freeloader and calling her "a hippopotamus." Annie S. yelled right back, saying she wasn't going to put up with such abuse, she was leaving right now, and she stormed out to her room. Thoroughly upset, Anne spoke quite sternly to Sis, telling her that Annie was Anne's guest and Sis should treat her politely. Reluctantly, Sis agreed but was never more than stiffly polite. Annie S. returned the next year and the year after that to finish two more books, and each time Sis was remote but civil. They even had a reconciliation of sorts, when Annie S. presented Sis with a flag that she flew next to the Irish flag.

Sis took much less a dislike to Margaret Ball, who then fit into a pattern of writers who spent time at Dragonhold. Anne and Margaret were less intense, and Margaret was easier to get along with, picking up after herself more than Annie S. had been inclined to do and giving more consideration to Sis. Anne was much easier to please, not knowing or caring whether guests were tidy. Margaret practiced her flute in the living room, a soothing beginning to every day she was there. In contrast to Annie S., who stayed for months, Margaret only stayed for six weeks; she and Anne had a fruitful collaboration with *Partnership* and the first two Acorna books, which are now being written by Anne and Annie S. Margaret was less able to travel, due to her teenaged children; and Annie S. was willing to continue the Acorna books, which have developed a strong following.

Co-author Elizabeth Moon is another collaborator who has turned into a close friend. Anne told Bill Fawcett that she admired Moon's work, especially her Serrano series, so Fawcett approached Jim Baen, Elizabeth's publisher. When Jim called Elizabeth with the invitation to co-write *Sassinak* with Anne, Elizabeth replied, "'Does water run downhill? Of course, I want to—I'm honored to be asked.'" While she was very conscious of working in Anne's universe, and "the need to make everything conform to her vision of her characters and their setting," Elizabeth described

Anne as "the perfect mix of strong creator and thoughtful collaborator. . . . [I]t's her universe and you can't forget it, but she's very generous in encouraging the co-author to be creative within the framework." Elizabeth learned a great deal from Anne, who told her, "in one memorable letter, to 'just have fun' with the aliens." She also appreciated the opportunities "to learn some of the technical bits I hadn't yet tried on my own, like multiple viewpoints . . . much easier to handle if you have an experienced co-author to lean on and to help with the inevitable difficulties." Elizabeth concluded, "What I found exciting, stimulating and just plain fun was being that close to a superb storyteller, someone who not only had the gift, but also the experience."

Richard Woods's experience in co-writing *A Diversity of Dragons*, a large-format nonfiction work, was similarly positive, perhaps because he and Anne were already such good friends before they collaborated. Anne also co-authored books with Jody-Lynn Nye, *Crisis in Doona*; with Margaret Ball, *PartnerShip*; with Mercedes Lackey, *The Ship Who Searched*; and with S. M. Stirling, *The City Who Fought*. Anne especially regretted never meeting Mercedes Lackey in person because she greatly admired Mercedes's writing, but not every one of her co-authors could or would travel to Ireland. In addition to the intellectual stimulation, the books were profitable. Anne's collaborative efforts explain, in part, her extraordinary productivity in the 1990s. Yet Anne was keenly aware that some of the collaborations were both artistically and commercially more successful than others. She wrote to Virginia, "The collabs are at least making money for both sets of folks [writers], though it's interesting to note which sets of us did better than which other."

In November 1990, before Dragonhold-Underhill was finished, Gigi returned home to Ireland, to live there permanently. She found a job and took classes as her health permitted. And perhaps most importantly, especially to her mother, who wanted Gigi to be happy, Gigi fell in love with Geoff Kennedy. The middle child of seven, from a large Catholic family, Geoff was a welder-artisan, attractive and attentive. Anne's letters reveal her delight in her daughter's happiness. In a letter to Annett, Anne mentioned that Gigi has "a boyfriend . . . who is quite faithful." In addition to boasting about her daughter's deft handling of her new job, Anne also lamented Gigi's illness and praised her strength: "As usual, and from some deep inner well of strength, [Gigi] managed to put her act together ONCE MORE! I don't know where she gets such inner fortitude from! She's amazing in that and I'm so very proud of her." In a later missive to Annett, Anne reports, "Todd has already met—and approved of—Geoffrey. I most certainly do. Mind you, I'm not saying a bloody thing but he has been making her quite happy for 14 months now." He continued to make Gigi happy, proposing marriage in August 1992. Planning Gigi's wedding enthralled Anne, not only because she loved playing fairy godmother, but also because she hoped the perfect wedding would somehow compensate Gigi for all her physical suffering. To Virginia, Anne confided her fears about the wedding: "Gigi has been so ill again. That alone is enough to drive me to tears when we can't be sure she'll be well enough to walk down the aisle a radiant bride. My local Tarot card reader has assured me she will." (The tarot card reader was right.)

Her son's and daughter's engagements made Anne reflect on her own marriage. As she wrote to Virginia, "Dearest Virginia dear, Today I would have been married 43 years. Glad I'm not. How time does fly! . . . (We've [Virginia and Anne] been 'married' at least 30 years now!)" Like her mother had done for her, Anne fussed, wanting her daughter's wedding to be spectacular, and it was. In August 1993, Gigi married in a gala wedding, with her attendants wearing designer dresses. Anne wore a red-flowered dress with a long, matching jacket, pearls, and pearl earrings. Two hundred thirty-seven guests enjoyed a sit-down meal. Richard Woods, Anne's good friend and co-author, officiated with a local priest, Father John Jacob. Gigi, beaming and beautiful in an off-the-shoulder, long-sleeved white gown of silk chiffon, carried an enormous bouquet of pink and white roses, stephanotis, and white freesia, lovingly arranged by her aunt Sis. Gigi said that she felt "like a million dollars in that dress." Her hair in an elegant chignon, Gigi's sheer voile veil was hidden in her hair by a clear comb, and the elegance of her outfit was completed by the gown's short train. When Gigi walked down the aisle on the arm of her brother Alec, Anne was so happy she thought her "heart would burst."

In 1993, Anne bought a Farrier's School, a setup with three barns where her future son-in-law, Geoff, could make horseshoes and shoe horses. It was a natural extension to Anne's extensive stables, and she enjoyed watching Geoff teach young people how to work iron for horses. This experience inspired Anne to write *Black Horses for the King* (1996), a short tale set in King Arthur's England. Unfortunately, this project, like Anne's dream for a writers' cottage named Dragonthorn, lasted only five years. But it was a sign of Anne's empire building, and her financial success, that she was willing and interested in setting up more projects to help two groups she favored—young people and writers.

The day after Christmas 1993, Todd married Jenna Scott in a smaller but no less festive wedding presided over by Richard Woods. One of Todd's Irish friends arranged for River Dance dancers to perform, and at the reception there were folk musicians rather than the rock group Gigi had preferred. Jenna and Todd had met at a Magicon in Orlando, Florida, when Todd had accompanied his mother and Jenna was the writer Lois Bujold's roommate. They had decided that instead of Jenna changing her last name, they would choose a common marital name. Jenna, who was enamored of being part of Anne McCaffrey's family, suggested they both adopt the McCaffrey name. Anne was flattered. Todd explained that changing his last name to McCaffrey was more than heeding his friend Scott McMillan's warning that it would mess up lineage to create a new surname. It was also to honor all his mother had done for him. There was another reason Todd changed his surname: he had been mistaken several times for a criminal named Todd Johnson, and once he was even detained at the Dallas airport. But, of course, his name change also signaled Todd's rejection of his father and Todd's desire to be a writer. He had published a few stories as Todd Johnson, but after 1993 he would write as Todd J. McCaffrey. Shelly Shapiro, Anne's and now Todd's editor, noted that his name change also meant his books would be shelved by his mother's—a huge boost for sales.

With the two weddings to pay for—and that included not only the meals but also the airfare and other expenses of all people in attendance—Anne needed her still-expanding advances and royalties. She had not only those expenses, but also back U.S. taxes to pay. "Gracious royalties this year. I can pay my horrendous tax bill," she wrote to her editor at Ballantine, Shelly Shapiro.

The year 1994 was memorable for the birth of Todd's daughter, Ceara Rose, and for a Worldcon in Canada for which Anne was GOH, guest of honor. The Worldcon always holds a party to honor its guest of honor; there were over a thousand people at Anne's party, which was run as a Pern "gather," based on the large social gatherings set on her fictional world of Pern. To a con organizer Anne wrote, "People have the weirdest ideas of what can/should/did happen on Pern and only I, the Dragonlady, can give definitive answers." As Dragonlady, she continued to receive awards. Shelly Shapiro wrote, "Congratulations! You've done it again! They might as well just call it [the SF Book Club Book of the Year Award] the Annual McCaffrey Award!" What didn't work out well was attempt after attempt to get the Dragonriders of Pern to film or television, in part because Anne wanted to be the one with "definitive answers." Although Anne had always wanted to see a film version of Dragonriders, and her books have been optioned seven times, including by Warner Brothers for a television series, she has turned down offers of a million dollars for the rights to *Dragonflight* because the contracts did not give her complete control. (Just recently, however, the rights to the Dragonriders of Pern were sold to an Oscar Award–winning firm, Copperheart Entertainment.) And while Anne is a heavyweight in the publishing world, in Hollywood her name carries no weight. For what are perhaps legitimate reasons, Hollywood is leery of authors who want to retain control over their novels. Novels, after all, are a very different form from film, and the collaborative process in filmmaking involves dozens of people, from the scriptwriters to the director, the producer, and the editor. Anne's desire to see a film version of Dragonriders remains a frustrated desire, but perhaps this latest option will satisfy her at last.

Also problematic was Anne's health. In March 1991, Anne experienced arthritis in her knee; in May, she endured surgery when her knee was replaced. She was pleased with the results and her improved mobility and lack of pain, but then she began to have hip trouble only a few years later. In April 1996, Anne began to rely on a wheelchair, and she was ordered to lose weight before the surgeons would operate on her hip. In September 1996, she had successful hip surgery, but she developed another physical problem, tinnitus, an inner-ear ailment that had plagued her mother. These signs of aging slowed Anne down slightly, but not her writing. Instead, she cut back on her traveling even more.

After 1990, Anne relied more on the computer to stay in touch with her friends and family. A consummate letter writer, Anne actually finds it easy to have e-mail friends. As you might expect from a science fiction writer, Anne was an early adopter of computer technology, encouraged by her two sons. She wrote with pleasure about how much faster electronic mail was, and she had obtained a "compuserv" account in the mid-1980s. In the 1990s, however, Alec set up an electronic chat room for his mother's fans, called "Kitchen Table Live" (KTL), in homage to her much-used kitchen table at Dragonhold-Underhill. The very first room on your right, as you enter Anne's house, is her sunny kitchen with its large table. It is there that most of her visitors settle in to talk to her. Anne's best friend, Maureen Beirne, who doesn't use the Internet herself, worries that Anne spends too much time with her electronic friends, but for a writer, especially a science fiction writer who has often written about transcending the limitations of the human body (especially in the Brain Ship series), the electronic world is just as real and compelling as the embodied world. In the electronic world, Anne is ageless and her skill at spinning words makes her a mistress of this venue. Not surprisingly, she often spent many hours a day or more online. It was becoming, in Anne's words, "addictive." To do a real-time chat, Anne would get on line at 4 p.m., so that it was early morning in America, late night in Australia. But she found the "adulation was too much of a good thing" and decided it was distracting her from her writing. After cutting back on KTL, Anne still devoted at least two hours online every day; she received more than twenty e-mails a day, and those just to her private mailbox.

Many people, of course, made a pilgrimage to see Anne, among them her co-author Elizabeth Moon. Like Anne, Elizabeth is horse crazy, and Anne arranged for Elizabeth to ride at Dragonhold Stables. Elizabeth raved about Irish horses, "Something to make any horse-lover go into a daze . . . silk and marshmallows and power underneath"; and Derval, who runs the stables, was "a force of nature, the good kind." In a later visit, Derval and Anne encouraged Elizabeth so much that after a lesson with Derval, Elizabeth felt prepared for a hunt she was to do in England. Anne was still riding herself then, and she reveled in sharing with another writer her superb horses.

Despite her disinclination to travel, especially long transatlantic trips, in May 1997 Anne gave a speech at her fiftieth college reunion. Anne followed Jessye Norman, whom she described as "a hard act to follow." Anne focused on a question germane to her own life: she asked her classmates, "What are we going to do with the rest of our lives?" Anne's life would be complicated by changes in children's lives. In 1998, Alec moved to Dragonhold-Underhill and divorced, but his wife and two children also moved to Ireland, living in Bray, a nearby town. In 1998, with a great deal of assistance from Anne, Geoff and Gigi adopted a child. Because of Gigi's health and her interfaith marriage (Geoff was Catholic), Gigi and Geoff had little chance of adopting a child in Ireland. However, just as Anne was lamenting her daughter's prospects of being a mother, two of Anne's friends in the United States knew someone whose daughter was dealing with an unplanned pregnancy. With a great deal of effort, an arrangement was made that allowed Gigi to be in the delivery room when her son was born, February 22, 1998. Anne's gratitude to the birth mother appears in the dedication to *Nimisha's Ship*: "To a courageous and generous young woman / For the greatest gift / One woman can give another." Anne had written to a friend, "For all that I have achieved I am helpless to give my daughter the one thing she wants, a child of her own." But as it turned out, Anne's money and, more importantly, her connections did provide the much-wanted child.

On January 30, 1999, Anne received the very welcome news that she would be the recipient of the Margaret A. Edwards Award for Lifetime Literary Achievement, presented by the American Library Association. Whenever Anne is asked about her many accomplishments and awards, she always singles out this award as the most meaningful to her. Receiving a significant award from a major literary association provided Anne with satisfaction that, despite her previous successes, she still craved. She noted that it proved her ex-husband, Wright, wrong on many accounts— she not only had made more than enough money to pay the telephone bill, but also had been recognized for her literary merit. Near the end of her career, Anne now looked to her literary reputation. Todd and Gigi were there to see their mother receive the award. During his visit, Todd explained his outline for a new Pern novel, *Dragonsblood*, to the two people in the world whose opinion was crucial—his mother and Gigi. They both liked it. During the trip, Gigi had a rather more hectic time than Todd because she was the designated "Mother Minder," as the kids named the role of protecting their mother at cons, intercepting fans and keeping their mother from getting exhausted. However, the American Library Association, while an enormous convention of ten thousand, seemed at first to be less frenetic and have fewer fanatics. But just when Gigi relaxed, a longtime fan approached Anne and became very emotional, to the point of tears, at being able to talk to her idol. Todd explained that "apparently this person had only survived her adolescence only by reading Anne McCaffrey." Very empathic, Anne has a hard time with inarticulate, crying fans, and Gigi had to come "peel her off Mum." Fortunately, Anne's acceptance speech went smoothly, with Gigi having some of the same feelings that her mother had had when Gigi married—"feeling as if my heart had just increased substantially in size."

While in New Orleans for the award, Anne celebrated, staying at the Windsor Court, the city's only four-star hotel. She and Gigi had dinner with me and my mother at Antoine's, an elegant

French Quarter restaurant she selected. Anne also took her friends Marilyn and Harry Alm out to dinner at Commander's Palace, another of New Orleans' world-famous (and very expensive) restaurants. The Alms not only were fans who had become friends, but also had become a part of Anne's writing world. Anne then went to visit her brother and his wife, Marcia, in St. Louis, finally ending up at Dragoncon in Atlanta in August. At Dragoncon Anne received two more awards, a Dragoncon dragon and the Julie Award for lifetime achievement in the field of the Fantastic Arts. While these awards might have suggested Anne could rest on her laurels, 1999 also saw the publication of a book with a new setting and heroine, *Nimisha's Ship*, and another novel in the Tower and Hive series, entitled (appropriately enough) *The Tower and the Hive*. Nineteen ninety-nine was the culmination of a very productive decade for Anne: She expanded her most famous series, the Dragonriders of Pern, with volumes entitled *The Masterharper of Pern* (1998) and *Dragonseye* (1996). She added to her Powers series, written with Elizabeth Scarborough, with *Power Play* (1995). In addition, she began a new series, the Freedom series, with the books *Freedom's Landing* (1995), *Freedom's Choice* (1997), and *Freedom's Challenge* (1998). This series follows up on themes characteristic of her work, but does so with a completely new cast of characters and setting, including an alien species of feline.

For Anne's fans, the only development more exciting than a new Dragonriders of Pern novel is the prospect of a new series. *Nimisha's Ship* draws on a concept from McCaffrey's other well-loved series, the Brain Ship series. The ship in the title is an experimental AI (artificial intelligence) vessel that has a personality. Nimisha, the human protagonist, shares many qualities of Anne's other heroines, such as Killashandra, being brave, talented, loyal, and a natural leader. *Nimisha's Ship* follows the life of a very young child through mature adulthood. Because Nimisha has inherited engineering and technological interests from her father, Lord Tionel, she has a somewhat difficult relationship with her mother, Lady Rezalla, who, despite her financial acumen, favors traditional views of femininity. Watching Nimisha negotiate this chasm between her masculine interests and her mother's insistence on the feminine is part of the pleasure of reading Nimisha's life story. While Anne did not write her autobiography, she created fictional biographies that reveal the tensions that marked her own life.

The next year or so was very stressful for Anne, and the stresses eventually told on her health. Always concerned about the quality of her work, Anne struggled, with Gigi's editorial help, to get the manuscript that would be *Skies of Pern* into shape. In a way, her Margaret A. Edwards Award from the American Library Association increased the pressure on her, as did concerns about her health. She worried, as she always did, whether she could still produce excellent fiction. Working very hard with Dr. Stephen Beard and Dr. Scott Manley, two astronomers, Anne also struggled to get the science right in this ambitious new Pern novel. She and Shelly and Gigi argued over aspects of the plot, with Gigi and Shelly wanting Anne to drop a subplot and simplify the narrative. Gigi eventually took post-it notes and placed them throughout the manuscript, directing her mother to what Gigi saw as the plot line. She finally persuaded her mother to streamline the novel, dropping a subplot about a census on Pern. The result was one of Anne's most successful novels in years, but at more of an emotional and physical cost than in previous years.

With thirty-nine of her books available for downloading, some without proper formatting, Anne was becoming more and more concerned about Internet piracy, With Alec's help she pursued and closed down some sites; but, for a woman who had always been generous and open to fans, this was a difficult proceeding. The downloading meant Anne had to recognize that she was being taken advantage of. Money again was tight (due to Anne's supporting her sons and their children's schooling), meaning that these pirated copies were especially aggravating. Anne identified the stress of the copyright violations as one factor that led to her heart attack. Being fairy godmother became a burden, too. Anne said of those years, 2000–2001, "Money was tight and slow to appear and I had so many people for whom I felt responsibility. There were other factors which resolved themselves later but nevertheless added to the pile so it was small wonder that I had a heart attack. In fact, I had two before the second one convinced even me that I should see a doctor. . . . [I]f you are stewing about a whole mess of things, it's difficult to find proportions properly . . . especially with my personality which has convinced me that only 'I' can solve these personal problems MY WAY!" Shelly Shapiro, Anne's editor, remarked that authors who are extremely successful, like Anne or Terry Brooks or Anne Rice, often have entourages of people they support. Being a personality and a successful writer and a wealthy individual can lead, as it did for Anne, to having tremendous financial responsibilities.

In 2000, Todd's marriage with Jenna was ending with a painful struggle, and Alec was trying to find ways to make himself useful to his mother. Anne supported not only Alec, but also his new partner and her children, one of whom Anne sent to an expensive private school. Anne also had to fight with the planning commission about building Alec a house. The film version of Pern seemed likely; then the negotiations bogged down, worrying and frustrating Anne immensely. Considering the stress she was under, with financial worries, Sis very ill, and a family history of heart trouble, it is not surprising that in September 2000 Anne was taken to the hospital with chest pains. In the emergency room, as she was hooked up to a heart monitor, a gentleman in a brown clerical robe came by. "I'm Father X," he said. "May I pray for you?" "Yes," Anne replied, "pray for a room for me." At that instant, she was rushed to ICU, as the monitor showed her suffering a heart attack. When the priest returned later, asking whether he could pray for her, Anne told him, "Yes, please give me another prayer—yours are so effective!" Anne had denied her heart symptoms in part because she had a trip planned to Florida that she did not want to cancel for any reason. "I was furious about the timing of this," she confided, "because I had been invited by Colonel Pamela Melroy to attend the launch of the [space shuttle] *Discovery*." Despite her disappointment, Anne found consolation in watching the shuttle pass over Ireland: "I got lucky, though, the nights in October in Ireland were amazingly clear so I could see, without benefit of binoculars, the blazing star of the *Discovery* as she made her orbits around Ireland each night. I could also see her disengage and pull away from the International Space Station." A regime of watching her diet and walking (which she hated) helped Anne gradually recover. The hardest part was giving up butter; she loved Irish butter.

On what would have been her fiftieth wedding anniversary in January 2001, in an irony that she noted, Anne suffered a small stroke. Although she had been put on medication after the heart attack to reduce the possibility of a stroke, she had "a TIA on the right side, which is motor control, but it [was] mild and I recovered after several days in hospital. I was assiduous in doing crossword puzzles to be sure the stroke had not affected language and memory." Anne recovered well enough to throw the party of her dreams in April. April 1, 2001, was Anne's seventy-fifth birthday gala. She was determined to have a spectacular event, and she did. She invited one hundred guests (fifty more than her for seventieth birthday party) and paid for many of them to fly over from the United States, including her ex-husband, Wright Johnson, and Vaughne Hansen, who worked with her agent Virginia Kidd. The enormous living room at Dragonhold-Underhill was emptied of furniture and filled with tables and chairs for a catered meal. Wearing "a very swanky red dinner gown from Harrod's," Anne was the belle of the ball. Tania Opland and Mike Freeman, who composed and performed music inspired by Pern's Harper Hall, flew over from the United States, bringing their instruments. The pianist Anne had hired was greatly impressed by Tania, who, in addition to having a magnificent voice, plays a hammered dulcimer and a violin. Tania set up the dulcimer so that she and Anne could sing together "Bells of Norwich," Anne's favorite song from the performers' latest CD.

Sis's gradually deteriorating health was one of the reasons that Anne invited Wright to visit. Until 1991, Sis had cooked for Anne, but as she grew weaker from osteoporosis, arthritis, angina, and pancreatic cancer, Sis herself could barely eat, and Anne fixed small meals for her. It was a role reversal that was keenly painful for Anne. Sis had a horror of hospitals and nursing homes, and Anne promised to keep her at Dragonhold in her own apartment. Sis began falling and would forget that she wore a medical pendant. At this time, Anne had Mary McCarthy, a local girl, move in to help with Sis. Maureen Beirne, Anne's good friend, visited daily. When Maureen went in to see Sis on June 27, 2001, she held her hand and said, "If you want to go, dear, today would be a good day." That Sis went so peacefully, with Maureen holding her hand, meant a lot to Anne, who still tears up at the recollection of Sis's death. The next year Anne tried to come to terms with this loss. Part of aging is dealing with the loss of friends and peers. The limited reconciliation with her ex-husband, Wright, continued, and Anne invited him to come over for Thanksgiving and this time he actually stayed at Dragonhold-Underhill in the guest room. While Anne still suffered tremendously without Sis at the first major holiday, Wright's visit kept her occupied and distracted from her grief. As Anne confronted the loss of Sis, she also faced and accepted her own mortality. Anne told me, not glumly, but cheerfully, "They'll probably find me slumped over my keyboard [dead]." In her brief stab at autobiography, Anne had written, "I shall continue to write—I can't NOT write anyhow—until I am too frail to touch the keys of my word-processor." By the next summer, Anne regained some of her characteristic good humor and optimism. Although she still missed Sis dreadfully, Anne was pleased that I was writing her biography. The loss of her dear friend Sis and two brushes with her own mortality (a heart attack and stroke) had left her focused in part on her literary reputation. When I had first asked to write her biography in 1996, she had turned me down, saying that Todd was going to write a biography (*Dragonholder*, 1999) and that she was going to write her own autobiography. Her fifty-page autobiographical essay was a start, but she soon found she simply didn't have the energy or interest. As she told me, "I bore myself." She welcomed me to her home, opened her files, and informed her friends and entourage to cooperate.

Uncharacteristically, in April Anne took a trip by herself to Sicily, a sort of therapeutic solace. She found a cab driver who drove her to all the places her father had been during his World War II stay in the town. She took a number of pictures, and the beautiful vistas seem to have provided comfort. In addition, just being away from all the demands of Dragonhold-Underhill, especially the financial pressures, was a relief. Anne needed to be away from the needs of others, and for once she wanted peace and quiet. She was also escaping family conflict, for, alerted by Gigi, Todd was flying over to confront his mother about her will. Gigi, who managed her mother's correspondence, had found a copy of a will that left more to Alec than to the other siblings. Part of aging and being wealthy is dealing with the dispersal of your wealth.

Being a world-famous writer means dealing with the dispersal of your ideas, your worlds. Gigi and Todd are the only two people Anne will allow to write in the world of Pern (her oldest son, Alec, has shown no inclination to be a writer). Gigi had collaborated with her mother in writing three stories, "Zeus: The Howling," "Bound by Hoof and Nail," and "Devil's Glen," and was centrally involved in editing the very successful *Skies of Pern* (2000). Derval, the family friend who runs Dragonhold Stables, admired Gigi's writing, praised her "incredible mind for detail," and explained, "She has a good way of telling things." Derval's opinion is corroborated by Shelly Shapiro, Anne's editor, who praised Gigi's work with the novel, saying, "She has talent as an editor." Although she is worried that "Mum would be a very hard act to follow," Gigi herself has said that she would "like to write more in the Harper Hall series." Todd had published short stories and a novel in David Drake's universe, *Slammers Down*. With Anne, he co-authored two young adult novels, *Dragon's Kin* and *Dragon's Fire*, and has published *Dragonsblood* (discussed in the next chapter). Todd described the novel as a "passing the torch story." The "torch passing" works in two ways: first, literally, because the book is set in time between two passes in Pern. In Todd's words, the novel is "a story about ancestors and their gifts to their descendants." But, of course, the other torch being passed, from Anne to Todd, is the gift of her fictional world of Pern.

I met with Todd at Dragon 2002 to interview him about his work and his mother. Like his mother, Todd is a charmer, and, like his mother, Todd enjoys telling stories. I attended three panels where he engaged fans with his wit and lively descriptions of his mom, her work, and his own work. As Prince of Pern, Todd has been groomed by his many appearances at cons with his mother. Whether he and/or Gigi will add to Pern remains to be seen. But Shelly Shapiro perhaps has it right when she says, "Pern will go on in, if nothing else, fan fiction." She further explains that Pern "will go on because it speaks to people's hearts. . . . [T]he market will tell if it [Todd's or Gigi's version of Pern] works or not."

Although Anne is prepared to hand Pern over to Todd, entrusting her legacy to him, or to Gigi if she so chooses, Anne still remains the Dragonlady in charge. Having built Alec and his partner, Trish, a house just up the hill (to which Trish contributed), Anne felt comfortable enough to tell Alec *not* to come down to Dragonhold-Underhill and raid the larder or expect meals. Todd arrived for a visit with Ceara Rose, and Anne enjoyed taking her to Dunn's, a leading Irish department store, and buying her a pair of stylish, fringed jeans and other clothes. (Being the fairy godmother to Ceara Rose that Aunt Gladys had been to her, Anne also paid for a week of horseback-riding camp.) Later, as Todd and his mother sat down to a dinner of pizza and wine at the famous kitchen table with Marianne McCarthy, an employee, and me and my husband, Les, their love and affection for each other was clear. Her bright green eyes gleaming, Anne bragged about her father's courage during World War II, landing in Italy as the wharf was being strafed and calmly smoking a cigarette to inspire courage in his men. Todd interrupted, saying, "Your father did a number on you. He cut you out of his will because you hadn't paid him back." As Anne and Todd reminisced about the early years in the States, Anne's enormous orange Maine Coon cat Pumpkin jumped on the table, sat, sneezed, and began to clean his face. Anne petted Pumpkin carefully as she spoke about Sis's dying and her own heart attack and stroke. As she poured her fourth glass of wine, Todd gently said, "Mum, isn't that enough?" Anne ignored him and continued to enjoy her wine. A close family friend explained that Anne is closest to Todd, an assessment corroborated by Todd, who explained, "Mum sympathizes and empathizes with me because I'm the middle child, the emotional barometer. Sometimes she gets angry with me because I'm male." Todd and his mother have a very affectionate, bantering relationship. For example, over pizza that first night, Todd said, "I was a spoiled teenager but I haven't changed much." With a smile, Anne replied, "Yes, you have—you're older!"

As we ate pizza and listened, Ceara Rose came in, curious about the visitor. A very pretty young girl, Ceara Rose was wearing a maroon sweater with sparkles and new jeans that her grandmother had bought her. With a wide sweep of her arms, she accidentally knocked a basket of apples off the counter, and Anne smiled at Ceara as she picked them up. In the other room, Jen Jen, Derval Diamond's daughter and Anne's godchild, watched a video with Ceara Rose, and she ran into the kitchen to give Anne a big hug on her way home. Then Trish, Alec's partner, an attractive Irishwoman with red hair, came by with her small dog, Zephyr, and Anne's grandson Owen Thomas. Trish and Alec were babysitting Owen while Gigi and Geoff spent the night out, seeing Paul Simon perform. Owen and Ceara were getting to know each other the way cousins do after a long absence, with Ceara being four years older and thus in charge. They went into another room to play, but Owen, clearly devoted to Anne, called her "Nanny" on his way out. Not only Owen but those who work at Dragonhold-Underhill dote on Anne. When asked to describe her work at Dragonhold-Underhill, Cyra O'Connor replied that her twenty-two years with Anne had been "a pleasure." Cyra's attitude seems typical of those who work at Dragonhold-Underhill, and certainly the large number of people who appeared during my most recent visit there gave me the sense that there was a magical draw to Anne McCaffrey's Hold. Janine O'Connor, a student and Anne's cook, twenty-six years old, with red hair and a big smile, was also in the kitchen. Barbara Callahan, a costume designer (who recently worked on the film *Reign of Fire*), popped in to say hi to Anne. Barbara's sister, Annie, lives in the cottage and maintains the gardens with her husband, Kohmang, so she came in to get their pay. Annie Callahan also has a business in crystal essences, but she specializes in essences for children. Anne told me that she had a "rescue kit" for kids and that Anne had sent one to Ceara Rose to help her get through her parents' divorce. I was bombarded not only with people, but also with a variety of ideas and experiences at Dragonhold-Underhill. As I prepared to leave, Anne walked me to the front door, picking up the bird feathers that were lying in the hall, one of Pumpkin's catches, and then stooped to pinch off the dead flowers in the big clay pots by the front door. It was a touching synecdoche for her care for all the people in her home.

On the second day of my visit, Todd was snuffling with a bad cold, and as Todd, Anne and I talked around the famous kitchen table, Todd asked, "What's that ringing?" I heard a faint sound, a "ding." Gradually the sound grew louder, and finally Antoinette O'Connell, Anne's homeopath, entered the room, ringing a small Balinese bell and spraying her own creation, crystal essences, to clear the air and to eliminate the possibility of infection. Antoinette said determinedly, "I am not going to get Todd's cold." Anne and Todd were nonplused, but I had the distinct feeling it was more than germs that Antoinette was trying to banish, a feeling that was confirmed a few days later when Antoinette told me in no uncertain terms that I was tiring Anne out. "She just gives and gives until she collapses," Antoinette said, warning me that I should not bother Anne. I realized this exchange must be typical of many that take place almost daily at Dragonhold-Underhill, with people vying for control of Anne's time, money, and energy. As Sis resented Annie, Antoinette resented me. I had repeatedly asked Anne if we should take a break, and took breaks myself to read the files. But except for one morning, Anne was always up waiting for me at the kitchen table, ready to talk. And her indomitable will prevailed. Later in the morning, with a whole group of us sitting at the enormous oak kitchen table, Gigi came in and gave her mother a kiss. She produced a few letters for Anne to sign. Todd, Todd's friend Bob, Gigi, and Anne sat companionably and opened the mail. Gigi told her mother a joke she heard at the Paul Simon concert exemplifying Dragonhold-Underhill's open conviviality. "What has ninety balls and screws old ladies? Bingo!" Everyone laughed, and by the glint in Anne McCaffrey's eye, I saw her pleasure in the magic of being in a circle of good friends and family, among whom she felt treasured, valued, and alive. This is the magic that she re-creates for her readers in her books.

CHAPTER 8

The Grand Master

My feet have yet to return to earth.
—Anne McCaffrey, Web page

A TIME OF GREAT ACHIEVEMENT and satisfaction for Anne, the 1990s were marked by the honors she received and her enjoyment of financial success. Yet more triumphs remained for the twenty-first century. Each represents an important milestone for Anne personally, as well as signifying her importance as a writer. The dream of many a science fiction writer or reader, seeing a space shuttle launch as an invited guest, came true for Anne. This event held special significance, for in her own life she enacted the plot of many of her novels: overcoming physical adversity to reach a desired goal. The permanence and power of Anne's fictional world Pern was solidified as she handed over the keys to Pern to her literary heir, her son Todd. As she has aged, Anne has worried about her ability to continue to take care of others and about the continuation of the fictional worlds she created. Todd's collaborations with his mother and his own Pern novel reassured her that Pern would continue to develop and that her literary creations would continue to provide support for her family. Finally, like so many of her heroines, Anne broke through barriers to receive a signal honor, one rarely awarded to women: she was named Grand Master by the Science Fiction and Fantasy Writers of America. All these events demonstrate the depth of Anne's literary accomplishments.

In October 2002, finally, Anne would get to experience something she had dreamed and written about, space travel. She had made arrangements to see a launch before, but had been bitterly disappointed when events made her trip impossible. Three years earlier, in 1999, she had been invited by pilot-astronaut Pamela Ann Melroy to see the STS (space transport shuttle) launch from the VIP pad. Such arrangements are always made well in advance of a launch date. Anne had planned to go to the United States for the fall 2000 mission takeoff, but a heart attack intervened. As a science fiction writer who had always written about space travel, Anne had always wanted to see a space mission up close. Now she could not only see a launch, but feel a part of it. Anne herself was increasingly "grounded" by her ill health, and her mind had always been able to travel farther than her body. As a girl during World War II, she could dream about worlds of great possibility, worlds in which women could be in space, women who had authority and power. Now Anne would be part of an exclusive club able to see a space shuttle launch up close. To Anne, the launch was more than a spectacle; this moment exemplified all that she had lived and dreamed and written. The experience had a personal dimension, too, for the space shuttle pilot, Pam Melroy, was a fan and friend.

A female pilot, a woman who achieved the rank of colonel, an intrepid spirit leading the way to humanity's future, Pam embodied the spirit of Anne's protagonists. A graduate of Wellesley, a sister college to Anne's alma mater, Radcliffe, Pam had been a fan of Anne McCaffrey's since graduate school. Pam explains, "It was when I read *The White Dragon* that I knew I had to have everything Anne had written!" Anne's depiction of "strong, talented women" has helped Pam "feel a sense of validation about being a strong woman (or at least a strong-willed one!). I feel like they are friends and try to emulate the best qualities in them. The fact that they are portrayed in a way that also stimulates my thoughts about science and technology is also really important." Her friendship with Pam confirmed Anne's faith in science and the world view she created in her fictions. In a letter to her, Pam praises Anne's writing, especially her depictions of women characters, which she described as "not sweet do-gooders or evil temptresses like you see in so much science fiction." Pam explained that she invited Anne to the launch in October 2000 in gratitude for "so much enjoyment for so many years."

When she returned to Houston after her successful mission, Pam found a letter from Anne saying that "she was sorry she didn't come to the launch, she decided to have a heart attack instead." Pam immediately wrote Anne, sending four photos of Anne's novel *Crystal Singer* in space. The photos show the book in Pam's hands in the International Space Station, floating in the air in front of Pam, her reading the book as she exercises in the shuttle and as she is settling into her sleeping bag. In the last picture, Anne's book has a Velcro patch so Pam can keep the book from floating away! In the accompanying letter, Pam explained, "Our storage is really limited in the Shuttle, and we can't carry up many personal items. . . . However, room is made for one or two personal items that the individual feels would be important to have. For me, I knew what that item would be long before I was even assigned. It would be a book." Like Anne, Pam would read to unwind before going to sleep. Like Anne, who also reads and re-reads her favorite books, Pam said, "When I am especially busy or stressed, I prefer to go back to books I have read before and re-read a favorite part. . . . I knew I simply had to have an old favorite to help me relax in that strange, busy environment so that I could sleep and be fresh for the next day. As you can tell from the pictures, it was my battered copy of *Crystal Singer*." Pam wrote about how hard it was to describe the feeling of being in space and concluded, "I guess we need to send a writer up, right?" But in Anne's description of crystal thrall, the trance-like experience of being one with crystal resonance, Pam found the perfect description of what she experienced, back on Earth, trying to describe space. She praised Anne's power as a writer to capture what Anne dreamed and Pam experienced: "Anne, I wish I could adequately thank you for the enjoyment that you have brought me as a master storyteller." Pam's words are a fine tribute, but her actions speak even more loudly: astronauts are only allowed to bring two personal items into space, and both times Pam chose to bring one of Anne's books (*Crystal Singer* in 2000; *The White Dragon* in 2002).

In March 2001, Alec sent Pam a note that his mother had had a stroke and invited her to come to Dragonhold-Underhill. Pam then planned to visit Anne in Ireland in the fall of 2001, but when she was chosen for her second shuttle mission, she had to move her visit to Dragonhold-Underhill forward to August 5–7, 2001. On Anne's Web page, you can see the pictures she has posted of Pam's visit to Dragonhold-Underhill. Anne wrote, "My feet have yet to return to earth after Pam Melroy's recent visit. . . . Having her as a fan is flattering indeed, but being able to honestly call her my friend is the far greater joy." The photos show Pam in Anne's office, in front of the photos Pam sent to Anne, in her study, clinking wine glasses at Anne's kitchen table, and talking at the table with Anne's good friend and co-author Richard Woods. Pam enjoyed her visit, describing Dragonhold-Underhill as "an incredible household. . . . When I got there I realized that Anne loves people and life and proceeds to encourage it in every way all around her. . . . [T]he sense I got was that Anne protects and cares for her family and friends and they reciprocate beautifully. Anne should install a revolving door on the front of her house because people are always coming and going!" Pam's appreciation of Dragonhold-Underhill marks her transition from fan to friend, a friend whom Anne treasures. Anne put the photos of Pam and her book on her Web site; the originals appear in a prominent place on her study wall. Befriending an astronaut was a thrill for Anne as well as a tribute to her work, but for Anne the culminating experience was to witness a launch herself.

At the Legible Leftovers bookstore in Longwood, Florida, Anne signed 170 books for fans. She stopped only briefly to pet the store's very large, friendly, all-black cat, regally ensconced in a large wicker baby basket. Wearing a white *Crystal Singer* T-shirt, Anne tucked her large sunglasses at the top of the shirt. Wearing only a little lipstick, with her hair pulled back, she was at ease and energized by the large group. Still adjusting to the heat, she had a small circulating fan nearby. Despite the huge crowd, Grainne

Sullivan, a fan, saw that Anne enjoyed the home-baked goods, including a delicious and not-too-sweet pecan pie, and that she was supplied with plenty of root beer to get her through the long lines of fans wanting Anne's autograph. She and Antoinette (Anto) O'Connell, the family friend who accompanied her to Florida, then had lunch with over a dozen fans.

The space shuttle was all set to go and the weather forecast for Florida was perfect. But Hurricane Lili intervened. For the first time ever, a space shuttle launch was postponed because of a hurricane headed toward Houston, where Mission Control was shut down. Anne and Antoinette were at a party thrown by Pamela Melroy's parents. The Melroy family was having a reunion, and they included Anne in their "gather." As usual, Anne found herself part of another family. She had to wait five more days until Atlantis finally took off. Anne spent part of the time at a Pernese Gather in Cocoa Beach, Florida. Anne had invited Elizabeth Moon, a favorite co-author of hers, who would also be going to the shuttle launch, to the luncheon. Anne wore a black T-shirt that bore the legend, "Anne McCaffrey/Elizabeth Moon, *Sassinak*," the first novel they wrote together. The T-shirt depicts a space-suited warrior. Anne was surrounded by her fans, some holding small stuffed fire-lizards, based on the small dragon-related creatures so important on Pern. The paraphernalia signified the importance of Anne's words, turned into icons by her devoted readers. At the gather, one of her fans, Robin (aka MasterHarper57, his Web-site name), presented Anne with a plaque in appreciation for her help with a post 9-11 fund-raising event. Robin wanted to raise money for a large American flag, and Anne had sent him autographed copies of some of her books for the auction. As a fan and observer of the space shuttle launch, Anne would purchase souvenirs and mementos, but she was constantly reminded that to her readers *her* presence was just as rare and engrossing.

Although she is a workaholic, Anne actually found it "kind of fun, not to have any things we had to do." As it had for Pam when the first shuttle was given extra time in space, Anne found herself suspended in time. For once, Anne was a member of a captive audience, waiting for the shuttle launch to be finalized. With

Anto, Anne went shopping, and she bought herself some lighter-weight clothes to help her cope with the Florida heat. She bought everyone at Dragonhold-Underhill T-shirts from the Space Station store; some listed this mission, "STS 121," and others proclaimed a motto that might be Anne's own: "Failure is not an option!" At the health store, Anne, who has sworn by vitamins ever since they helped her cope with insomnia and depression, frugally stocked up on vitamins that are cheaper in the States than in Ireland. After she shopped, Anne and Anto toured the NASA museum with its impressive display of rockets, including a shuttle. The line of people waiting to sit in the model cockpit was too long, and since Anne had already had the pleasure of sitting in a space shuttle cockpit in Houston in the 1980s, she skipped that part of the museum. With her avid interest in food, Anne particularly enjoyed the display of food that the astronauts would eat. Pam had told her that all astronauts bring Tabasco sauce "to spark up the rather bland prepackaged food." As enjoyable as all these activities were, they were all just marking time until the big event, the actual launch. After the delay of five days due to Hurricane Lili, on October 7, 2002, the launch was finally ready to go. The usual crowds of tens of thousands of spectators gathered for a several-mile radius. A lucky couple of hundred, including Anne, would watch the launch more closely, from the VIP stands.

From their hotel in Cocoa Beach, Anne and Anto drove over to the Space Center, whose immense parking lots seem enormous enough for a shuttle to land on. At the protocol office, Anne stood in line to sign in, get her hand stamped, and receive the ticket for the bus ride to the launch site. In an enormous, air-conditioned building, there were food, rest rooms, and displays for those waiting until the launch was imminent. The day's beautiful 84 degrees was far too hot for Anne, used to Ireland's cool and misty weather. Across a lagoon, on the Banana River bleachers of Pad B, Ann, Anto, and a large crowd gathered to watch the launch. The national anthem was played, which got Anne in a festive mood, except she found she had forgotten some of the words, a sign both of the momentousness of the occasion and her Irish citizenship. It had been a long time since Anne had sung the national anthem or even heard it. With Anne's journey back to the United States, the McCaffreys had come full circle. A large timer lit up and all eyes watched the countdown and the shuttle, in place and ready to be launched. When the countdown reached 10, the huge crowd counted along with the timer. "10, 9, 8 . . . , Liftoff!" At 3:46 p.m., the shuttle took off. Clouds blossomed from the end of shuttle, then flames appeared, and slowly *Atlantis* glided from the launch pad, with the crowd cheering wildly. Shock waves appeared in the lagoon, and the noise of the engines, while not deafening, filled the air. Close to tears, Anne controlled herself, not wanting to cry: "It was so incredible to be there, seeing it happen, hearing the noise and feeling the burst of pride and achievement as the *Atlantis* continued happily upward, swirling the clouds at its tail and gradually veering westward to get in line for its orbital adventure." As the *Atlantis* rose into the skies, Anne's book was along on the journey. The shuttle rose and then rolled on its back as it must to continue its flight. The sky was so clear that Anne saw the booster shell as it separated and turned end over end and fell into the sea. From her tour, Anne knew they would send a ship out to retrieve it, and her practical mind approved and noted the recycling. Far too quickly, though, *Atlantis* was out of sight and the space launch was over. Back at the hotel, Anne turned on the in-house NASA channel, watching the replay of the launch constantly over the next few days. She had originally scheduled her trip so that she would be able to see the *Atlantis* land as well as take off. But because of the delays, Anne decided to return home as scheduled. The *Atlantis* would arrive back in Florida after she was back in Ireland. At home in Ireland, she would relive the launch in her heart and imagination.

And she would return to her computer to write, creating worlds in which space travel is routine and peaceful, sharing her elation at the space launch in fictional worlds even more powerful than the real thing. She would do so in concert with her son Todd, producing their first joint novel, *Dragon's Kin*, in 2003, and *Dragon's Fire* in 2006. Dedicated to Anne's brother Kevin and Todd's daughter Ceara Rose, the first novel bears all the hallmarks of Anne's fiction, but its publication marked a very public passing of the torch to her son. *Dragon's Kin* reads very much like Anne's much-acclaimed Harper Hall Trilogy and, like that series, features very young protagonists (ten years old at the book's beginning). With a very accessible prose style, the novel could easily be characterized as young adult fiction. Yet the messages and patterns are demonstrably part of Anne's fictive universe. The novel employs epigraphs from Pern ballads, as Anne's first Dragonriders of Pern novel, *Dragonflight*, did. The protagonists are juvenile outsiders, struggling to find a place in their society and, in the process, resisting authority figures. Characteristic elements of physical disasters, the traumatic loss of family members, the saving grace of a dragon's love, political infighting, and the centrality of music as a redemptive element appear in this novel, as they do not only in Anne's Pern series, but in her other series as well.

Anne and Todd have developed a new twist on Pern society (rather impressively so, for this is the sixteenth book in the Dragonriders of Pern). Where other books have focused either on dragons or fire-lizards, here Anne turns to a creation present in the first Dragonriders of Pern novel, *Dragonflight*, the Watch-whers, dragon-like creatures that are telepathic to a degree, can fly, go *between*, and, perhaps most importantly, bond with human beings. While not as awe-inspiring as dragons or as beautiful as fire-lizards, Watch-whers have an important role to fulfill. Focusing on Watch-whers' ability to sense heat, young miners' children save their families during a mine disaster. In her other Dragonriders of Pern novels, Anne focused on guilds and activities near to her heart: Dragonriders (like equestrians) and Harpers (singers and musicians). This book bears the impress of Todd's engineering training in the focus on mines, barely mentioned in any other book. Family allusions also pepper the book, including, most notably, the appearance of a character nicknamed "Sis." Sis, of course, is the name of Anne's sister-in-law, who lived with her for many years, dying in 1996. Terregar, the smith who marries the main character's sister, seems a likely parallel to Geoff Kennedy, who married Gigi, Anne's daughter (to whom this book is dedicated). And it is perhaps not too farfetched to see in a brief reference to a man who drank and beat his children a sign of

Todd's lingering bitterness at his own father. But the fun of spotting family references or inside allusions pales beside the pleasure, for most readers, of entering another Pern community. If this novel seems a bit sketchy in terms of the great emotion that Anne's characters usually evoke, it may be ascribed to the difficulties of co-authorship, also noted in some of Anne's other collaborations. The plot, mise-en-scène, and features, though, are all palpably Pern.

Dragon's Kin, the most recent collaboration of Anne and Todd, was crowned with the signal success of being on the *New York Times* best-seller list for several weeks. Focusing on a wide range of characters from childhood to adulthood, this novel contains many deaths of sympathetic characters, far more than in other Pern novels. Taking place in Pern history when Thread is soon to appear, the narrative wrestles with the plight of the "Shunned," characters exiled from Holds and society, and hence starving and in great danger of perishing when Thread finally does arrive. A young orphan who cannot speak, Pellar, provides narrative focus, another typical McCaffrey feature, focusing on a character with a difference. Pellar's other skills more than compensate for his inability to speak. This novel expands the Pern base of knowledge, as a new form of firestone is discovered and the Watch-whers' importance is understood. The events of this 2006 novel bear the guiding hand of Todd, as many of the characters and plot elements are drawn from his own, single-authored Pern novel, *Dragonsblood*. Todd's *Dragonsblood*, appeared in fall 2005, and it is dedicated to his sister, Georgeanne Kennedy. *Dragonsblood* is a four-hundred-page-plus adult novel, including references to sexuality, complex and violent conflicts, and many deaths, both of dragons and people. It is easy to see how *Dragonsblood* evolved from Todd's collaboration with his mother. Many of the same characters appear in both *Dragonsblood* and *Dragon's Kin*, most notably Kindan and Dragonrider J'Trel and his dragon, Talith, among others. The plot follows that of Anne's first Dragonriders of Pern novel, *Dragonflight*, including the focus on an orphaned young woman with special Talents, a queen dragon, a mystery solved by attention to Pernese ballads, and chapters with epigraphs from Pernese ballads and books. But while he relies on his mother's framework, Todd creates a Pern novel that is more integrated, less romantic, and more conflict based. His complex alternating structure, taking two narrative strands, one following events four hundred years in the past as the Pernese begin losing their technology and one set in a future where medical and technical knowledge has been lost, allows the reader to experience the span of the planet's history. The intense yearning of characters for connection appears in the novel, but Todd's interest seems to lie more with the science than with the characters. Though he develops a couple of romances, they seem almost perfunctory. And while especially in recent years, Anne has been reluctant to kill characters off, Todd covers the events of the Plague years, killing off a large percentage of the population, and then follows that up with an epidemic among the dragons that decimates both the animals and their riders.

It is tempting, too, to see, in Todd's portrait of an older female scientist, a version of his relationship with his own aging mother. While their relationship is more positive than the one depicted between Wind Blossom and her daughter Emorra, the depiction of aging is heartfelt and compelling, especially of Wind Blossom's awareness of the aging process. Of course, it is just as likely that Todd is recalling his grandmother McCaffrey's difficulties as she aged. But that he includes an older woman as a heroine, key to solving problems not only in her own time, but even four hundred years in the future, suggests the degree to which he loves and admires his mother. After all, she has been a heroic figure, creating and solving problems on Pern and her other fictional worlds and in her real world, helping friends and family and fellow writers. Perhaps the most important aspect of *Dragon's Kin*, *Dragon's Fire*, and *Dragonsblood* is whether they meet the readers' test of acceptability. As Anne and Todd's editor, Shelly Shapiro, told me, "the marketplace will decide" whether Todd is a worthy heir to his mother's worlds. Both books have sold well. Certainly anyone who saw Todd clutching his mother's Grand Master Award could see that he liked the feeling, and no doubt yearns for a Nebula Award of his own. After all, as a young boy, he helped his mother create the first trophies, so a Nebula Award for Todd McCaffrey would certainly seem to be not only in his blood, but also in his history.

In February 2005, Anne McCaffrey learned she received the only major award that had still eluded her grasp—the coveted Grand Master Award, presented by the Science Fiction and Fantasy Writers of America for lifetime achievement. The award brought Anne McCaffrey to the United States again—this time to Chicago, where the presentation of the Grand Master Award was the highlight of the Nebula Award weekend. In the announcement of her selection, the Science Fiction and Fantasy Writers of America praised Anne McCaffrey for having "done much to bring new readers into the genre" and also for having "nurtured the careers of many writers." "Her groundbreaking literature and service to SFFWA" were also cited. Only the twenty-second writer to be recognized by the SFFWA as a Grand Master, Anne McCaffrey is only the third woman writer to be so honored (the others are Andre Norton and Ursula K. Le Guin). In concert with the SFFWA meeting, at a Border's bookstore, along with many other authors, Anne autographed books. In her new, shorter haircut and a peasant Indian blouse, Anne was surrounded by friends. Her good friend Marilyn Alm literally covered Anne's back, standing behind her and keeping a hand on Anne's chair to block out fans. To Anne's right, her co-author and friend Elizabeth Scarborough looked on as Anne chatted with Lois McMaster Bujold. In addition to Bujold, who had won a Nebula for best novel, Anne also got to see her old friend Frederick Pohl. As they posed for a group photograph, Anne again let Todd hold her Grand Master Award as she leaned over to talk to a handsome young Neil Gaiman, the ceremony's toastmaster.

At the Grand Master reception, Anne was toasted by a number of writers, and she was presented with a large cake with a screened Michael Whelan design of her dragons. The cake read, "Congratulations Anne McCaffrey Grand Master 2005," and like a wedding or birthday celebration, Anne did the honors of cutting the cake. A large poster board of *Dragon's Kin* stood to the right of the cake. Of all her many books, Anne chose to feature her last, written with Todd. Anne was resplendent in a purple shell and a bright, multicolored, sequined jacket with matching pants. The Grand Master Award provided a fitting tribute to Anne, and one that meant a great deal to her. As one of the early officers in the Science Fiction Writers of America, Anne had been the first woman to win both the Hugo and the Nebula (for "Weyr Search"). As Neil Gaiman explained, "People who make up sf are still a family and fundamentally supportive. . . . [T]he Nebulas are our way of saying 'thank you' to those who produce sterling work."

Throughout the SFFWA meeting, this theme was repeated. But the evening presentation of the Nebula Awards was more formal. Catherine Asaro, herself a Nebula award winner and the president of the Science Fiction and Fantasy Writers of America, came to the podium; she praised Anne, saying, "For most of my life I have admired Anne McCaffrey. I have loved her work unabashedly. . . . Miss McCaffrey has offered untold readers the joy of her work." As Catherine announced that Anne was the 2005 Science Fiction and Fantasy Writers Association Grand Master, the assembled ballroom rose and gave a standing ovation. Catherine presented the Lucite award containing images of the earth, a nebula, and stars to Anne, and the two hugged. Todd reached over to take the award, saying to his mother, "Can we hold it so it doesn't drop?" and commenting, "This is the first time I've ever seen anybody willingly hand over a Nebula or Hugo."

Diana Tyler, Anne's longtime agent, rose to speak next. She had flown over from England and in her clipped British accent praised Anne as a person and as a writer: "There is little to say about her writing that this distinguished gathering doesn't already know: brilliant, imaginative, and sensitive are just three words that come to mind. But I know Anne not just as a writer but as kind, generous, and warm-hearted, and someone who extends a helping hand to those in difficulties." Diana cited Anne's legions of fans as evidence of her good-heartedness, explaining, "Many a time I have watched her sign bag-fulls of books with real pleasure." She concluded, "Anne is a wonderful person who has created worlds from words and gives such pleasure to so many people. Thank you, Anne. You richly deserve the distinction of Grand Master. We all love you." After Diana's accolade, Anne moved to the podium and, in a characteristically self-effacing fashion, praised another Grand Master, Andre Norton, who had recently died. Holding up the jade bead necklace she was wearing, Anne told the crowd, "Andre Norton made this necklace for me after she heard I had been named a Grand Master. It was probably the last thing she made. As you know, she was responsible for my writing *The White Dragon*. We all miss her—she was a marvelous person." Anne broke off and, seemingly at a loss for words, held up the necklace again, nodded, and stepped aside.

Then Todd moved over to the podium and said, "We here in SFFWA have a history of helping each other. I've had the honor of knowing Anne McCaffrey from inside and out for forty-nine years," which produced titters. He continued, "I would like to remember those who helped raise Mum up." As he named each person, he explained how each had contributed to Anne's success: Andre Norton, A. J. Budrys, Ed Firman, Judith Merril, Virginia Kidd, Damon Knight, everybody at Milford, John Campbell, Frank Kelly Freas, Judy Lynn Benjamin Del Rey, Gordie Dickson, Ian Ballantine, Betty Ballantine, Isaac Asimov. At Asimov's name, Todd stopped and smiled; demurring, "I am a baritone," Todd proceeded to sing the words Isaac had sung to Anne so many years ago at a Worldcon: "Anne McCaffrey, Open your golden gates." The audience, familiar with this science fiction anecdote, began to chuckle, anticipating the punch line, Todd repeating Anne's words to Isaac: "Ten minutes alone in a room with me, and you'll know I'm no Tinkerbell!" Anne and the crowd laughed together. Then Todd turned more serious and announced that he also wanted to remember people who weren't in science fiction and said that he would do his best to give them voice: he named John Greene; Colonel Hugh McCaffrey; Sis, Anne's beloved sister-in-law; and Anne's father, G. H. McCaffrey. At each name, Anne covered her face with her hands, somewhat overcome, and wept gently. Todd gave his mum a hug and kiss and handed her the Grand Master Nebula Award (a Lucite block), announcing, "There's one final ceremony to commemorate [this occasion]. In your honor, and in honor of Pern—there was a moment of silence as Todd and the three granddaughters shook cans of silly string—THREADFALL!!" And they showered Ann with the silly string, festooning her hair, the award, and the general area, to the audience's applause and laughter. It was very clearly Anne's crowd and Anne's night.

The future of Pern seems set; Anne and Todd have three collaborations, and Todd has two more solo novels under contract. Having sold the rights to the Dragonriders of Pern to Copperheart Entertainment, Anne hopes to have a dear wish fulfilled: to see *Dragonflight* on the big screen. Her eightieth birthday, April 1, 2006, was a gala affair with eighty people at a large, catered affair at Dragonhold-Underhill. A few days later, she had another knee replaced: as she herself repeatedly says, "I can't recommend aging for the faint-hearted." Yet as she deals with aging and its stresses, she has the consolation and reward of her life's work. In June 2006, she was inducted into the Science Fiction Museum Hall of Fame—significantly, she was the only inductee present (two of the other inductees were deceased, and the third, George Lucas, sent in a video acceptance speech). As Anne's own fiction offers alternative endings for her characters' lives, so her own life defies a conventional conclusion. Engaged and active, she knows that her hopes, fears, and dreams will remain alive in her books and her son's books.

In her eighth decade, Anne McCaffrey can look back on a life well lived, a life that has had an impact far beyond her circle of family and friends. Anne brought emotion and heart to science fiction, and she exerted a powerful influence on more than one generation of readers and writers. Any convention appearance by Anne provides overwhelming evidence of her impact on the lives of her readers, who thank her for providing them with support and hope, often when they were going through difficult times in their lives. The extensive fan community and fan groups testify to the passion and dedication of her readers to her fictional worlds. As Anto O'Connell describes, "She opened so many young people's minds to limitless possibilities." Not only for young people, but also for adults, especially women, Anne has provided alternative narratives. Her collaborator Annie Scarborough concurs, explaining, "I believe in dragons more than Prince Charming." Jody Lynn Nye praises her as "one of the first women since Mary Shelley . . . to use her own name to write science fiction [and create] strong and effective women heroes." In 2006, we take for granted the world that women like the ground-breaking, "bucking the system" Anne McCaffrey helped make possible. Astronaut and pilot and soon-to-be shuttle commander Pamela Melroy may be one of the most famous of Anne's readers to give her credit, but many of the rest of us, less heralded, acknowledge the meaning and inspiration her books have provided. Anne's life bears testimony to Carolyn Heilbrun's assertion that "women come to writing . . . simultaneously with self-creation." As I hope this biography has shown, Anne's life reflects the passion and commitment so evident in her books, and she herself remains as effective and compelling a model as any of heroines.

SOURCE NOTES

Anne McCaffrey's personal papers at Dragonhold-Underhill, her first literary agent Virginia Kidd's collection of correspondence and papers, and numerous interviews provide the major sources for this biography. Included are interviews with Susan Allison, Marilyn and Harry Alm, Maureen Beirne, Jean Bigelow (by phone), Derval Diamond, Annett Francis, Vaughne Hansen, Alec Johnson, H. Wright Johnson, Georgeanne Kennedy, Virginia Kidd, Anne McCaffrey, Kevin and Marci McCaffrey, Andi McCaffrey, Todd J. McCaffrey, Pota Meier (by phone), Antoinette O'Connell, Elizabeth Anne Scarborough, Shelly Shapiro, Richard Woods; and mail or e-mail interviews with Betty Ballantine, Jody Lynn Nye, Pamela Melroy, and Elizabeth Moon. For literary analysis of her work, see my previous book, *Anne McCaffrey: A Critical Companion*, and its CD updates.

INTRODUCTION
Quotations

"A blazing fire . . . too." Elizabeth Moon, e-mail, 1-28-03.

"Horses help you . . . slightly humble." E-mail from Anne McCaffrey, 3-5-02

"It was such a surprise . . . in my hands." Interview with Anne McCaffrey, 7-14-01.

"HE didn't believe . . . support." A. McCaffrey, "The Self-Made (Wo)man," 1.

"I made this . . . your books" Comments at signings at Dragoncon, 8-30-03 and 8-31-03.

"It is great . . . emotions." Lefanu, 24.

"as a tongue-in-cheek . . . on the spot." A. McCaffrey, "Hitch Your Dragon to a Star," 282.

"from margin to center." Donawerth, 45.

"The dragons offer . . . relationship." Ibid., 55.

"The hero . . . planets." Ibid., 27.

"After seven . . . women." A. McCaffrey, "Hitch," 283.
"Emotional content . . . elements." Ibid.," 283.
"With the . . . literature." Ibid., 287.
"It became . . . to." Larbalestier, 179.
"I bore myself." E-mail from Anne McCaffrey, 4-24-02.
"I feel like . . . part of it." Dragoncon, 8-31-03.

CHAPTER 1:
AN IRISH FAMILY HERITAGE

Selina Perkins is remembered in a way that suggests that she was dominated by her husband, who was an imposing presence. While Grandfather McCaffrey was both large and tall, his wife was a petite four feet high. While Selina herself was a native Bostonian, her family had emigrated from England in 1632. This date is recorded in McCaffrey family lore, but Selina's English heritage and Pilgrim status appear to have had little effect on the McCaffrey family. The *Statistical Abstract of the United States* provided the information about educational degrees in 1936.

In *Dragonholder*, Todd McCaffrey tells a wonderful story of his grandfather, the Kernel, defying George Patton, who made an unreasonable request that the Italians not use the main road into Agrigento because their water carts were slowing down military traffic. G. H. countermanded the order, hence ensuring he would remain only a colonel for the rest of his career, but doing right by the Italian people. In so doing, he followed the pattern his father had set of challenging authority for a good cause. According to Todd, the reporter John Hersey created his famous Colonel Joppolo in *A Bell for Adona* based in part on G. H. McCaffrey. *Dragonholder* is also the source for other examples of McCaffrey premonitions.

In her famous study, Helen L. Koch found that "birth order interacted most frequently with the factor of sex. When a child and his or her sibling were of the same sex, there were few differences in characteristics that could be attributed to birth order; when they were opposite in sex, there were many differences" (see Yahraes, 2). Martha Trachtenberg describes Anne's dressing up her cat in clothes.

Quotations

"Help Wanted: . . . apply." Ryan, 14.
"Protestant foreigners." Ryan, 42.
"still . . . jobs." Ryan, 14.
"My grandfather . . . him." E-mail from Anne McCaffrey, 8-26-01.
"The old house . . . around it." E-mail from Anne McCaffrey, 8-26-01.
"Irish policemen . . . Sunday." Ryan, 137.
"No one . . . beat." E-mail from Anne McCaffrey, 8-26-01.
"Grandfather . . . complaints." Ibid.
"a family trait . . . son." Ibid.
"had also . . . lifeboat." Ibid.
"a hedgerow . . . Catholics." Ibid.
"I cannot . . . plagues me." Ibid.

"Bad food . . . industry." Brizzi, 48.

"it would do." E-mail from Anne McCaffrey, 6-20-02.

"If I . . . status." A. McCaffrey, "Retrospection," 20.

"parade ground voice" E-mail from Anne McCaffrey, 10-20-01.

"different . . . 'odd.'" Ibid.

"My parents . . . color." Ibid.

"were sent . . . ignore." Ibid., 9-5-01.

"Once we . . . might not." Ibid., 8-28-01.

"Dad and . . . other." E-mail from Anne McCaffrey to Todd, 2-5-98.

"had a . . . phrases." Ibid.

"he had. . .scarce." Ibid.

"A precise. . .disorder." Ibid.

"As the . . . pet." A. McCaffrey, "The Self-Made (Wo)man," 2.

"Dad . . . him." E-mail from Anne McCaffrey, 9-5-01.

"He pushed himself hard." Interview with Kevin McCaffrey, 6-18-03.

"how . . . superiority." A. McCaffrey, "The Self-Made (Wo)man," 2.

"Gruff . . . humor." T. McCaffrey, *Dragonholder*, 26.

"PATERNAL . . . PERFECTLY." Ibid., 39.

"My Dad was the famous one" Letter to Virginia Kidd, 6-22-67.

"Whatever bonding . . . by me." E-mail from Anne McCaffrey to Todd, 2-5-98.

"was the first . . . troops" A. McCaffrey, "The Self-Made (Wo)man," 12.

"was a . . . his kids." Ibid., 4.

"I think . . . on the spot." E-mail from Anne McCaffrey, 2-5-02.

"I got . . . fixation." Letter to Virginia Kidd, 6-22-67.

"His life . . . inconceivable." Woolf, 208.

"My father's death . . . wobbled." E-mail from Anne McCaffrey, 8-28-01.

"Is it . . . women?" A. McCaffrey, "Retrospection," 22.

"because . . . them out." E-mail from Anne McCaffrey, 10-02-01.

"Was in . . . life." Ibid., 10-14-03.

"The Depression . . . crashed." T. McCaffrey, *Dragonholder*, 22.

"Mother paid . . . support." E-mail from Anne McCaffrey, 8-28-01.

"two . . . me about." Ibid., 8-28-01.

"The most . . . neglected." Yahraes, 4.

"middle . . . around." Hall, 25.

"They're . . . care of." Ibid.

"'I . . . different.'" Ibid.

"allowed . . . team." E-mail from Anne McCaffrey, 9-5-01.

"to melt . . . toys." Ibid.

"I'll . . . with me." Ibid., 8-29-01.

"I think . . . the girl." Ibid.

"Hugh . . . on him." Ibid., 9-5-01.

"To my . . . write." H. McCaffrey, v.

"I was . . . circumstances." E-mail from Anne McCaffrey, 9-5-01.

"I remember . . . it over." Ibid.

"devised . . . table." E-mail from Kevin McCaffrey to Todd, 3-10-98.

"parents . . . her wrists." Ibid.

"a godawful, ego-centric extrovert" E-mail from Anne McCaffrey, 9-5-01.

"I made . . . profiles." Ibid., 8-29-01.
"had a . . . knew it." Ibid., 9-5-01.
"the least popular." Yahraes, 6.
"[I] would talk . . . young life." E-mail from Anne McCaffrey, 9-5-01.
"I remember . . . Grandmother." Ibid.
"skivving . . . fun." Ibid.
"would thump on the wall." E-mail from Anne McCaffrey to Todd, 3-28-98.
"It was . . . completely." Ibid.
"When . . . lives it." Interview with Shelly Shapiro, 9-26-02.
"was always . . . munitions." E-mail from Anne McCaffrey, 9-5-01.
"I remember . . . group." Ibid.
"remember[s] . . . future." Ibid.

CHAPTER 2:
ADOLESCENCE AND A TIME OF WAR

Many of Anne McCaffrey's characters, such as G-D, who reclaims her given name of Cita in *Powerlines*, and Helva, the Brain Ship who changes her designation when she partners a new brawn or partner, rename themselves

The Negro in New Jersey (by the Interracial Committee of the New Jersey Conference of Social Work) singles out Montclair, Anne's hometown, for having an integrated community center.

Anderson's *Wartime Women* provides the context to understand women's workforce participation during World War II (4).

In *Dragonsong*, for example, the main character is a strong runner. Her speed saves her as she sprints to safety from the life-destroying Thread. In *Damia*, the title character saves her brother from being struck on the head by a rock. This second example may be a fantasy on Anne's part, to be able physically to protect her brothers—one deathly ill, the other at war.

Quotations

"writes . . . fit in." Interview with Susan Allison, 9-26-02.
"I . . . I was." Anne McCaffrey letter to Hutson, 4-21-93.
"'under control.'" *Pueblo Chieftain*, 4-27-85.
"She . . . girlfriends." Interview with Kevin McCaffrey, 6-18-03.
"also not . . . much." E-mail from Anne McCaffrey, 10-02-01.
"adolescent girls . . . appearance." Pipher, 55.
"With . . . time." Bro, 3.
"not a pretty girl." E-mail from Anne McCaffrey, 10-02-01.
"one of . . . Mother." Interview with Kevin McCaffrey, 6-18-03.
"much nicer." E-mail from Anne McCaffrey, 12-17-01.
"I wished . . . distinctive." Ibid.
"I think . . . time." E-mail from Anne McCaffrey, 12-19-01.
"a good . . . writer." Ibid.
"We are . . . master." Snedeker, *Forgotten Daughter*, 18.
"Unselfishness . . . cure." Ibid., 123.
"about a very . . . place." E-mail from Anne McCaffrey, 10-02-01.

"he wrote . . . view." *Contemporary Authors Online.*
" 'I'll die . . . knees." Grey, 77.
"a normal . . . associate with." Radcliffe sophomore questionnaire.
"The school . . . no difference." E-mail from Anne McCaffrey, 10-22-01.
"eighty-six . . . white women." Interracial Committee of the New Jersey Conference of Social Work, 25.
"Ella . . . work with." E-mail from Anne McCaffrey, 10-22-01.
"also had . . . they had." Ibid.
"decided . . . weren't." Ibid., 10-17-01.
"women could . . . children." Ibid., 4-11-02.
"we just . . . weekends." Ibid., 2-26-02.
"sort of . . . me in." Ibid., 10-22-01.
"I wasn't . . . she was." Ibid.
"pretty self-reliant . . . did fine." Ibid.
" 'a southern . . . Weyr." Brizzi, 48.
"It was difficult . . . assignments." E-mail from Anne McCaffrey, 10-2-01.
"When our history . . . class." Ibid., 11-27-01.
"not an Old Family." Ibid., 1-7-02.
"In a group . . . by doing so." Stuart Hall file.
"She has some . . . poems." Ibid.
"She is . . . resentment." Ibid.
"very much . . . available." E-mail from Anne McCaffrey, 10-2-01.
"a sport . . . player." Ibid.
"We were . . . could play." Ibid., 10-16-01.
"The Army . . . quack." Montclair High School Yearbook.
"I knew . . . unscathed." E-mail from Anne McCaffrey, 10-16-01.
"Never . . . enough." T. McCaffrey, *Dragonholder*, 25–26.
"dancing . . . with mother." E-mail from Anne McCaffrey, 10-2-01.
"a good . . . illness." Ibid., 10-16-01.
"He was . . . movies." Ibid.
"whereas . . . antediluvian!" Ibid.
"I don't . . . home." Ibid.
"I had a . . . Moultrie." Ibid.
"[I] enjoyed . . . Society.)" E-mail from Anne McCaffrey, 10-2-01.
"strong hands . . . concert." Ibid.
"lunch . . . them." Ibid.
"imperative . . . career," Ibid.
"*is* Annie." Interview with Vaughne Hansen, 2-18-02.

CHAPTER 3:
COLLEGE DAYS AND MARRIAGE

Quotations

"the right college for me." E-mail from Anne McCaffrey, 10-22-01.
"to have . . . abroad." Radcliffe college file.
"I . . . studying." E-mail from Anne McCaffrey, 11-27-01.
"We landed . . . upperclasspersons." *Radcliffe 1947 50th Reunion*, 1997, 3.

"Poise . . . tabu." "Do You Know the Answer? Public Appearance and Poise at Radcliffe," reprinted in *Radcliffe 1947 50th Reunion*, 1997.
"especially . . . them." Radcliffe college file.
"Lee . . . deep." Ibid.
"still . . . conscientious." Ibid.
"Too show-off . . . nice one." Ibid., 1-6-47.
"A little . . . deficiencies." Ibid.
"trimming her down." Ibid., Appointments Bureau, 3-18-47.
"Of course . . . can I?!" Interview with Todd McCaffrey, 5-7-97.
"in God . . . call it" E-mail from Anne McCaffrey, 1-14-02.
"the trappings and the rituals." Ibid.
"God did . . . hypocritical." Ibid., 1-13-02.
"for his . . . corrections." A. McCaffrey, "The Utopian Novel," i.
"unfortunately . . . work" Ibid., 19.
"To be frank . . . experience." E-mail from Anne McCaffrey, 11-27-01.
"once . . . other girls." Ibid.
"He would . . . was concerned." Ibid.
"plenty of makeup." Ibid.
"[she] had . . . fun." E-mail from Anne McCaffrey, 4-6-02.
"I was . . . there." Anne McCaffrey, interview by Todd McCaffrey, 5-7-97.
"Chickory . . . Brazil." Ibid.
"an imposing . . . character." Phone interview with Jean Bigelow, 1-3-03.
"expected . . . did." Phone interview with Jean Bigelow, 6-25-03.
"he didn't . . . over." E-mail from Anne McCaffrey, 12-17-01.
"an extremely . . . conspicuous." Interview with Todd McCaffrey, 5-7-97.
"She seems . . . the salt." Radcliffe college file.
"ahead of its time." Interview with Todd McCaffrey, 5-7-97.
"Her discussions . . . as [she] did." E-mail from Anne McCaffrey, 10-16-02.
"But I . . . Circus." Ibid.
"I was . . . ballet." Ibid.
"met . . . picky." Ibid., 12-17-01.
"Mother . . . roses." Ibid.
"I did . . . everything." E-mail from Anne McCaffrey, 1-14-02.
"Robert Goheen . . . students." Letter from Wright Johnson, 1-11-02.
"Granville-Barker . . . throughout." Johnson, 22.
"a small group . . . history." Letter from Wright Johnson, 1-11-02.
"shook up . . . factual." Ibid.
"good-looking . . . attraction." E-mail from Anne McCaffrey, 12-19-01.
"hav[ing] . . . lunch." Ibid.
"Mother . . . disagreed." Ibid., 1-8-02.
"felt no hurt or rejection." Ibid., 1-14-02.
"one of . . . accents." Ibid., 1-8-02.
"I never . . . anybody." Interview with Pota Lewis Meier, 1-30-03.
"got so . . . hooked." A. McCaffrey, "The Self-Made (Wo)man," 3.
"I . . . City." E-mail from Anne McCaffrey, 2-3-02.
"[I] did . . . drink." Ibid.
"You'll go . . . your life?" A. McCaffrey, "Retrospection," 22.
"alone . . . work." E-mail from Anne McCaffrey, 1-8-02.

"a strange . . . all?'" Friedan, 11.
"I knew . . . credit for." E-mail from Anne McCaffrey, 2-3-02.
"She . . . activity." Ibid.
"She . . . be." Ibid., 12-18-02.
"I was . . . moment." Ibid., 2-3-02.
"a very . . . delivered." Ibid.
"Having . . . did." Ibid.
"knocked out." E-mail from Anne McCaffrey, 3-5-02.
"a beautiful . . . dainty." Ibid.
"Clearly, . . . child." Ibid.
"dad . . . said." Ibid., 4-12-02.
"I try . . . child." Ibid.
"found she . . . antics." Hargreaves, 4.
"Anne, . . . write." Interview with Todd McCaffrey, 5-7-97.
"I never . . . typewriter." E-mail from Anne McCaffrey, 2-4-02.
"'just . . . things." Ibid.
"wriggly." Ibid.
"the facility . . . kitchen." Ibid., 4-9-02.
"sending . . . ships." Letter from Virginia Kidd, [2-30-02].
"perfect." Letter from Wright Johnson, 1-5-02.
"'That's . . . tell.'" E-mail from Anne McCaffrey, 2-4-02.
"How I . . . man want?" Letter to Virginia Kidd, 5-16-02
"something . . . hoped for." E-mail from Anne McCaffrey, 2-4-02
"Boys . . . by women." *60 Minutes*, 2-3-02.
"I thought . . . sf, too," E-mail from Anne McCaffrey, 2-4-02.
"We would . . . Earth." Ibid.
"With . . . of things." A. McCaffrey, "The Utopian Novel," 1.
"a strong . . . about it." *Radcliffe 1947 50th Reunion*, 3.
"wish[ed] . . . better place." Ibid., 28.

CHAPTER 4: ANNIE AND VIRGINIA

See the letter quoted in Judith Merril and Emily Pohl-Weary's *Better to Have Loved: The Life of Judith Merril* (56), where Merril describes a similarly unsupportive situation An interview with Virginia Kidd (2-17-02) informed much of this chapter. The term "Milford Mafia" is cited in Clute and Nicholls's *The Encyclopedia of Science Fiction* (807). The 1970 divorce statistics are from Jones, 157.

Quotations

"had . . . humor." E-mail from Anne McCaffrey, 1-12-04.
"she . . . dislike." Ibid., 1-26-04.
"Boys . . . chance." Letter from Virginia Kidd, [2-30-02].
"purely . . . outrageous ones)" E-mail from Anne McCaffrey, 1-10-02.
"especially . . . talking about." Ibid., 1-26-04.
"Virginia . . . great writers." Merril and Pohl-Weary, 57.
"diaper copy." Interview with Virginia Kidd, 2-17-02.
"we . . . followed." E-mail from Anne McCaffrey, 1-26-04.

"my relationship . . . maturity." Ibid., 2-21-02.

"post . . . differences." Letter of Virginia Kidd to Anne McCaffrey, 10-1-65.

"the blanket . . . the changes." Ibid., 10-15-65.

"I decided . . . editors." Ibid., 9-14-65.

"It was . . . novel-writing." A. McCaffrey, "The Self-Made (Wo)man," 10.

"that old . . . DRIVING me." Letter of Anne McCaffrey to Virginia Kidd, 9-20-65.

"My dear . . . Old Me." Letter of Virginia Kidd to Anne McCaffrey, 3-2-65.

"THE GOLD . . . his/her agent." Ibid., 3-28-67.

"innumerable . . . concern." Ibid., no date.

"when . . . slower." Ibid., 12-5-67.

"Art . . . vaguely." Ibid., 9-6-65.

"I tried . . . long-suffering, etc." Letter of Anne McCaffrey to Virginia Kidd, 1-6-67.

"Have I . . . income." Ibid., 8-18-66.

"I, too, . . . spiritually?" Ibid., 1-6-67.

"I have . . . good." Letter of Virginia Kidd to Anne McCaffrey, 12-5-67.

"we have . . . add." Letter of Anne McCaffrey to Virginia Kidd, 1-6-67.

"I discovered . . . for me." Ibid., 3-22-67.

"Peg . . . feet." Ibid., marked "received," 9-13-65.

"Peg . . . from now." Letter of Virginia Kidd to Anne McCaffrey, 9-14-65.

"until . . . royalties." E-mail from Anne McCaffrey, 8-28-02.

"my biggest . . . analysis." Letter of Anne McCaffrey to Virginia Kidd, 5-22-67.

"My aunt . . . loved them." Ibid., 12-6-67.

"was perfect." Ibid., 1-5-02.

"Being . . . space." Hargreaves, 6.

"Johnson . . . watching tv . . ." Letter of Anne McCaffrey to Virginia Kidd, 5-16-66.

"Helva . . . that scene." A. McCaffrey, "The Self-Made (Wo)man," 8.

"I'm going . . . this matter." Letter of Anne McCaffrey to Virginia Kidd, 5-16-66.

"Johnson's . . . Pern #2." Ibid., 1-31-68.

"It's a . . . with him?" Letter of Virginia Kidd to Anne McCaffrey, 5-19-66.

"Irish Annie." Letter of Anne McCaffrey to Virginia Kidd, 6-22-67.

"loved . . . other officers." E-mail from Anne McCaffrey, 2-5-02.

"wishful . . . me home." Ibid.

"You're . . . Wright)?" Letter of Virginia Kidd to Anne McCaffrey, 1-27-69.

"that his . . . SFWA." Letter of Anne McCaffrey to Virginia Kidd, 12-20-68.

"I remember . . . leave." T. McCaffrey, *Dragonholder*, 67.

"It got . . . divorce." A. McCaffrey, "The Self-Made (Wo)man," 18.

"Wright . . . monster." Interview with Virginia Kidd, 2-17-02.

"The Wright Johnson story." Interview with Vaughne Hansen, 2-18-02.

"the corporate. . . fussy." A. McCaffrey, "The Self-Made (Wo)man," 19.

"good company . . . fabulous." E-mail from Anne McCaffrey, 1-12-04.

"Anne . . . Tinker Bell." T. McCaffrey, *Dragonholder* 66.

"he was . . . Me." E-mail from Anne McCaffrey, 1-10-04.

"Peggy . . . godawful." Letter of Anne McCaffrey to Virginia Kidd, 5-25-70.

"much . . . I did!" Ibid., 8-20-70.
"had a . . . heartbreak." E-mail from Anne McCaffrey, 1-10-04.
"maybe . . . quite yet." Letter of Anne McCaffrey to Virginia Kidd, 5-16-66.
"it was . . . pattern." E-mail from Anne McCaffrey, 1-10-04.
"It surprised . . . nasty." Interview with Virginia Kidd, 2-17-02.

CHAPTER 5: EMIGRATION AND A BEST-SELLER

That there were two Anne L. McCaffreys in Dublin led to some confusion—they received each other's mail. In addition to the hassles of relocating, Anne had to fulfill a contract with Doubleday for a cookbook of recipes by science fiction writers. Anne was the editor; being an editor is always difficult, but doing so across the ocean meant the job involved more than the usual difficulties.

Significantly, Anne's publicity photo of herself after moving to Ireland was a picture of her with her horse, Mr. Ed. In the hall of her home is a large portrait of Anne with Mr. Ed. It is an engaging portrait in which Mr. Ed appears as an equal. Anne holds his reins in her hands, and both Mr. Ed and Anne lean over a white picket fence. Mr. Ed's white coat and Anne's silver hair makes them a matched pair.

Quotations

"The fact . . . practiced." Interview with Shelly Shapiro, 9-26- 02.
"deepened . . . there." Interview with Virginia Kidd, 2-19-02.
"the first . . . [she] met." Interview with Antoinette O'Connell, 7-28-02.
"on the strength . . . Haughey." A. McCaffrey, "The Self-Made (Wo)man," 19.
"a backlog . . . notions." Letter from Anne McCaffrey, 4-21-02.
"In case . . . leave it." Letter of Anne McCaffrey to Virginia Kidd, 12-27-70.
"You . . . Ireland." Ibid., 2-21-71.
"I do . . . money." Ibid., 5-27-71.
"the [publishers'] . . . never arrives." Ibid., 10-21-71.
"Mucking out . . . on time." Ibid., 10-28-71.
"In my . . . again!!!!" Ibid., 11-10-71.
"he was . . . no, no." Ibid., 1-6-71.
"I'll show . . . otherwise." Ibid., 5-27-71.
"I developed . . . living in." A. McCaffrey, "The Self-Made (Wo)man," 21.
"wild gang" T. McCaffrey, *Dragonholder*, 76.
"a real . . . tales." Interview with Alec Johnson.
"It is . . . jazz." Letter of Anne McCaffrey to Virginia Kidd, 12-2-70.
"fluttered" Ibid.
"If Todd . . . ears in." Ibid.
"Do I ever . . . ALL.." Letter of Virginia Kidd to Anne McCaffrey, 12-8-70.
"true to . . . Dun Laoghaire." Letter of Anne McCaffrey to Virginia Kidd, 3-12-71.
"I shall . . . can." Ibid.
"without leaving me . . . unfriendly." Ibid., 5-11-71.
"Alec . . . muchly." Ibid.
"Jan-who-is-Lessa." Ibid., 9-3-71.

"Lessa is my landlord." T. McCaffrey, *Dragonholder*, 76.

"My Jan-Lessa . . . spare)." Letter of Anne McCaffrey to Virginia Kidd, 12-6-71.

"who helped abused women." E-mail from Anne McCaffrey, 4-17-02.

"who is . . . manner." Ibid., 4-6-02.

"in a . . . meeting." A. McCaffrey, "The Self-Made (Wo)man," 23.

"excellent frame . . . cookie." Letter of Anne McCaffrey to Virginia Kidd, 11-10-71.

"My new . . . attentive." Ibid., 11-23-71.

"You may . . . for play." Ibid., 12-28-71.

"everyone . . . book, however." Ibid., 4-6-72.

"I shall . . . at that time." Ibid., 8-14-72.

"has made . . . future." Ibid., 10-19-72.

"gave Interpol . . . a fluke! " Ibid., 10-19-72.

"mentioned my . . . has tried!" Ibid., 5-7-73.

"Mabel started . . . campaigns." Ibid., 12-16-73.

"had always . . . younger woman." Interview with Anne McCaffrey, 8-2-02.

"another Aries . . . occasionally macho." Ibid.

"I didn't . . . another Aries." Ibid.

"He didn't . . . different." Ibid., 7-29-02.

"Derek was . . . comfort." Ibid.

"'this story . . . Jaxom.'" Letter from Betty Ballantine, 4-21-02.

"She is . . . bitter." E-mails from Anne McCaffrey, 4-17-02, 3-12-71.

"job is . . . her books." Letter from Betty Ballantine, 5-17-02.

"a state of mind," Letter of Anne McCaffrey to Virginia Kidd, 10-19-72.

"everyone liked . . . after that." E-mail from Anne McCaffrey, 4-22-02.

"an autobiography . . . real world." Interview with Todd McCaffrey, 8-31-02.

"voracious reader . . . style." E-mail from Anne McCaffrey, 4-22-02.

"ravening fan public." Hodge, 7.

"not only . . . needed money." Ibid., 23.

"religion . . . exist," Ibid., 32.

"created her . . . readers, too." Ibid., 132–133.

"The gothics . . . writing them." E-mail from Anne McCaffrey, 4-12-02.

"the project . . . of choices." DuPlessis, 4.

"share a . . . of control." Longnecker, 1.

"Ed . . . toes." E-mail from Anne McCaffrey, 4-17-02.

"cart before the horse thing." Ibid., 4-15-02.

"Ha! . . . world!" A. McCaffrey, *The Mark of Merlin*.

"is no . . . my friends." Letter of Anne McCaffrey to Virginia Kidd, 1-6-71.

"Mother . . . I think." Ibid., 8-14-72.

"Between the noise . . . myself." A. McCaffrey, "The Self-Made (Wo)man," 24.

"The woman . . . hulk." Ibid.

"[Why] my own . . . only the character." E-mail from Anne McCaffrey, 5-22-02.

"is probably . . . to her." Ibid., 4-17-02.

"Such antics . . . in culture." A. McCaffrey, "The Self-Made (Wo)man," 24.

"I have . . . *Kilternan Legacy*." E-mail from Anne McCaffrey, 4-17-02.

"I'm not . . . as Simon." Letter of Anne McCaffrey to Virginia Kidd, 11-22-75.

"in the Dark ages." A. McCaffrey, *Kilternan Legacy*, 512.
"I hope . . . under discussion." Letter of Anne McCaffrey to Virginia Kidd, 11-22-75.
"on the strength. . . next year." Ibid., 5-3-74.
"I have never . . . Texas A & M." Ibid., 4-7-76.
"The tour . . . on." A. McCaffrey, "The Self-Made (Wo)man," 36.
"not much . . . who she is?" Ibid., 38.
"a fan . . . needed one." Ibid., 39.
"salvation . . . lunch pail." Ibid., 38.

CHAPTER 6: STRUGGLING WITH SUCCESS

Anne's sales hit their high of around 100,000 hardcover, 125,000 paperback. Her preferred title for the book is its British title, *The Carradyne Touch*, which she describes as "a MUCH more informative title." "The Lady" is a more traditional phrase, whereas "The Carradyne Touch" evokes the physical connection to animals that is so central to Anne's fiction and her life. "Carradyne" is the name of a character and the "touch" skill with horses. The story of Anne's paying the dinner bill at a convention appears in *Locus* #287, vol. 17, no. 12, December 1984.

Quotations

"disconnected from her imagination." Trachtenberg, 62.
"keeps the . . . chaos." Silverberg, 4.
"he's never asleep." Ibid., 22.
"had stage . . . persona." Interview with Harry and Marilyn Alm, 8-17-02.
"I always . . . writing." Letter of Win Catherwood to Anne McCaffrey, 5-13-84.
"W. . . . bathtub." Ibid., 7-31-84.
"Wright moved . . . I did." Letter of Anne McCaffrey to Win Catherwood, 10-5-85.
"One never . . . books." Letter of Virginia Kidd to Anne McCaffrey and Lynn Del Rey, 2-17-83.
"I thought . . . her touch!" Letter of Virginia Kidd to Anne McCaffrey, 4-25-83.
"Fat and . . . I lead." Letter of Anne McCaffrey to Joanne Forman, 7-16-83.
"I gave . . . of me." Letter of Anne McCaffrey to Win Catherwood, 11-16-87.
"utterly, completely and thoroughly drained." A. McCaffrey, *Stitch in Snow*, 137.
"I don't . . . protect her." Interview with Todd McCaffrey. 9-1-02.
"Mum and . . . my opinion." Email from Georgeanne Kennedy, 1-28-03.
"great rapport . . . Fist of Bray" Interview with Anne McCaffrey, 7-8-02.
"appalled at . . . man's chattel." A. McCaffrey, *The Lady*, 408.
"You men . . . previously appreciated." Ibid., 418.
"Some are . . . in Ireland." Ibid., 237.
"I dearly . . . love it" Letter of Win Catherwood to Anne McCaffrey, 7-23-84.
"How the . . . at once?" Ibid., 11-5-82.
"I understand . . . of Win." Interview with Anne McCaffrey, 7-30-02.

"I'm sort . . . that quarter!" Letter of Anne McCaffrey to Win Catherwood, 2-24-84.

"young men . . . of sexuality." Interview with Anne McCaffrey, 7-28-02.

"She made . . . a writer." Letter of Anne McCaffrey to Joanne Forman, 5-19-83.

"Annie McCaffrey . . . lesbian." Interview with Maureen Beirne, 8-4-02.

"he has . . . helping her." Interview with Shelly Shapiro, 9-26-02.

"Are these all . . . fathers." Interview with Marilyn and Harry Alms.

"nice to . . . dithering." E-mail from Anne McCaffrey, 9-5-01.

"She reminded . . . at once." E-mail from Elizabeth Moon, 2–11-03.

"a keen . . . character." Interview with Richard Woods, 8-1-02.

"she was . . . always right." Interview with Derval Diamond, 7-31-02.

"enjoyed playing . . . be good." Interview with Anne McCaffrey, 7-31-02.

"Sis was . . . an American." Interview with Maureen Beirne, 8-4-02.

"Because I . . . the trade." *Women Writers: Anne McCaffrey*, Thames Television, 1988.

"If we . . . your own?" Ibid.

CHAPTER 7: BEING A FAIRY GODMOTHER

In the 1990s, four books on Anne McCaffrey were published: Mary T. Brizzi's Anne McCaffrey, Matthew Hargreaves's *Anne Inez McCaffrey: Forty Years of Publishing, an International Bibliography*, Robin Roberts's *Anne McCaffrey: A Critical Companion*, and Todd J. McCaffrey's *Dragonholder: The Life and Dreams (So Far) of Anne McCaffrey*.

Quotations

"a house . . . writer resides." Letter of Anne McCaffrey to Annett Francis, 7-28-86.

"By playing . . . very expensive." Interview with Anne McCaffrey, 8-3-02.

"It is . . . six months." Fax of Anne McCaffrey to Virginia Kidd, 6-13-93.

"taking care . . . to her." Interview with Shelly Shapiro, 9-26-02.

"Dearest Virginia . . . rolls in!" Fax of Anne McCaffrey to Virginia Kidd, 2-25-93.

"Mom likes . . . to her." Interview with Georgeanne Kennedy, 8-2-02.

"did not . . . had finished." E-mail from Anne McCaffrey, 1-5-03.

"as near . . . could get." Ibid.

"KWITCHURBELIAKIN . . . a necessity." Fax of Anne McCaffrey to Virginia Kidd, 6-17-93.

"What a . . . so now." Ibid.

"publishing had . . . merchandising considerations." Interview with Anne McCaffrey, 7-28-03.

"Taking . . . niceness." Interview with Vaughne Hansen, 2-18-02.

"suggested the . . . already liked." E-mail from Anne McCaffrey, 6-18-02.

"I got . . . damned outline." "Anne McCaffrey: Life with Dragons," 5.

"it's good . . . a book." Interview with Anne McCaffrey, 7-27-02.

"It's flattering . . . your universe." Interview with Susan Allison, 9-26-02.

"on the . . fortunately are." Fax of Anne McCaffrey to Virginia Kidd, 2-9-93.

"'Ms. Nye . . . McCaffrey waters." Fax of Virginia Kidd to Anne McCaffrey, 2-12-92.

"Well, honey . . . PTB trilogy." Fax of Anne McCaffrey to Virginia Kidd, 2–12-92.

"That's a . . . wants to." E-mail from Anne McCaffrey, 6-13-03.

"much more . . . Irish!" Interview with Elizabeth Ann Scarborough, 5-25-03.

"it was . . . true collaboration." "Anne McCaffrey: Life with Dragons," 5.

"'Does water . . . the experience." E-mail from Elizabeth Moon, 2-9-03.

"The collabs . . . . which other." Fax of Anne McCaffrey to Virginia Kidd, 6-1-93.

"a boyfriend . . . months now." Letter of Anne McCaffrey to Annett Francis, 1-20-91.

"Gigi has . . . she will." Fax of Anne McCaffrey to Virginia Kidd, 6-17-93.

"Dearest Virginia . . . now!)" Ibid., 1-14-93.

"like a . . . that dress." E-mail from Georgeanne Kennedy, 1-3-03.

"heart would burst." Interview with Anne McCaffrey, 7-28-02.

"Gracious royalties . . . tax bill." Letter from Anne McCaffrey to Shelly Shapiro, 2-3-93.

"People have . . . definitive answers." Letter of Anne McCaffrey to Veronica Yaworski, 2-8-93.

"Congratulations! . . . McCaffrey Award!" Fax of Shelly Shapiro to Anne McCaffrey, 7-1-93.

"addictive . . . good thing." Interview with Anne McCaffrey, 7- 28-02.

"Something to . . . the good kind." E-mail from Elizabeth Moon, 2-11-03.

"a hard act to follow." E-mail from Anne McCaffrey, 1-14-03.

"What are . . . our lives?" Interview with Anne McCaffrey, 7-28-02.

"for all . . . her own." Ibid., 8-2-02.

"apparently this . . . Anne McCaffrey." E-mail from Todd McCaffrey, 2-10-03.

"peel her . . . in size." E-mail from Georgeanne Kennedy, 2-11-03.

"Money was . . . MY WAY!" E-mail from Anne McCaffrey, 9-10-01.

"I'm Father X, . . . so effective." Ibid.

"I was . . . Space Station." Ibid.

"A TIA . . . and memory." Ibid.

"a very . . . Harrod's" Ibid., 1-22-03.

"If you . . . good day." Interview with Maureen Beirne, 8-4-02.

"They'll probably . . . keyboard [dead]." Interview with Anne McCaffrey, 7-28-02.

"I shall . . . my word-processor." A. McCaffrey, "The Self-Made (Wo)man, 42.

"I bore myself." E-mail from Anne McCaffrey, 4-25-02.

"incredible mind . . . telling things." Interview with Derval Diamond, 7-31-02.

"she has . . . an editor." Interview with Shelly Shapiro, 9-26-02.

"Mum would . . . Hall series." E-mail from Georgeanne Kennedy, 1-30-03.

"passing the torch story." Interview with Todd McCaffrey, 8-31-02

"a story about . . . descendants." outline for *Dragonsblood*.

"Pern will . . . works or not." Interview with Shelly Shapiro, 9-26-02.

"Your father . . . him back." Todd McCaffrey, 7-27-02

"Mum sympathizes . . . older." Todd and Anne McCaffrey, 7-27-02.

"I was . . . older!" Anne McCaffrey, 7-27-02.

"a pleasure." Interview with Cyra O'Connor, 7-30-02.
"I am not . . . collapses." Interview with Antoinette O'Connell, 7-29-02.
"What has . . . Bingo!" Anne McCaffrey, 7-28-02.

CHAPTER 8: THE GRAND MASTER

Anne's witnessing of a space shuttle launch was delayed first by her heart attack, then by technical problems with the shuttle. Originally scheduled for August 22, 2002, this flight was postponed when, in late June, cracks were discovered in propellant lines in all the shuttles. The shuttle *Atlantis*'s launch was rescheduled for September 26, then September 28, when cracked bearings in the crawlers that carried the shuttle to the launch pad were found, it was delayed again until October 2. For Anne, the wait seemed interminable. In summer 2002, Anne eagerly counted down the weeks until her trip. Although she had taken a bad tumble in July, she wasn't going to let a little thing like a broken arm derail her.

The 2005 Nebula Awards Cermony is available on DVD from www. alphavideoproduction.com. All quotations from the ceremony are from this DVD.

Quotations

"It was . . . really important." E-mail from Pamela Melroy, 3-17-03.
"not sweet . . . science fiction." Letter from Pamela Melroy to Anne McCaffrey, 12-11-00.
"so much . . . many years." quoted on www.destinationspace.net/escape/evtests/launch.asp, 9-12-00.
"she was . . . attack instead." E-mail from Pamela Melroy, 3-17-03.
"Our storage . . . master storyteller." Letter from Pamela Melroy to Anne McCaffrey, 12-11-00.
"My feet . . . greater joy," www.annemccaffrey.net/index.html 10-15-01.
"an incredible . . . and going!" E-mail from Pamela Melroy, 3-17-03.
"kind of . . . to do." Ibid., 1-23-03.
"to spark . . . prepackaged food." Ibid., 1-28-03.
"It was . . . orbital adventure." Ibid., 10-23-02.
"She opened . . . limitless possibilities." Interview with Antoinette O'Connell, 8-2-02.
"I believe . . . Prince Charming." Interview with Elizabeth Anne Scarborough, 5-25-03.
"one of . . . her heroes." E-mail from Jody Lynn Nye, 5-11-2004.
"women come . . . self-creation." Heilbrun, *Writing a Woman's Life*, 117.

WORKS CITED

Interviews (2000–2003) with Susan Allison, Maureen Beirne, Derval Diamond, Annett Francis, Vaughne Hansen, Alec Johnson, H. Wright Johnson, Georgeanne Kennedy, Virginia Kidd, Anne McCaffrey, Kevin and Marci McCaffrey, Andi McCaffrey, Todd J. McCaffrey, Shelly Shapiro, Antoinette O'Connell, and Richard Woods.

Alpern, Sara, et al., eds. *The Challenge of Feminist Biography*. Urbana: University of Illinois Press, 1992.

Anderson, Karen. *Wartime Women: Sex Roles, Family Relations, and the Status of Women during World War II*. Westport, CT: Greenwood Press, 1981.

Andrews, Benjamin J., ed. *The Girl's Daily Life*. New York: J. B. Lippincott, 1944.

"Anne McCaffrey: Life with Dragons." *Locus* (March 1993): 5.

Arbor, Rosemary. *Brackett, Bradley, McCaffrey: A Primary and Secondary Bibliography*. Boston: G. K. Hall, 1982.

Brizzi, Mary T. *Anne McCaffrey*. Starmount Reader's Guide 30. Mercer Island, WA: Starmount House, 1986.

Bro, Margaret Harmon. *Let's Talk about You*. New York: Doubleday and Company, 1943.

Brody, Jane E. "Photos Speak Volumes about Relationships." *New York Times*, July 17, 1943, section C., page 1, column 2.

Clute, John, and Peter Nicholls, eds. *The Encyclopedia of Science Fiction*. New York: St. Martin's Press, 1993.

Contemporary Authors Online. Gale Group, 2000. Reproduced in *Biography Resource Center*. Farmington Hills, MI: Gale Group, 2001. (http://www.galenet.com/servlet/BIORC).

Donawerth, Jane. *Frankenstein's Daughters: Women Writing Science Fiction*. Syracuse: Syracuse University Press, 1997.

DuPlessis, Rachel Blau. *Writing beyond the Ending: Narrative Strategies of*

Twentieth-Century Women Writers. Bloomington: Indiana University Press, 1985.

Friedan, Betty. *The Feminine Mystique.* New York: Dell Publishing Co., 1963.

Grey, Zane. *Riders of the Purple Sage.* 1912. Rpt., New York: Grosset and Dunlop, 1940.

Hall, Trish. "As Middle Children Become Rarer, Society May Miss Their Influence." *Wall Street Journal.* August 21, 1986, 25.

Hargreaves, Matthew. *Anne Inez McCaffrey: Forty Years of Publishing, an International Bibliography.* Seattle: Hargreaves, 1992.

Heilbrun, Carolyn *The Last Gift of Time: Life beyond Sixty.* New York: Dial Press, 1997.

———. *Writing a Woman's Life.* New York: Ballantine Books, 1988.

Hodge, Jane Aiken. *The Private World of Georgette Heyer.* London: Bodley Head, 1984.

Http://popularmechanics.com/automotive/collector_cars/2001/11/its_all_here.

Interracial Committee of the New Jersey Conference of Social Work. *The Negro in New Jersey.* New York: Negro Universities Press, 1932. Rpt. 1969.

Johnson, H. Wright. "Harley Granville-Barker, 1877–1946: A Critical Biography." AB thesis, Princeton University, 1948.

Jones, Mary Somerville. *A Historical Geography of the Changing Divorce Law in the United States.* New York: Garland Publishing, 1987.

Larbalestier, Justine. *The Battle of the Sexes in Science Fiction.* Middletown, CT: Wesleyan University Press, 2002.

Lefanu, Sarah. *Feminism and Science Fiction.* Bloomington: Indiana University Press, 1999.

Longnecker, Marlene. "Introduction: Women, Ecology, and the Environment." *Natural Women's Studies Association Journal* 9, no. 3 (fall 1997): 1–17.

McCaffrey, Anne. "Hitch Your Dragon to a Star: Romance and Glamour in Science Fiction." In *Science Fiction Today and Tomorrow,* ed. Reginald Bretnor, 278–294. Baltimore: Penguin Books, 1974.

———. *The Kilternan Legacy.* New York: Dell, 1975.

———. *The Lady.* New York: Ballantine Books, 1987.

———. *The Mark of Merlin.* New York: Dell, 1971.

———. "Retrospection." In *Women of Vision,* ed. Denise Dupont. New York: St. Martin's Press, 1988.

———. "The Self-Made (Wo)man," manuscript.

———. *Stitch in Snow.* New York: Tor, 1986.

———. "The Utopian Novel with Special Emphasis on Eugene Ivanovich Zamiatin and His Novel *WE.*" Manuscripts and Archives Division, New York Public Library, Astor, Lenox, and Tilden Foundations.

McCaffrey, Hugh. *Khmer Gold.* New York: Ivy Books, 1988.

McCaffrey, Todd J. *Dragonholder: The Life and Dreams (So Far) of Anne McCaffrey.* New York: Del Rey, 1999.

Merril, Judith, and Emily Pohl-Weary, *Better to Have Loved: the Life of Judith Merril.* Toronto: Between the Lines, 2002.

Ortner, Sherry, "Is Female to Male as Nature Is to Culture?" *Feminist Studies* 1, no. 2 (autumn 1972): 5–31.

Pipher, Mary. *Reviving Ophelia: Saving the Selves of Adolescent Girls.* New York: Ballantine, 1995.

Radcliffe 1947 50th Reunion, 1997.

Roberts, Robin. *Anne McCaffrey: A Critical Companion.* Westport, CT: Greenwood Press, 1996. CD updates, 1999, 2000, 2001.

Rosenfeld, Jeffrey P. *The Legacy of Aging: Inheritance and Disinheritance in Social Perspective.* Norwood, NJ: Ablex Publishing, 1979.

Ryan, Dennis. *Beyond the Ballot Box: A Social History of the Boston Irish, 1845–1917.* East Brunswick, NJ: Associated University Presses, 1983.

Silverberg, Robert. *Lord Valentine's Castle.* New York: Harper Collins, 1980.

60 Minutes. CBS. February 3, 2002.

Snedeker, Caroline Dale. *The Forgotten Daughter.* 1929. Rpt., Garden City, NY: Doubleday and Company, 1966.

——. *The Spartan.* Garden City, NY: Doubleday, 1936.

——. *The White Isle.* New York: Doubleday, Doran and Co., 1940.

Statistical Abstract of the United States, 1939. No.61. Washington, DC: U.S. Department of Commerce, 1945.

Trachtenberg, Martha P. *Anne McCaffrey: Science Fiction Storyteller.* Berkley Heights, NJ: Enslow Publishers, 2001.

Turner, Barbara F., and Lillian E. Troll, eds., *Women Growing Older: Psychological Perspectives.* Thousand Oaks, CA: Sage Publications, 1994.

Woolf, Virginia. *The Diary of Virginia Woolf, 1925–1930.* Ed. Anne Oliver Bell. Orlando, FL: Harvest, HJB, 1981.

Wright, Austin Tappan. *Islandia.* New York: Farrar and Rinehart, 1942.

Yahraes, Herbert. "What Research Shows about Birth Order, Personality, and IQ." *Science Reports.* Rockville, MD: National Institute of Mental Health, May 1979. 1–10.

INDEX

Index

Index

Kennedy, Owen Thomas, 201
Kennedy, Robert, 74
Kennedy, Rose Fitzgerald, 20
Kidd, Virginia, 72, 92, 93, 96–114, 116–
18, 119, 120, 122–24, 126, 130–31,
135, 157, 169, 176, 182, 188, 197, 216
Kipling, Rudyard, 26–27, 49–50, 71,
184; "The Butterfly That Stamped,"
45; *Jungle Tales*, 92; *Just-So Stories*, 45;
Kim, 49
Kiss Me Kate, 85, 90
Kissimmee, Florida, 80
Knight, Damon, 98, 100–1, 216
Korea, 31

Laban, Mare, 150
Lackey, Mercedes, 187
Lambertsville Musical Circus, 79, 82
Larbalestier, Justine, 11
Le Guin, Ursula K., 8, 52, 97, 214
League of Women Voters, 34
Lefanu, Sarah, 8
Legible Leftovers bookstore, 207
Leinster, Murray, 94
Let's Talk About You, 47
Lewis, Pota, 67, 75, 76, 78, 83
Liberty Music Shops, 78–79, 87
Lone Ranger, The, 41
Longfellow, Henry Wadsworth, 26–27
Lucas, George, 217
Ludus De Nato Infante Mirificus, 90

Manley, Scott, 195
Marsh, Ngaio, 34
Massachusetts Institute of Technology
(MIT), 76
Massey, Raymond, 78
McCaffrey, Anne: adolescent self-image,
46–48, 64, 146; book tours, 149–50,
155, 160; chat room, 191–92; childhood, 36–43; collaborators, 13, 180–
87, 199, 204, 210–13, 217; cooking
and food, 23, 62; courtship and
wedding, 83–84; dancing, 62–63,
76; depression, 142–53; divorce,
116, 117–18, 121; earnings and finances, 113, 120–24, 152, 162, 176,
178, 190, 195–96; education, 57–61,
62, 66–68, 70; emigration, 118–21;
extracurricular activities in college,

74–76; generosity, 7, 165–67, 215;
illnesses, 12, 175, 191, 195–97, 205;
influence of agent/editor, 96–97,
99–102, 104–6; influence of father,
24–27, 30, 31–33, 72, 146; influence
of mother, 24–26, 32, 33–36, 59, 86;
influences, literary, 48–52, 71–72,
94; Irish heritage, 5, 16–24; jobs
after college, 78–79; lovers, 126–33,
161; marital problems, 109–11,
113–16, 124; middle age, 152, 158;
as middle child, 36–37, 40; motherhood, 88–89, 91–92, 93, 114; musical
interest, 24, 49, 60, 63–64, 75, 76–
77, 79, 82, 85, 89–90, 116, 135, 146,
172, 184; political interests, 54–55,
74; pregnancy and childbirth, 85,
87–88; religion, 71; social life in college, 73–74, 76–77; at space shuttle
launch, 207–10; sports, 60; tolerance,
163–65; as tomboy, 37, 41, 60; **Characters:** Brains, 89; Brawns, 89; Brizzi,
58; Catriona, 161–62; Cita, 89, 185;
Clodagh, 126, 160, 185; Damia, 36;
Dan, 159; Dana, 159–60; dragons,
9, 38, 42, 146–47, 172–73; Emorra,
213; F'lar, 32, 134; F'nor, 126–27,
134; Helva, 13, 33, 35, 39, 58, 63,
110; Hivers, 72; Isabel, 161–62;
Jaxom, 134; J'Trel, 212; Keevan, 141;
Killashandra, 20, 50, 56, 77, 105–6,
119, 157, 194; Kindan, 212; Kylara,
58; Lady Rezalla, 194; Lessa, 13, 15,
20, 36, 50, 56, 58, 70, 89, 110, 126,
127, 134; Lord Tionel, 194; Menolly,
15, 40, 64, 89, 119, 125, 128, 146–47,
148; Moreta, 14, 39, 61, 130–31, 144,
155–57; Niall, 138; Nialla, 139–40;
Nimisha, 13, 70, 119, 194–95; Pellar,
212; Rene, 145; Robinton, 13, 32, 64,
89; the Rowan, 13, 36, 40, 56, 58,
89, 105, 180; Sara, 110; Selina, 162;
Simon, 145; Sis, 211; Talith, 212; Terregar, 211; Thread, 11, 23, 72, 212;
Watch-whers, 211, 212; Wind Blossom,
213; Yana Maddock, 64, 185; **Works:**
Acorna series, 183–84, 186; *Alchemy
and Academe*, 122; *Black Horses for
the King*, 189; "Bound by Hoof and
Nail," 199; Brain Ship series, 89, 191,

Index